Spirit Guides a
Death and Taxes

Wayne R. Cesaro

Contents

Dedication

Immerse yourself. This is dedicated to you. The slightly different. You are sensitive enough to feel colors, hear thoughts, see orbs and sense a psychic reality. Does it make you feel alone? Like, you can't relate. Or those around you can't relate to you? You can live a continuous communion with nature's forces and with the common life force that flows through all creation knowing that you are different. You can see and touch the heavens and interact with the life celestial, its thoughts and energies and live an anchored, successfully peaceful, contented future and you'll know that you are not alone. Learn from my successes. Immerse yourself. Succeed with the help of this uninhibited, raw look at what it takes to fully live in both worlds; the celestial / spiritual world while succeeding in the modern, work-a-day, reality that we call a rat race.

This is not a time for preconceived opinions or biases. The world is going crazy and we've no idea where it will end up in our lifetimes or our children's. Get all the input you can about your psychic, metaphysical, spiritual gifts while you can. Immerse yourself and free spiritual prisoners.

Spirit Guides and Angels

About the Author

An active metaphysical practitioner and instructor from his mid-twenties through his late fifties, an Internet ordained Reverend, and a one-time co-pastor of a Spiritualist church and flowering, regional Spiritual Center.

Professionally, a licensed ship's master then technology teacher, high school through graduate level programs, settling down with technology manager of professional staff. Now retired and motivating clients as fitness advisor and certified personal trainer.

Death and Taxes

Chapter 1: Cesaro

Life is — NOT— just as I see it. That's my biggest leap of faith. My faith directs that I am enfolded in a spirit of benevolence, love, and creation. Celestial beings and angels exist and are involved with my life for my greater good. Within me resides the spark of life that binds us together, in common, in life, and in the afterlife.

So, I have faith, and I keep the faith. Does faith in the spark of life within me help? Is it good for me to feel this spark? Are there certain kinds of faith I should have? Is the spark of life within the spark of a god? What good is faith in anything, anyway? Does faith bring me comfort? How? Does it smooth my days and give me hope and a purpose? Is it something to help me through the hard and troubled times or to get past my challenges? And when all is lost, does it give me the license to hope for mercy?

I am a hearty and independent sport. Throughout my life, I maintained one common core principle that stuck with me no matter how I tried to shake it: the existence of the spirit that I experience within my heart and throughout all my life is real and expresses the fact that there is a continuity of life that transgresses the experience called death of the body.

Spirit Guides and Angels

If I am going to have faith in the spark of life within, what should be my goal? Should it be the salvation of my soul and the receipt of the "Crown of Life"—eternal life? Do I need to live by one specific, defined faith to attain the glory of heaven and to share at the table? Do I get eternal life if I don't? Faith in the spark I carry within is my confidence that after leaving this life, I will receive the life everlasting that I hoped for. My hope is my desired wish that after this body turns to ashes and dust, there will be life eternal, and I will rest, learn, and be free of fear and any electrical and chemical reactions, and I will communicate with those souls I love, honor, and respect freely. Above all, my hope is the knowledge that I will know the mystical secrets that have long remained hidden from me.

If I express this confidence in the way I live, then my confidence is an expression of my living faith—my belief that I am an eternal being and, in Christian terms, will inherit the kingdom of God.

Is that something that interests you? Are you looking for eternal life or just the hope that it provides? Would it do you any good today, here and now, to know that you are an eternal being of light, hope, and love? That you are loved unconditionally by guides, guardians, gods, angels, and sainted beings that interact with you as they do with me through my clairvoyance, personal meditations, and in many cases, my visions of a spiritual world? And let me not forget the communications that come to me within my dreams.

I must be prepared and willing to accept that faith is a living thing and, like life, can go through many stages. Faith for me will never stay permanently fixed after a single vision, experience, or discovery, no matter how genuine or sincere that experience. My faith can be shipwrecked, departed from, disowned, wandered from, missed, and lost. No one—not Christians, Spiritualists, Buddhists, Jews, Hindus, free thinkers, or anyone else—has a "waiver" that exempts them from such vexes.

I voiced my soul's first expression of my faith, living as a child, arriving at adulthood. I was not immune to the confusion and anxiety of my years. I experienced all that any person of contemporary times would undergo. I questioned my destiny and my reason for being. I wondered in my silence what my part would be in the nurturing of my world and my relationship with those about me.

It was during my early years, before I was eighteen, that I came to instinctively grasp the true but vague nature of who I was then and who I was to become.

It was through experiencing life on my own, of that I was sure, that I will truly understand the trials of my earthly sojourn. Leaving the family home and striking out on my own,

I will eventually and naturally be saddled with the responsibilities of caring for a family and becoming a wage earner. I will likely undergo hard times and work my way through debt to feed my family.

It will be during this struggle that I will determine to become generous yet practical. I will experience the contradictions of daily life and choose to be kind, loving, compassionate, and even entertaining and recreational while still consigned to living within the yoke of my responsibilities and station.

I will eventually come into my own. I will speak of Spirit and own the decision of my existence. I will not wish to rend the wicked and punish the oppressors in battle and war but mend the meek and bind the brokenhearted.

In my assertions, I will entreat the heavens and all about me to comfort all who suffer and to return hate with love, the ugliness of the treatment some would receive with the hope of beauty and the tools of happiness. In worship, I will assert chanting of admiration over expressing sorrow, such that we are pyramids of virtue and therein glorify life. My living is for my soul. I will seek not material beauty but will look into the eyes of others and see the beauty of the spirit. I will come to know that I am an eternal being, given life and a chance to do my part on this green earth. I will work to plant the seeds of wonder that I may glorify the spirit and soothe the soul.

At the age of eighteen, I affirmed to be positive and to seek good and not evil, to do good works, but above all, to create good thoughts, thereby filling the voids of my spirit with hope, happiness, and enlightenment. This is the key to doing, as my contentment requires: walk honestly, love mercy, and tread humbly, holding the spark of life within me.

I would find that my physical manifestation, my ego-driven self, in this life would place many roadblocks into my path of fulfilling my early heavenly entreaties. As I started out on my own, I found that my initial choices were limited to those presented during my formative years. I only knew what I knew by observing the world around me. A world that was defined by the norms of this local, close-knit society and by the people who were influential throughout my early years: family, friends, and challengers. I would find that culture and station would be as restrictive as a snake confining my chest while I instinctively aspired to breathe clear, fresh air.

I may not know exactly what the afterlife or that heavenly hierarchy is all about, but I shouldn't let that little detail keep me from seeing the forest for the trees. Enlightened people actively lived their faith as children of a higher god and glorified the connection to heaven. They apparently came to understand all the divine mysteries. The Buddha and the Christ, for instance, with their continuous acts of self-purification, provided the motivation for hope and living evidence that we carry the spark of a god within.

What I do know is that I am a medium and clairvoyant. I walk in two worlds. I live in this physical illusion while simultaneously keeping a spiritual presence in the heavenly world. My spiritual presence is mindful. Cultivated. Ambidextrous. I have three dimensions to my otherworldly presence.

First, my clairvoyance is always on. I mask the projection of my vibration and energy when out and about or whenever feeling oversensitive or uncomfortable. There is no turning off sight from a clairvoyant perspective. Reading emotions, energy, vibration and frequency, inspirational thoughts, and thoughts that are best to be ignored on multiple levels of perception throughout my day require attentive navigation. I have no choice in the matter. I'm always on.

Second, I live in a continuous communion with nature's forces and with the celestial beings that inhabit this universe. The common life force that flows through all creation speaks to me *telepathically*, for lack of a better word. Seeing the branch of a tree wave in the breeze and its leaves take flight in freedom gives me insight and information on all levels of existence regarding the tree, leaves, and wind. Each entity has a being; I recognize their being, and they acknowledge mine. I respect and pay homage to nature, wind, water, and the force that binds us in common. And they return the gesture. The celestial beings that are no less about me and within my mind intermingle with my spirit. As I sit here in the flesh, I also stand in the presence of my brethren in spirit. Thus is the duality of my soul and of my earthly experience. As is here, so is above. I am here in the flesh while I am also in spirit essence, singing right along with the choir.

Third, I am one with the central sun, the four pillars of creation, and the one source and center of all creation. My active and conscious participation in such a state of being requires sitting in meditation and stillness. Occasionally, I will slip off in a trance. I become free of all physical distractions and chemical and electrical reactions while placing the focus of my soul on mind-driven collaboration with heaven and earth. I align my spirit, soul, and body with the vibrational rate of the one source and center that is everywhere, within all things, and I become one with it. I become the child returning to the womb of creation.

I don't choose to be so out there with the properties of my living experience. Living a multidimensional life is all I know. For me, it is simply the way it is now and has been throughout my past. Once I experienced first seeing, and then living in each successive dimension, I could not go back to the forced blindness that brings me some contrived peace of mind. The impacts upon my personality living this reality, per my experience, produce vulnerability and ultra sensitivity, most felt when going about my worldly activities, interacting with others of this concrete, everyday living. And in the everyday living of this wondrous life, I know that I am different. I see and touch the heavens. I interact with the celestial life, its thoughts, energies, and inhabitants. It is what it is. I have seen it. And I know it.

The ancients knew it and held fast to open communication with the dead. The Romans believed in regular communication with their ancestors, as did the Chinese and the Japanese. The Egyptians believed in three bodies: one to walk the earth, one to guard the personal portal into the afterlife, and one to live in the afterlife.

The ancients were not the only ones to take up the concept of the existence of spirit and the heavenly hierarchy of life after death. Religions also had belief systems incorporating various aspects of life after physical death and the existence of the spirit and of soul. The Christians based their concepts on the life of Christ, while the early Hindus developed a sophisticated concept of the continuation of energy in which once something is created, it cannot be destroyed, only changed. They believed that the soul was a "something" that was created and lived on in as many other forms as necessary for spiritual development.

My interpretations of my spiritual life motivate my activities of socialization and service and bring about the exchange of ideas with others and knowledge from the whole as opposed to the self. As such, my pursuit of knowledge in this realm is prime, and I desire to apply the acquired knowledge to the service of others and to the pursuit of personal growth and advancement. In return for my service to the community, I experience inspiring love and fellowship.

After all my fears and worry about where I will end up today, next year, or when I pass from this life, my realization holds fast that life is eternal. My faith in that conviction brings a balance and perspective to my daily routines. It puts into perspective a stubbed toe, a lost job, and that controversial election result.

As the spark of life works within me, I have no alternative but to spend time in fruitful service to others, pursuing true knowledge, and engaging in honest communion with all.

Spirit Guides and Angels

Chapter 2: Formative Years

Different

Riding around my arena putting my horse Spike through his paces delivered me a surprise when the neighbor drove down our common private road in haste. Walking the horse through the course of cones and barrels that we would eventually canter around, Spike startled. And quickly, suddenly, he shifted three feet to the right while I stayed in the physical space I was then occupying. Lacking a horse under me, I dropped to the ground with a thud. The last thing I remembered seeing while on the way down was one of Spike's eyes looking at the neighbor's truck traversing the road quickly, too quickly. The thud landed me on my hip and very close to freshly planted horse manure. The hip was knocked out of whack. The local chiropractor was new to the island. I that day became one of his newest patients.

On my first trip to the doc, it was apparent that my sciatica was the root of the issue. X-rays confirmed the fact, visually, while the pain and weakness in my left leg were all that I needed to know that something was not right in that region of my body. The chiropractor adjusted me and brought some relief and then sent me off with the instructions to take it easy, ice my lower back, and report back the following week.

Death and Taxes

Taking it easy is not something I can do when I have a few acres, horses, and a work list that would take me a full-time job to complete. Before reporting back to the good doctor, I spent my days in hard physical labor clearing downed trees from my woods in preparation for turning a small clearing into a round pen for horses' exercise. The tractor did most of the work, but I still had to hump chains, set the chokers, and walk through the underbrush. Add to the planned labor the weekly horse manure patrol (cleaning out the fields) and digging in a few new fence posts. I was spent and stiff at the end of almost every day. These were atypical days at the ranch, but ones that rear up on you when the sun is shining and there's work to be done. And that's just the way I like it.

I reported to the chiro doc the following week and provided a summary of my week's physical labor. He took me to task before conducting the exam to address my deteriorating condition that he was sure to find. He was startled to find that I was completely healed. The strength in my legs returned. The pain in the lower back and throughout my legs was gone. My posture was back to normal, and my gait was as quick as ever. He was stunned.

Searching for some rationale for this unexpected health and healing of my body, he inquired into the family history. He proceeded to postulate that I had good genes. "How healthy are your parents?"

I answered, "My mother and father are both deceased. My father and his father never made it to their sixties, having both succumbed to heart disease and cancer. My mother had three siblings. Each sibling had multiple instances of cancer. One uncle had it four times and eventually succumbed to the last instance. My mother had cancer four times and beat each one, only to be taken out by Alzheimer's and respiratory failure."

He looked perplexed.

Reading his face and seeing obvious confusion, I added, "I'm different. I'm not one of them."

He took my offhanded comment at face value and proceeded with the adjustment, saying nothing more but still marveled, nonetheless.

I'm different. I'm not one of them. I never could understand how I was born of these, my parents. I never could understand why I turned out the way I did. It didn't make sense. Everyone else around me turned out differently. *Everyone.* Friends, family, the kids down the street—they all grew into their very predictable outcomes. They were who they were as culture and ethnic requirements dictated. I turned out strikingly dissimilar to my origins and bloodline. The contrariness was evident in almost everything about me and particularly in something as singular as my health. I just don't get sick.

It was not always that way. I was plenty sick when I was younger, living in the family home. My sophomore year in high school saw some of the sickest days I could count. I was to leave the private school I attended, St. Benedict's Prep, for failed attendance. Keeping up with studies was difficult for me. I was rarely at school. That year I had strep throat, pneumonia twice, the flu that was going around, some typical colds, and fevers. One instance of absence lasted six weeks to cover the span of Thanksgiving, Christmas, and New Year's Day. It was difficult to follow algebra and Latin from the sickbed to which I was confined.

My path to health would require leaving the family home and striking out on my own. I knew there was something to life that I wasn't seeing. I needed to leave and become my own man. I had no clue what that meant or what it looked like or what it would mean to my mind and body. My first attempt didn't work.

With my first attempt, I had no idea of what nutrition was, and I remember one particular outcome of an evening meal. I was sitting in a tub of lukewarm water at 2 a.m., having consumed a six-pack of Coca-Cola after 10 p.m. I didn't know there was caffeine in Coke! To this day, I cannot drink coffee past 11 a.m. lest I stay awake half the night. The resulting level of self-care I provided during that first attempt landed me back at the family home, coughing blood, and getting transferred to a hospital bed for the next three weeks. No one knew the cause of my distress. This was the second time in my young life that family members were concerned to the point of calling on the local priest to deliver me the last rites. But I made it, and I'm still here. My grandfather attributes my survival to my strength. I now attribute my survival to my soul's origins and to the fact that it simply was not in my karma to pass from the earth at that time.

My second attempt at leaving the family home succeeded thanks to the help of friends whom I met through other friends. These new friends I would keep for half a century or more. When we first met, they inhabited an old farmhouse on many acres in Pennsylvania. I asked if they had room, they did, and in I moved.

The stability, social comfort, friendly atmosphere, and the local, small-town community helped set the stage for my successful transition. It also brought about opportunities to experiment and find my identity. Forming one aspect of my newly discovered identity, I developed a foundation of practices I would keep for the rest of my days. This was where I taught myself how to meditate. This was where I started to clearly see beyond the veil into the neighboring dimensions associated with the celestial hosts and the metaphysical aspects of life in this illusion.

Originally, I was a city boy born of parents who were products of their environment and culture. My character was contrary to the world they brought me into, and upon this second foray into freedom, a spark emerged from within to display an unmistakable outward strength. From Pennsylvania and self-taught meditation onward, sickness was not to plague me again, lest it be associated with incalculable lesson material for my development and advancement.

I was different from the start. Unmistakable. I played alone as a child. I couldn't find too many little friends who would engage in play that required the make-believe roles of countless historic and imagined personalities. My kind of play, I would painfully come to learn, was not one that children of my age and culture should engage in. That pain was not the emotional pangs of social solitude. The pain often came in the form of a backhanded blow to the back of the head or a sudden pulling of my hair around my ears counter to the grain. Who was the dispenser of this physical pain? Sister Some Name. My play was counter to our culture and the expected topics I should be concerned about as a child when in the first grade. My teachers regularly reinforced the dogma. I remember to this day some of those hair pulls and the circumstances that called them.

While in the first grade, my desk mate—there were two to a large desk at St. Paul the Apostle school—could not get the technique I was attempting to teach by demonstration. Our play for the recess hour that day was levitating the sheet of paper that sat before each of us on our desks. "It's simple!" I would exclaim. "Look at the paper and squint your eyes. Try to look under the paper and lift it up with your mind. It will look like this when you do it." I exhaled softly onto the desk surface, and the sheet of paper, slightly, perceivably rose on the layer of expelled air. I would have explained to him that he needed to be relaxed, reach a meditative state, and raise his vibrational level before he would be able to lift the piece of paper. But at the time, I didn't know what all that meant, and I couldn't imagine that that was not something everybody naturally knew and practiced. I did mention that he would create a layer of air between the sheet of paper and the surface of the desk, but without breathing it, by thinking it instead. At the time, I did not know the worldview on meditation and changing vibrational rates. I was just being a kid and playing some interesting games.

So, I demonstrated. Ever so slightly, the edge of the paper curled up just a fraction of an inch. He turned quickly to look at me, then again at the paper. While I couldn't and shouldn't have acknowledged his surprise, I was weak in concentration while in this classroom environment and eventually flashed him a smile. The break in concentration was enough to stop the works from developing, and the edge of the paper sheet noticeably dropped back to the surface.

Concurrent with my diverted attention to my friend's reaction, the recess hour ended, and the lessons were to begin. Our topic that day was astronomy. We were taught astronomy in the first grade. It was just a smidge of astronomy. Even first graders need to know about the stars and planets above. As presented, it was all in God's glory, as this was a parochial school and the heavens were His creation. There may have been stars and planets above us; I hadn't really noticed. *I may one day really see them,* I thought. As it was, I lived in the city and wasn't allowed out at night. Were I to be out on any nighttime sanctioned occasion, I would have noted that the light in the city obscured any true sign of the stars. And if I were out at night and it was sanctioned, then I would likely be herded about under tight instructions to not get lost or placed into jeopardy. "Stay close, dammit." The close management of my movement would take my mind from the stars for sure. It was likely the same for all other first graders at St. Paul the Apostle. We learned about the stars and planets on this day in class.

This lesson, then, was the only real way for us to learn of God's glory in the heavens. Mastering the subject matter set us up for the coming required Catechism classes that fill every other period of the second grade. Sister, in her habit, would teach us about the cosmos today, and Father, with the collar, would teach us catechism next year.

Perhaps I was flushed from my interaction with my desk mate and having personally risen to the levitating vibrational rate. I felt empowered by Sister's topic, the cosmos. Sister didn't teach me the astrological characteristics, personalities, or legends of the planets that day. Sister stuck to the physical basics regarding relative size to Earth and the sun, the number of moons, and the general climate environments. Then she got to Pluto. Pluto was a planet in those days, still way out there and the last one in our solar system lineup. Pluto could never sustain life, she said. It was too far from the sun.

In all sincerity, I stood, wanting to ask a question. Our astronomy topic postulated the aspect of the other stars being suns like our sun. As Pluto is the farthest away from us and closest to the stars, was it not possible that Pluto was lighted and warmed by the other suns out there? The hypothesis was grounded in the fact that when we look up to see the stars, we note that the planets are visibly comparable to the stars in brightness. As I was unable to visually distinguish the difference between a star and a planet, they must be near each other. If they, the stars that are suns, are that close to Pluto, might they not serve as the planet's sun? No. No! No was the answer.

Initially, Sister's reaction to my question, a question I stood up to speak as opposed to sitting at my desk, was not measured but delivered with a full load of impatience. I was interrupting the class, diverting her from delivering the lesson. But I was persistent. I wanted to know. After all, hadn't I just taught my desk mate how to raise a sheet of paper off the desk with his mind? I never said that. I never mentioned that to Sister. I would likely get my knuckles rapped with a ruler. But I was flush with the aspect and activity of being the teacher of interesting topics to another person. All sincerity resided in my hypothesis and my explanation, and after the initial reaction and record, Sister brightened. She took a step back. She breathed a deep breath and answered with even tones, pleasant body language, and precise information. She explained that although I see the lights of the planets and many separated stars appearing as if on one canvas, the two are many, *many* miles apart from each other.

I remember this day as the day my purpose was revealed and, for that day, fulfilled. True to the aspect and execution of my purpose, I was to learn in later years, the lessons I teach, the questions I ask, and the observations I conclude are typically met with shock and consternation, leading to disavowal and discrediting. My purpose, therefore, was to think and expostulate. Only to have my words and ideas met with rejection. The rejection forged my purpose.

Sister gave me a taste of what was to come. Many are the times I recoil and retreat as the objections and obstructions I encounter take their toll. Yet it forced me to know my mind and my visions. I have since grown tired and keep my observations, gifts, and questions to my own counsel. Much that comes at me in this physical, social, and political world of man distracts and overpowers me. Often, it is painful to experience, bringing impactful emotions that weigh heavily upon me. I am inhibited by the social interaction associated with discourse on the topics of my gifts and my being different. The predictable results: I cannot bear my heart, soul, and mind to others. I cannot speak with others of my visions and dialogue with the heavenly host and hierarchy. My words never seem to be accepted for what they are, from someone seeing things differently. While I require neither a following nor agreements in principle or practice for what tidbits I bring to the conversation, I found it best to simply keep my mouth shut. Regardless of the acceptance or lack thereof, I desire only to question, converse, observe, and share with others when invited.

Death and Taxes

I am different because I was such from my very beginning. The manner in which I was treated throughout childhood reinforced the introverted activities and mindset that I would maintain throughout my history. I never knew why I was in that family, school, or social circle. Why should I be experiencing cosmic boredom while slowly plummeting into an angry, simmering quicksand? Why? Because that's the way it is, and it was all that I knew.

I played alone much of the time till I was in the eighth grade. I noticed girls in the eighth grade and started looking for my piece of the popularity mystique.

Popularity was relative. I never got the hang of it. I became not the butt of jokes but not one of the "together" kids or leaders of the social circles. It was to follow that this was my place in the normal social life of the material world about me. My role was to be there, sitting, yet participating in an offhanded, 50 percent fashion, with an afterthought presence. It was the social norm that I fell into, and it was reinforced by the familiar cultural norm I grew up with at home. I traversed my childhood as no one's priority, who played well when left on my own.

I was not taught or mentored in the ways of the world or the habits congruent with creation and intention. Children of this era, in many instances, were literally left in front of the TV set, an innovation, to occupy themselves. TV left an indelible impact. My foundational ideals, values, and role definitions were determined by the movies I watched on TV. *Lost Continent of Atlantis, Great Expectations,* and *North by Northwest* all held some foundational pieces of my character's puzzle. Sadly, away from TV, I cannot recall one person who had a lasting influence on me stemming from my childhood years. Growing up, I had no choice but to develop my own personality and character and to fill my considerable need for content in these areas. I recognized neither limits nor norms that I had to observe. I had a mind that could levitate paper. I would release my imagination and see where it took me.

Different. It's not like I had a choice. I am grateful for the opportunities I had to choose and be tested. I am happy with my efforts and with the results my efforts have produced. In the beginning, I was young and did not know my own mind. And at times, I was likely out of my mind. While in my younger days, popularity and social interaction were important at a limbic level, today I welcome those who wish to interact, knowing that they expect nothing from me and will accept me for who I am. I am lucky in that regard. My mind now knows neither bounds nor restrictions, limitations passed on by cultural norms, or religious dogma. The world, though cruel it may be to those born different, provides opportunities that chisel out the rough edges from granite dispositions, producing works of art and wonder. Oh, happy I am that I was different.

My First Out-of-Body Memory

Squirming in bed and looking up, I see the heads in a circle above me. The light from the ceiling punctuated the free space between their heads and alternately blinded me from the brightness while casting shadows upon their faces, making their identities indistinguishable. They were a coven of witches cackling around a cauldron, stirring up some sort of trouble. However, there was no cauldron on this occasion, and they were no witches; they were my maternal family members. I was the center of their attention as I lay squirming and screaming on the bed that took the space a dining table once occupied.

I couldn't understand what the entire hubbub was about that evening as I lay there. Leave me on my own, and all would be quiet and peaceful, for I had the comfortable warmth and glow of a high fever. That is what brought me such attention and ministrations from those surrounding me. Their cackling continued as they were preparing some pleasant surprise that night. I was the object of attention and the one to be surprised.

No one understood the cause or the why of it, but here I was at four years of age with a fever that topped 105 degrees Fahrenheit. The understanding was that my body would burn up if the fever did not abate. The potion the witches were stirring was a tub of cold water. But the water was not cold enough. "Get some ice from the icebox," I heard someone say. "There's not enough ice to make it cold enough. Go! Run over to your aunt's and get all her ice," someone was commanding another in the circle. I lay there squirming, confused and concerned about the potential outcome of all this chatter and upheaval.

After some amount of noise and clambering, the potion was ready. Lifting me up in a swaddling cloth, I was suspended over this washbasin tub that was placed on a makeshift table in the bedroom I shared with my mother. The bedroom that until recently was my grandparents' dining room.

Amid all the activity, my grandfather would travel between the kitchen and the living room, the room hosting our large, black-and-white console TV. "Can you keep it down in there? I'm trying to watch my show!" They would be done with their work soon enough.

At the drop of a hat, off came my swaddling clothes and down into the tub I was lowered. Needing to break the fever or my system shutting down may become inevitable, the family called upon their traditional training in the healing arts from the old country. Back in the day, healing traditions were handed down from grandmother to granddaughter. My great-aunt was the recipient of that training. Where or when this tradition originated is beyond me. For how long it was in effect, no one knows. The assumptions are that between AD 500 and 1200, the Christian movement obliterated the Celtic traditions of the European countries and regions. If the movement to Christianity was not enough, the coming of the Roman popes, with their armies bringing reform to the heathen, would ensure that any practitioners of the traditional healing arts were eradicated as a scourge. Somehow, my ancestors maintained their traditions and arts and passed them down in secrecy from grandparent to grandchild. And here, in 1950s America, was the enactment of a longtime response to high fevers. That response was to place the child in a cold bath until the fever broke. My ancestors never had the benefit of a Westinghouse refrigerator. They would typically place the child in a cold mountain spring. Here in the 1950s, they placed the baby in a tub filled with cold water and ice.

I can't say that I have a clear memory of all the events that day. Being immersed in freezing water brings much to the mind in a very short amount of time. It separated me from my skin and took my mind to a place that is not rooted in current events or the concrete physical representation of the world. The initial shock blended away to a peaceful and quiet place. While there was much going on about me—much activity, shouting, handwringing, and that ever-present murmuring of a lone great-aunt in the corner doing what I would come to understand as "the Eyes"—I was in calm waters where the world and all its trappings faded away. Floating, looking down on the scene, I remember judging the medical practice with a knowledgeable eye and remarking how well my great-aunt remembered her grandmother's lessons. This technique would heal the body, and I knew that it was in this body below me that I was to continue residing for the time being.

Eventually, the out-of-body bliss would end as they pulled me from the ice tub. No one knew how long I was to stay immersed, so the immersion was likely longer than needed. That requirement was never passed down in the teachings. I enjoyed the experience I had with the immersion into the icy waters. I ceased my crying and lay still and quiet. This brought about the oohs and ahs of those around me working the spell. My crying started as soon as I was pulled out of the tub. Screaming, I was later told. Screaming intolerably. Could it have been a second birthing for me? At the time, I was too distracted to think of the particulars. My screaming set off a chain reaction as the witches around me started to debate the instructions of my ancestors and the method applied: the water was too cold; I would come to harm and be damaged for life. For me the experience of pulling me from the frigid water was a traumatic ripping me from the world I had temporarily resided within to be met face-to-face with the protestations, consternations of grandmother, great-aunts, aunts, and now a grandfather who left the living room in disgust and protest as he was not able to hear his show with all this screaming and general volume of complaints going on. He, in his wisdom, decided to go hang out with his friends on the corner.

Whatever the roots or the object lesson from the old traditions, the ice bath worked. My temperature immediately lowered to a manageable level. Eventually that sickness would pass, eventually to be replaced by another, but not before the prayers of thanks to God and to our ancestors who once again provided us with the skills to combat the unknown and to reign, again, over Western medicine and those quack doctors. Especially, my mother would say, that quack Dr. Monetti. He, it was felt, was the one who started all the sickness that I would experience throughout my life by the very act of giving me a tetanus shot when I was a wee lad, less than one.

This all occurred in my new home. My grandparents owned the first floor of a medium-sized duplex. Having only two bedrooms on this first floor that were already occupied, one by my grandparents and the other by my aunt, who was yet to marry, the dining room remained available. When my parents separated, my mother moved in with her parents. The dining room sat between the kitchen and the living room. Out went the china closet, dining table, and chairs, and in went the queen-size bed, dressing table, vanity, and chest of drawers that my mother listed as her last possessions. This was where I was to reside for several years, at the time, as I processed being a new child of divorce.

The sickness of the moment passed, and I advanced another year in age. I was eventually allowed out of the house to play with my new friends and neighbors.

The house we lived in sat on a city street with a steep hill that terminated at the freshly commissioned Garden State Parkway. During my fifth year, I was playing with my neighborhood friends under the cherry tree in the vacant lot four houses down the hill. Someone's mother called. My friends left me so they could get home right this instant. I was alone, but not completely. With me were four of my large trucks and earthmovers. My friends left me alone with all of my trucks that they originally helped me carry down to the vacant lot. I had to get home, but I had a dilemma. I had to get my trucks home with me.

As I could not bear to have any of them leave my sight, I managed to ferry them one at a time to a series of waypoints. Each waypoint was within line of sight of the previous one. Carrying one at a time, I stockpiled the four work trucks at a waypoint, and then one at a time, I would advance to the next point. After five such waypoints, I was able to arrive at home on the front porch together at once with my vehicles at my feet. And none of them left my sight for an instance as I had been instructed by my grandmother.

That night, I slept restlessly. The stress of the predicament and the efforts I expended taxed my five-year-old body and mind. Up to that point in my life, there weren't many problems hitting me up where Grandma wasn't there, on point and handling it as needed. I would just go with the flow. This time, however, I was presented with a complex set of priorities and requirements. Face it: the concepts of priority and requirements were a first for this five-year-old. In all, I found the experience to be one of growth that required some out-of-the-box thinking. For that one afternoon, the bar was raised for me, and I triumphed.

Eventually, sleep was to find me. Perhaps it was my fitfulness that brought on a series of dreams, but considering the day's efforts and stresses, my dreams were lucid and clear, and I remember them still to this day. I dreamed I was at the cherry tree in the vacant lot. Looking down from above the tree, I assumed I had climbed the tree into the branches. How else could I be looking downward from above? I saw my trucks and earthmovers drawn in a pile waiting for the trip home, where I wanted to be at that moment. And the very next instance, I was on the porch of my house, standing at the front door with my trucks and earthmovers at my feet. There was no discernable transit of me and my cargo from one place to the other. I thought of being home with the trucks, and there we were, the very next instant.

Even though this was a dream, I knew of the physical requirement that to move things from one place to another, I must pick them up and carry them; one doesn't skip from one place to another without first carrying the stuff. I thought it odd that we all were standing at my front door, and I did not accept that these trucks were really mine. In this instance of this dream, I did not carry these things here; they and I just appeared here at the front door with a mere thought. I decided to retrace my steps, thinking that I left my real trucks at the tree and that these and such at my feet were not really mine.

In my dream, I walked down the steps from the porch and got to the sidewalk. I turned and started down the hill to return to the cherry tree. I took the first step forward and, quite naturally, lifted myself up while spreading my arms and took to the air. Looking at myself, shocked and awed like any five-year-old would be knowing that he can now fly, I noticed that I looked just like Rocky the Flying Squirrel, a character from a favorite TV cartoon show. My legs and arms were spread wide-open and webbed like ducks' feet, and my body was paper-thin as I floated down the hill high enough off the ground to look directly into our neighbor's second-story window. I arched in flight while carried on a current that was not wind and alighted right next to the cherry tree in the vacant lot.

To my chagrin, I noted that the trucks and earthmovers were not there at the foot of the cherry tree. I then surmised that the ones on my porch were truly mine and that they really did arrive with me at the front door, propelled by the spontaneous thought that I had at the time: to be home at the front door with my trucks and earthmovers at my feet.

Then Came the Visions

The neighborhood I was living in was multi-ethnic. There were several nationalities abundant in the neighborhood. They all were quite distinct in their own way. Although all the residents looked pretty much alike, European.

Since, in most cases, their parents or grandparents emigrated from their native lands, the people who made up my childhood maintained their roots. These roots stretched back decades and centuries. Lore, skills, and gifts handed down from parent to child and grandparent to grandchild.

I was a part of that diverse community and of Italian descent. I attended Catholic school and hung around with the neighborhood kids. We had Protestant neighbors who didn't go to the Catholic school. Going into their houses was always a time of discovery. I never got too emotionally attached to the Protestants. Perhaps it was because they weren't Italian and watched different TV than we watched.

Irish, Polish, Ukrainian, Hebrew, and Italian were the major nationalities represented by some very fine, hardworking, and honest individuals. And our looks, mannerisms and personas were much like any stereotype imagined, the true stamp of our roots. Roots that, again, were planted in centuries-old traditions.

One day, while attending that Catholic school, two classmates and I stole away and went snooping about the school building. The school was a two-story building. The church was in the middle of the first floor, with classrooms on either side of it and above it.

We three were reaching or had just entered the age of reason; we were seven years old. Or at least I would be in a few days. At the age of reason, we receive our first Holy Communion. We just started our religious instruction on the topic. The priest would come into the class and give us an hour of his time to deliver that instruction. We were all to be taking our first Communion in a matter of two weeks.

As my classmates and I were horsing around in the hall, we passed the doors of the church and found one open halfway. I had been in a church before. My aunt would bring me with her.

But I had never been in a church that was empty before. And one where we could walk wherever we wanted.

What's a group of seven-year-olds to do but enter? And we did, separating into different groups, with them in one and me in the other. I walked down the right-hand aisle. The others went elsewhere. As I walked down the aisle, I focused on the altar, changing course accordingly to reach my destination.

I met up with one of my mates at the center, right before you open this low gate and walk into the altar area. Just last week, the priest came and taught us about the altar. But the aspect that interested me was the structural and physical details of the layout, including the layout and the purpose of each accoutrement placed where it had to be according to ritual.

We looked over and affixed on this little structure that holds the chalice. "That's where they keep the body and blood of Christ. The hosts are stored there till they're needed, that and the chalice," my friend informed me.

The box was located on the left side of the altar. We were still some paces distant from it. I replied to his marking of the host's location, "Yeah. And they have a painting of Christ in front of it."

At the very moment I blurted out my observation, we heard a door close hard and footsteps coming. We stared at each other, mouths wide open, and turned tail to run. I don't remember whether we got caught or not. And if we did, it would not have turned out badly because it would have been the young priest who would have caught us. And he was cool.

That afternoon in class, the other priest, the older one, came to give us instructions. We talked about the procession we'd exercise when we were in the church in two weeks' time, receiving our first Holy Communion. After he finished giving us the processional route and timing, he started again giving us the details and design of the altar. Along with his instructions, he covered the hosts and chalice. As he told of the ruby-red silk covering, I got the bug in me to be the center of attention and help him along with the details. I did, after all, get a private showing of the altar and toured till my heart's content. Or at least till the young priest came in. And I did see the painting of Christ that was apparently brand new, having been just placed there the moment before I saw it. For what I saw could later be described as watercolor silkscreen on a transparency. The skin tone coloring of the silk screen did not match other depictions of Christ that I had encountered in books and pictures displayed in the church proper. Yet I was sure of whom the individual's image represented. Something about it rang true, and I was sure my identification was accurate.

"In front of the ruby-red silk cover, that's where they have the painting of Christ. Don't they, Father?" I said out of turn.

"They have no painting of Jesus on the altar."

"But Father, I was in the church in front of the altar, and I saw a painting of His face in front of where the hosts are kept."

"There is no painting of Christ on the altar."

"But Father, it was right there in front of me and—"

"Quiet! Sit and be still!"

There was no more talking about altar design. He probably told the principal that I interrupted him and that I had been in the church. I likely got in trouble.

The next day, I was home with my great-aunt. We all lived in the big duplex, all nine or ten of us. On the first floor were my grandparents, my aunt, who was their daughter, my mother, and me. The second-floor apartment had my great-grandfather, who was from Italy. He was Etruscan from Tuscany, or so I was told. With him were my two great-aunts. The third floor was like an upgraded attic with a large, single bedroom and sitting area. My uncles lived on the third floor.

That day, I was feeling a little under the weather. Not sick but low energy and feeling heavy-headed. My malaise may have had something to do with the abrupt rejection of my vision the previous day in school. My great-aunt Rose was the one to always fix me up. I called for my great-aunt Rose. Rose was born in the United States, but her mother and grandmother were born in the old country and immigrated to America together. Great-Aunt Rose would do the Eyes for me.

Great-Aunt Rose learned the Eyes from her grandmother. Her grandmother learned the Eyes from her grandmother. And so it stretched back in time for some hundreds of years. We never really knew how far back the gifts from Aunt Rose's grandmother originated.

Aunt Rose would sit next to me on the couch. She would tell me to close my eyes. Then she would close her eyes and whisper prayers or healing statements. I never could understand the words, but they had a healing ring. She would move her hand up and down my body, seven or ten inches from it. Palm open. She would then touch my crown and then forehead with her right hand. All the while with her eyes closed and whispering her prayers. Then she'd do a small sign of the cross on my throat and then my chest. She'd open her palm again and hold it over that achy spot right in the middle of the chest. And lastly, she'd hold her palm about one foot over my belly button and somewhere below that I could not see.

Stopping, she'd sit up straight and give a real good exhale before she opened her eyes.

Now, what really was Great-Aunt Rose doing? And what are the Eyes as taught by a Tuscan great-great-grandmother who traced the skill back to her great-great-grandmother and beyond?

Later in life and after much study, I was to discover that it was a healing of my core and spirit that Great-Aunt Rose gave me. Opening and clearing my energy centers all the while whispering loving, healing words, and calling the angels, saints, and the Holy Trinity itself to come and render me assistance. And it worked. It always worked on me. I'd be up and feeling good in just a short while. To make sure the healing would stick, she always required me to sit or lie still for a little while longer and yawn.

The skills that Great-Aunt Rose learned during her childhood are those very same skills taught by many spiritual healers today. How would a nice, respectable, churchgoing, Italian, Roman Catholic bookkeeper know about clearing chakras and calling loving and healing energy from the Celestial? Some things never change. Western medicine can rebuke the healing arts that worked for centuries, but natural laws will always show through and work magic on a sensitive soul.

My Living Reality

There is a star on my body. The star is located on the inside of my left elbow. It is not a novelty. Not a mark of the heavenly or the beastly. The star is a scar, a remnant of a surgical procedure that was long ago cut into that section of my body when I was just a baby. The story of the star was not one that I came to know easily. There were abject lessons that had to first come to light before I would learn the secret of the star.

The entire sixth grade of St. Paul the Apostle lined up one day to get shots. They were free and provided by the school that I was attending. I was deathly afraid of needles, but I remember no nervousness on this one occasion. There was no way I was going to show any fear or worry with this shot. The entire sixth grade was lining up in the hallway. The queue started at the nurse's door and wound down to the principal's door. All the kids were there. And all the kids were aware of what was coming. I didn't learn the type of shot it was to be, only that it was something we had to have. I didn't know of the negotiations or the notes home to parents. Just as well that I didn't, as I was deathly afraid of needles. My guardians and those adults who cared for me likely knew not to tell me about the nurse's office visit that I would be making in school the next day. "Better to let him not worry. He can learn about it when they take him and the class to the nurse's office to get the shot." They thought they were doing me a favor, and they likely were.

Death and Taxes

There was a spattering of nervous stammers, a twitch here or there. Every now and then, someone would walk out of the office, being guided by one of the more compassionate nuns. One girl was crying intently. Passing the line, she got some notice, and the nervous stammering increased. Still, all were showing a brave front and taking care not to break down in front of their peers. A few would even boast that they *weren't afraid of no needles.*

Got the shot and showed no fear. All was well, and for whatever reason, I satisfied the requirement.

That night, I started to feel out of sorts. My arm, where I received the shot, was swollen. That was nothing new. The arm was expected to swell up a little when given a tetanus shot. It was a tetanus shot that I got, I learned. I had no idea what a tetanus shot was, only that it prevents lockjaw. I had no idea what lockjaw was either. Once your arm is swollen, you simply work it off by moving the arm about like a chicken. To help it along, my uncles would punch me in the arm. That would break the bubble or move the tetanus medicine out of the arm faster. It also hurt like hell getting punched in the arm.

Awaking in the morning, I found that my arm was still swollen. But in addition to the arm, the swelling traveled into my chest and down to my wrist. After closer inspection, my entire left side above my waist and below my neck was swollen like a balloon. The doctor was called. This was Dr. Silverstein. Dr. Silverstein was a good Jewish doctor. Not like that pig Monetti, who ruined my health so long ago when I was just a little baby. Or so my mother would chant.

After several such questions were passed between Dr. Silverstein and my mother, it was determined that I was having an allergic reaction to the tetanus shot—just like what happened when I was a little, little baby. Dr. Monetti gave me a tetanus shot back then. That time, the shot was in my hip. That time, my entire body swelled up, and I received my star, I was to finally learn.

The star was a cut-down. When my body was swollen, they found it necessary to give me fluids to hydrate me, as the fever was quite high and they were worrying about burnout. I am sure they tried several times to find a good vein. Having no luck, they cut down the skin on my inner elbow, sighted a vein, and started an IV. It's not a mysterious mark after all. It was simply a marvel of medicine.

"I got a tetanus shot when I was a baby, and swelled up all over?" I asked my mother.

"Yes. It was a very trying time for me. We were all nervous and worried for you. You were very sick."

"Dr. Monetti gave me that shot?" I asked.

"Yes," my mother said. "We thought it was the reaction from dirt, as he was always picking his nose and wiping it on his pants. But it wasn't from dirt. It was from the tetanus shot. You were allergic."

"Well, I got a tetanus shot yesterday and I'm all swelled up and feeling like I have a bad fever now."

"Yes. You must still be allergic."

"Why did you let them give me a tetanus shot if you knew I was allergic to them?"

"I thought you grew out of it. And besides, they said you had to have one and it was while you were in school, so I would not have to take you to the doctor's office, and it was free."

I was later to learn that I was truly allergic to tetanus toxoid after being given an allergy test by a Navy medic. He asked me if I was allergic to any drugs. I said that I was likely allergic to tetanus shots. They tested me and, as sure as you know it, the test sight expanded. It was a textbook case of an allergic reaction.

I've never had a tetanus shot since the sixth grade.

Angelic Intervention Begins

I wanted to be popular in the seventh grade. I didn't know why it was important, but it was something I wanted to do.

There was a difference between me and the popular pillars of the seventh grade. I felt it was time for me to integrate. This was school, and the students hailed from different neighborhoods. I was safe in the bosom of my circle of earlier childhood friends who all lived on the same block as me, but my friends were not in my class. School was the big apple, and things were different at school than in the neighborhood. I felt it would be beneficial for me to become more worldly-wise by extending my circle of friends into the classroom.

Having lifted above some ceiling in the social aspects of life as I integrated into this new circle, I wanted to be accepted by the here-and-now movers and shakers of our school's seventh-grade society. I realized now that at the time; I was emerging from the shell of my early childhood perspective. These classmates were here, concrete and in your face, up to date and ranging from far and wide, and I saw them every day. I sought the perspective of this diverse group. They were in my life, and I had to be a part of it. So, I extended myself thus.

Being new to the practice of being in society, I casted about for a friend with whom I could hang out and mirror, if need be, to better understand the customs and mannerisms of the local popular here-and-now folk. The fates brought me Eddie.

The region I lived in at the time, urban Newark, New Jersey, in the early sixties, had a certain attitude that Eddie consumed and exuded. He was quite good at it, too. You couldn't really call it meanness because it was simply the way people interacted on a personal level at that time and place. You could call it something on the order of meanness, perhaps, at face value, but it was life as I knew it at the time. It was the hallmark and essence, and attitude of my local civilization.

There were many pranks that were played on me by the seventh-grade society, usually at my expense. It was to be expected. For me, being the newly emerging popular guy who came up from the fake-sword player cast and crew, this was to be my initiation. However, I was to learn, as everyone's behavior remained steadfast and quite natural, my relegated role in the local society was to remain in this initiation phase. I was to be the focal point of everyone's typical and accepted East Coast, Newark's, interactive attitude. Eddie perfected the operationalization of this attitude. With Eddie, and I must admit with mostly all the other people I interacted with of this culture, both family and friends, there appeared to be a certain personal satisfaction and relish when the punch line landed, and I was coughing up the cost.

One day, I was visiting Eddie's house. We were hanging out. There was something really, *really* neat that he wanted to show me in the basement. I'd really enjoy seeing this, and then I'd want to do it also. That's how neat it was. All right, I figured, may as well see what's so great to see. So into the basement we strode with Eddie enthusiastically leading and me close behind as we noisily descended the old wooden steps into the basement.

Eddie's parents' house, like every other house in the neighborhood, was coal heated. Built in the early part of the century, they all had coal bins that held the coal to fuel the furnace that provided the steam for heating the radiators. You've probably seen some of these old furnaces in the basement with their expanding networks of ducting. From the furnace emerge these giant, long octopus tentacles. It could be scary looking if you were young and impressionable and had never seen one before.

The furnace had a firebox. Now we're not talking just a little pilot light to light the gas from time to time. We're talking a pile of coal on fire sitting inside this iron box behind this iron door that you would open to expose the fire and pile more coal into it to keep the house warm. I'm telling you I was nervous, but not about the fire and the firebox. At my house, like Eddie's parents' house, we had the same type of furnace, but a newer model, circa 1940. At my house, the only ones who were allowed around the firebox were my great-aunt Annie or my grandfather. Kids were to keep away. That's what got me nervous. There had to be a similar rule in effect here because we all knew that kids were to stay away from the firebox. But here I was taking another step into the "this is what popular kids do" world. I decided to go with the flow.

Where there is coal, there is coal oil. Not that I knew what coal oil was, having never been allowed to go near or to tend the firebox. But evidently there was such a thing. "Come here and take a look at this."

"What?"

"This. Come closer and look at this. It's really, *really* neat."

At that, Eddie opened the heavy, iron door of the firebox. And there were the glowing red-hot coals and the wisps of fire and sparks that powered the boiler to make the steam to warm the house.

"All right. It's the firebox. And there's the fire. So?"

"No. Keep looking at it. Look into it."

"I am, and it's just a fire."

Am I supposed to investigate the element and life of the fire? I wondered. *Am I supposed to bring the fire into myself and become one with it to some extent? Did Eddie know all about that level of familiarity I had with elements? What? What am I supposed to do with this fire that I am staring at while I inch my head closer and closer to the opening of the firebox?*

From the corner of my eye, I see Eddie take up an old, used tin soup can. I glance at it and then at Eddie. He glances back at me, half smiling while keeping his focus and attention on the can and contents. A liquid.

Eddie tosses the contents of the can into the firebox.

Yellow. All around me was yellow. I initially had my eyes open to see the effect of what Eddie was hyping as "really, *really* neat." Yellow. I don't know what prompted me to close my eyes, but I eventually did. I didn't really feel the need to close my eyes because I did not in the least feel threatened. I was going to see something really, *really* neat. My eyes closed automatically. I believe I closed my eyes in recognition of the intense color that was about me, enveloping me. But it was the sound that first caught my attention. Whoosh!

Thinking back, it was the sound that first came to me, a low, emerging expansion of an initial "booh." The "booh" turned into a "whaaah." The "whaaah" brought the expanding orb of bright, intense, celestial, yellow light immediately toward me. As it filled my field of vision and flew past my periphery, it became time to close my eyes. And so I did.

Then the sound ended. It just went away. Coolness. The sensation on my skin was a dry coolness. The basement was damp and not very warm. Yet this coolness was dry and calm, much different from the mustiness of the old basement. I was now relaxingly invigorated and felt much different from the environment of that basement and of every other environment and atmosphere I could ever before remember experiencing. When the time was right, I would open my eyes. I didn't give it another thought.

I opened my eyes. Eddie was to the right of me. I turned to him. A shrug of my shoulders and a "What?" What was it that was so neat he couldn't wait to get me down here? I felt inconvenienced. Eddie was not initially glancing over at me directly, yet in the next flash of an instant, he would stare over at me with his mouth wide open and slowly, or relatively so, bringing his hands up to his face. He looked rather odd and contradictory for someone who was to have just seen something that was really, *really* neat. As he brought his hands up to his face, he was nervously turning his head from left to right. In quick jerking motions, he looked left and right and up to the ceiling and down. Then back to me.

After he made a quick survey of the perimeter and area where we were standing, he flung out his arms and, racing to me, embraced me in a shaking, or shivering, bear hug. A quick bear hug. Eddie was doing everything very quickly at that time for some reason. He released the grip of his shivering, quick bear hug and grabbed my shoulders, pinning me back at arm's length. He had the oddest look on his face. Whatever it was that spurred it was a mystery to me, but he had quite the look of surprise on his face. He almost looked as though he was surprised to see me or that I was a long-lost cousin newly found.

Gripping me, he stepped back and began to quickly survey my entire body and the clothes I was wearing while using that same quirky, jerky head movements he used when I saw him upon first opening my eyes. He was also biting or chewing on his lips.

Evidently, he was satisfied with what he saw as he finally, for the first time since I opened my eyes, shifted his attention and sight to something that was not me. He looked up above me and to the side of me, where the furnace stood. I followed his eye movement as he looked up and over. Then I saw it too. The beam of the floor directly above the firebox opening was on fire. Not badly on fire, but there was definitely a flame that had better be extinguished right now. I continued to follow Eddie's lead and focus of attention. My attention moved to a point behind me where a wall stood. There were points of flame loosely scattered from an area that was equal in height from my waist to the ceiling. Not an immediate concern. The floor beam above the firebox was more of a priority at this point, I thought. Eddie brought his attention to the ceiling immediately above and behind me, and again, there were small specks of flame. Not too much to worry about at this time because they were scattered like the flame on the wall, but the floor beam above the firebox was definitely the more important flame, and, gee, did it grow since I last glanced at it.

With a spontaneous thrust, we realized "sink" and grabbed the nearest anything to fill with water. With water splashes and his mother's freshly laundered towels, we beat down the flames and averted any real imprint of our neat experience. Several of the beams looked worse from the wear, but why would anyone notice?

Now was as good a time as any for me to mooch a glass of grape juice from Eddie and his mother. Up we went to the kitchen, and after a hearty glass of Welch's Grape Juice, it was off to the bathroom I went. Passing the mirror, I took the opportunity to arrange my wavy hair, ensuring I was complying with the grooming standards of the popular seventh-grade society. Good. Not a hair out of place. Eyebrows fluffed. Eyelashes were as long and as wavy as usual. Wavy hair was a boon and a blessing at the same time. How I wish I had straight hair so I could comb it straight back with Vitalis like all the other guys. Looking good.

Business done, it was time I started my walk home. "Be home by five" was the instruction. With nothing really being neat enough for me to risk going over the time restriction, I conveniently bid my leave to Eddie's mother. "Yes, Mrs.

Huston. I enjoyed myself very much. Thanks for letting me hang around with Eddie."

"Come back any time."

"Yes. Thank you. See ya', Eddie."

Eddie tossed the coal oil contents of the old, tin can into the firebox as I was peering into the opened door to get a better look at what was so neat about the coal fire in the firebox. As Eddie flung the contents and stepped back to see the effects of his prank, he observed a fireball emerge from the firebox, enveloping me from the waist up to the ceiling above me and to the wall behind me. The lateral extent of the fireball scorched the adjacent wall that was just beyond arm's length from me and to my left, opposite Eddie and his empty tin can of coal oil.

Typically, when a person is enveloped in a fireball, their first reaction is to quickly inhale in surprise and terror. Inhaling the fire into the body incinerates the lungs. Without functioning lungs, suffocation occurs. This did not happen with me at this time. Rather than becoming enveloped in a fireball and suffering the consequences, I was protected by a bubble that fit loosely around my skin. Instead of feeling the heat of the fire, I felt calm, serene, and quiet. It was quite peaceful, actually. The bubble covering did not just protect me from the ignited coal oil but brought me into what seemed like another existence. Maybe even another dimension. But let's not call it a bubble. Let's call it what I was to discover decades later: the layer of protection was provided by an angel's wing.

What is the feeling one gets when held in the loving arms of a loving mother: comfort and warmth? The child so held will experience and register physical sensations, such as comfort and warmth, yes? There is more to the experience, however. The child cradled in Mother's loving attention receives the subliminal impulse of security and stability that all is right with the world, and they are home safe. Feeling at home, safe in the right world, has nothing to do with the physical sensations as much as it speaks to the very core of our needs. Satisfying our needs for safety and security elicits from us a peace of mind that transcends all physical sensations and renders us into a higher dimension or vibrational level, if you want to call it as such. Why is the crying baby comforted and quieted when cuddled by a loving mother? And raising that question to the next relevant level, I ask, "How would one feel when wrapped within a loving angel's wing?"

That is how I felt when enveloped in a coal oil fueled fireball. It took me some time and experience to understand the dynamics of that early afternoon in the musty basement. And as I progressed in the world, I was to experience that feeling of security and safety, often to the point of immediate, real-time acknowledgment.

My First Girlfriend

As I have since come to understand the dynamic, life begins with the first breath of air. That is when the issuance becomes an independent, living being. It is on the first breath that soul and celestial components take residence; the first breath brings life and grounds the spirit, the spark of life. We are children of creation, and it is this first breath that establishes the celestial and physical relationship of the life in question.

These days, I tend to think of political issues, hot buttons certainly, in personal and individualistic terms. I tend to consider the direct effect and impact of the pros or cons upon myself, loved ones, and the individuals living in my community. I try to consider the emotional, spiritual, and physical attributes of the policies involved.

My first girlfriend was a sixteen-year-old girl living in our society and time. We didn't know where our innocent relationship would lead us. She didn't have the experience of a worldly-wise matron. We were both young and dumb, going out with each other for over a year. We loved each other. We loved that innocent, naive, sixteen-year-old kind of love. What we had was sincere and true. What did we know about anything? Parents and teachers of our culture never spoke of the physical aspects of love. People of our culture never spoke of love in any aspect.

I was a good kid. Her parents liked me. They felt I came from a good, common stock family. We didn't know what we were in for with this love thing. And we couldn't help but express ourselves physically as we taught ourselves that love and physicality could be a blessing and a vexing. Our love just evolved as we spent time together, alone, in our very adult-like relationship. We had no role models or mentors. We were on our own. I didn't know what I was intending or doing, and she welcomed my embrace, naturally, just as innocent and ignorant as I was. Our very first time in direct intimacy, after more than a year collected, we lay together.

She gave the issuance of that night's romance much thought. Her parents would support her in whatever she decided. They respected her and would respect her decision. They were saddened that their innocent child had to make such a grown-up decision so early in life. They had hoped to spare her from grown-up decisions of any kind this early on. They were bringing her up to the perspective slowly, wisely. They knew what they were doing, and they were doing it lovingly and respectfully. She was the one living her life, and every decision she made, from choosing breakfast to selecting a major, was her decision. And she, as a person, willingly and dutifully, takes responsibility for all her decisions and actions. The blessings and consequences are joyfully hers and acceptably so. They taught her that. They showed her how to walk the talk. And she was an apt student.

She had to live in this society, and she had yet to establish a life to call hers. In Polynesian society, two hundred or even one hundred years ago, living was different. Children were cared for by the community as the lifeblood of the future they were. There were people aplenty to care for the children and teach them the ways of society. Things were different there and then. This was here and now. She didn't ask for this society with its customs and norms established by others. This—early 1970s, small, New Jersey hamlet—is the society that others gave her upon her birth and childhood. She would think and figure this thing out with what she must work with.

She must survive, thrive, and create a life and family or community within this world, she observed. And within this life, she will obey the laws of the land she resides within. That's understood. Her commitment as an active and growing member of this community will be to live by our laws and do as the law allows.

She then made her decision. She's going to finish her childhood and transition out of the home when she is prepared and ready to take on the challenges of living in this society. She's going to attain an education and become learned in the ways of commerce, emotion, gratitude, and living in general. She will learn how to excel and approach the future with the power of education, parental love and support, and experience a healthy body and mind. Then afterward, she would have a family of her own.

Her requirements, establishing the criteria, led to her responsible decision.

Others will choose how they will. And well they might consider the impact of their decision. For this decision lay not lightly on her shoulders, as well as the many others of her caste, age, and circumstance at this crossroad in their lives. Yes. There are those who would abuse or take lightly the import of their decisions. There will always be those such as they. Throughout the course of time, known as far back as the pharaohs of Egypt and the citizens of Rome, there have always been those who have had choices such as hers and made decisions like hers. There have always been and there will always be. The decisions will be cherished for those who bear a child as well as for those who do not.

Those who must choose similarly do so with tender blessings. Their way is written within the law of the land. The law is out of necessity in recognition of how it is now and how it has always been for child bearers throughout time. And so, it is. The choice becomes law, enhancing the emotional, physical, and spiritual health of society.

Beliefs come and go. Cultures always pass. When healthy, they evolve as new truths are understood and new customs are integrated into the fabric of society. We'll never know what the truth of the matter is when it comes to life's beginning. Will we? So, what's left for us when we are met with an opposing viewpoint or opinion on the issue drawn from alternate beliefs long held by many? Actions resulting from decisions on this issue are personal. They are never taken lightly. They are made by other bright and shiny beings while all others stand aside and observe. We don't have to know the truth about when life begins to trust and respect the decider. It is the decider's life. It is the decider's decision. It is the burden and exaltation of the gender.

Wandering

Sickly and of ill health for many of my young years, I thought that was how it was always to be. Perhaps it was the environment. I infrequently go back to that region of the coastal country and see old friends, those who are still alive, at any rate. People age over there on that coast. Forty looks fifty, and sixty looks like seventy for those always residing there, but not with me. I don't reside there in that world anymore, not since I was twenty-one years old.

When living my own life for the first time with friends in Pennsylvania, I often traveled east to visit the family home and family. At times, I'd give a hitchhiker a ride along the way. This one ride I remembered provided much good conversation. This was the time of year when I was drawing my residence in Pennsylvania and the "farm" to a close. I was soon to travel out west and relocate to Oregon. My conversations were animated and usually about the attributes of living away from family and from the city. This one fellow had the year before left his family home and struck out to make it on his own, away from cities and corresponding contrary attitudes. For all intents and purposes, then, he was the mentor and I the mentee. The sage spoke one word of advice that entire trip. "Stay out of the cities." I followed the advice as well as I could for the next decade or less. Was the advice really about cities? Or were we speaking and communicating on a different level where innuendo and subtleties of symbols and juxtaposition are the true topics of conversation? Stay out of the cities. Or stay out of the mindset cultivated by living in a city, family, social circle, church, or community. While intended to be the bedrock of societal membership, the cultures of family, social circle, church, and community produce limitations that inhibit seeing light in a dark tunnel.

Following my interpretation of the sage's advice freed me from dogma and normal expectations. The lifestyle I then pursued sparked some spirit that I had simmering inside. The simmering poured forth into a lifestyle that produced renewing energy within me. The lifestyle and its energy were to stay with me forever. And this energy transmuted all my illness and the effects of sicknesses that came my way into health.

The effects of my spark of health energy continued throughout the convening years and through to the recent present. While in my senior years, attending a speakers association meeting, one of the members started coughing uncontrollably in the small kitchenette. I was concerned for her. She sounded like she was choking. "Are you all right now?" I asked when there was a break in the sputtering.

"Not going to be. I have a bad cold."

I wasn't happy to hear that. There was now the confirmed presence of germs in the small conference room we inhabited. Germs. They were lurking in wait for me to inhale and plant themselves in the warm moisture of my lungs.

As one would expect, three days later, at 5 p.m., I felt the symptoms of a cold. *It is going to be a miserable night,* I thought. It wasn't. The symptoms were mild, and by noon the following day, all trace of the cold was gone from my system.

Energy came and went from me throughout my life, and its intensity and impact produced varied effects and states upon my body and mind. Balance. Balance was the key to my health riddle. Balance is the key to many mysteries when working with energy.

Balance of energy always seemed like such an arbitrative and remedial concept. What should be the proper mix of energy for any of my given experiences? Surely, my mental and karmic states may influence the energy balance scales, altering the quantity and intensity in one direction or the other. Balance of my energy and mind bring about the balance of my health systems and my ability to ward off colds, ignore cancer contrary to every one of my living relatives and ancestors, and maintain a level of physical strength not seen by many in my age demographic, as exhibited in my typical ranch day work list. I am in balance now, today. I was not always able to maintain an acceptable level of energy and holistic balance. Like a formula concocted by a mad scientist, I had to experiment on the dosage levels. Experimentation takes time. It took me over four decades to learn the dosages. My failures were opportunities for success and provided valuable lessons.

Experimentation takes a toll, but once success arrives, if it ever arrives, life gets a degree more comfortable and to my liking.

Life wasn't always balanced. That was not through my intention but through my fault. Energy is a substantial part of life, and just as the body functionality is critical for running a well-oiled host, the manifestation of energy requires the foundation of a balanced and well-grounded life. I, the initiated neophyte, work energy over the course of a season or a year or more. Moving energy produces an effect upon every aspect of my life. Suddenly removing the energy for any reason produces a rebound effect. In many ways, manifesting and moving energy is like having a prescription of psychotropic drugs. While I have little significant experience in taking antidepressants or mood stabilizers, I have still experienced the effects of ceasing the occasional prescription and the rebound that can send me, the patient, into the depths of mental and emotional probabilities.

Commencing life on my terms, I initially selected to be that of a hippie and lived a ragtag life. Socializing, working in a factory, and being in the swing of things with all the other hippies and young adults of our era. The lifestyle practiced by my housemates and me was mellow.

I was living on a two-hundred-acre "farm" in Pennsylvania. Or at least it was a farm at one time. It had a main house, barn, pump house, and corral. Looking off the porch to the west and down the other end of a low field was the Conodoguinet Creek. To the east was a new development of suburban homes. Every few months, a new row and street would be added to the development, and the acreage belonging to the farm would decrease. The farm's days were numbered. But we didn't mind; the rent was super cheap. And it wasn't a permanent thing anyway.

Working the graveyard shift at a factory making grinding wheels, I would get off work at 8:00 in the morning. I could have joined my coworkers to meet at the local bar for a shot and a beer. Instead, I would go home and walk down to the creek and sit a while.

I would say to my housemates that I would go down to the creek to meditate, but I really didn't know what that meant. I heard of meditation paired with the word transcendental. But never engaging in the practice, reading about it, or knowing anyone who meditated regularly, I really didn't know what I was going to do once I got down to the creek to sit a while.

Reaching out over the creek was a tree. The tree, at one time, must have been pulled off the bank by a flood. Pulled but not quite uprooted, the tree lay parallel and four feet above the creek. There were sparse branches and leaves, but all in all, a perfect place to sit and relax. It had a perch to sit in. All was quiet except for the sounds of moving water. The creek was about thirty-five to fifty feet wide. Its velocity was a quick walking pace.

So I sat. My initial plan was to sit and relax while being attentive to my breathing. I didn't know whether to close my eyes or not. I wanted to think of nothing and empty my mind as much as possible. And as luck would have it, there's not too much in a twenty-one-year-old mind to clear out, so the task was all the easier. I eventually settled on keeping my eyes open. For this city-bred boy, there was much to see in the nature of the place.

What first caught my attention was a catfish skimming the bank for food. Slowly, swimming slightly against the current to travel slower than the creek, he was better positioned to eat what he could find on the bank. He had in his attendance a smaller and differently colored catfish. I never saw a catfish in real life. I was in a deeply relaxed state of mind as I studied him. The keener the interest I took in the catfish, the more I identified with it. My immediate sensations were those of mud and water slowly moving over my skin. I attained a level of awareness that was attuned to what was of interest on that muddy bank. My eyes were opened, looking intently at the catfish and seeing all that was around me, yet my awareness was attuned to the creek's movement, the bank, and the relaxed and meandering hunt for something to eat. Nibbling and rustling this mud on the banks of this creek would find that something. My mind took command of the pathway to sight, smell, touch, and texture. That pathway gave me the creek from the perspective of that catfish. For that is where I was.

Eventually, the water flow carried the catfish away and out of the radius of my attention. I continued with my relaxation and concentrated on my breathing. I still didn't know why I needed to concentrate on my breathing or exactly how I was supposed to be breathing, but I did anyway.

Birds would swoop down and glide low over the creek. The banks of the creek were treed. With the creek being wide enough to have clear air space, the local birds would swoop down and glide over the creek. Usually, buzzing in zigzagging clumps just above the surface of the water were insects of all types. The birds would come off their tree branches and swoop down with their beaks open, taking in the local fare. The birds caught my attention.

As I kept my attention on the swooping birds, I was caught with the sensation of air flowing over my skin and feeling light as a feather. Flight was the first word that came into my mind. My mind carried the image of looking down directly over the creek and the tree. Then, with one last swoop and a climb before my mind's eye returned me, I was again sitting here on a tree looking over to the other side of the creek.

Escaping deeper into my breathing and concentrating on every breath, I wondered what it would be like if I added sound to the breath. Around me, the scene had a tone. Not being a musician, I didn't know what note, key, or harmonic matched the environment. But exhaling, I matched the tone and the harmonic that I felt. In a short period, the tone I emitted was in complete harmony with the vibration coming from the life around me.

My breathing became more defined. I was most definitely aware of each inhale and exhale. I emitted my harmonics in the form of a humming, long, drawn-out note. My throat vibrated. The vibration continued affecting the rest of my body. First my throat, then my chest, the vibration spread to every part of my body. My head was vibrating, and my vision blurred in response to the sensation I had throughout my body. I was losing physical definition as the vibrations increased.

The trees about me, as well as those on the opposite bank, were also vibrating. I had an impulse to go over to the trees on the opposite bank and touch them. A part of me, I did not know which part, stood up and moved over to where this one tree was standing. As I looked about from my position on the opposite bank, everything around me was in this blur of vibration. The sound of the tone I was emitting was felt everywhere as I repeated the vibrational tone with every breath. And with every breath, the dynamic was reinforced.

All definition of the physical greenery around me blurred, obscured by what seemed to be a haze or fog that sapped the definition out of every edge till the whole scene blended into one living mass. It appeared that nothing about me had an edge to define the boundary of what it was and where it ended.

I reached out to touch the tree to feel whether it was there or not. Well, apparently it was not. Because what I thought was a tree's trunk was just more space I could occupy. And occupy the space I did by moving into the space that looked like a tree but was blurred as it vibrated to the frequency of the tone I was emitting.

And as I stepped forward, I stood in the space that was also occupied by the tree. Movement again was my first sensation. Not the movement of air over my skin or water flushing about me, but of something at a molecular level. I was met with the sensation of an unseen upward flow. Like a tide of water flowing through every cell in my body, upward it moved. Slowly upward to some point where it was warmer, lighter, and airy and filled with a swaying movement. And this, too, I felt as though I was a part of the movement as experienced by my muscles and nerves. In this world of edgeless blurred vibration and vision, I could not tell what part of the tree trunk was the tree and what part was me. Don't ask me how or why this was the case. It just was.

That evening, I dined with friends. It was a lighthearted evening. Much merriment, laughing, and pleasant conversation were had by all. I was in the company of good friends I knew for a length of time. We all cared for each other, and it was evident in our moods and deliberations.

Somehow, the conversation turned to guardian angels and guides, and I don't remember whether we were debating the existence of each or of their attributes, as they existed. As I looked up from my plate to my friend opposite me, I remember saying, "And your guide is a Southwestern Indian. He is a golden Indian. And he's standing right behind your left shoulder." I said it nonchalantly, off the cuff, and without thinking. That's how it came up in the conversation.

After my experiences at the tree and creek in the morning, I was up for anything—sight, sound, revelation—anything. I was no longer surprised at what I would see, nor would I ever be again. After a morning of flying with crows, swimming with fish, and standing in the middle of a tree trunk, my mind was conditioned for accepting whatever would flash before my eyes.

Death and Taxes

The golden Indian stood about five feet seven. He wore a buckskin vest. Or so the vest would have been buckskin. It was this vest that shimmered like it was gold. His trousers were blue and tan. Not blue and tan together, but either blue or tan. From time to time, the color would turn blue to tan and back with the same shimmering hue of his golden vest. His skin and all other attributes were crystal clear. My sight here was clearer than it had ever been. Not even the air between us obscured the sight I had of this guardian.

There were no shimmering lights about him. No halo or light rays radiating outward from him. He stood there as though he were a waiter waiting upon our need or nod. He was standing there as whole and present as either of us at the table, except that his clothes were shimmering, and I saw him clearer than I saw the others. I pointed to him as I was speaking. I looked down again at my plate, and when I lifted my head, I no longer saw him.

Later that evening, my friend came to me and asked a bit more about what it was I saw. He didn't ask me any detailed questions at the time we were dining because the conversation was of a jovial nature. It was later, when we were quietly sitting around the house that evening, that he came to me with questions.

I gave him a detailed description of the guide. I knew this Southwestern Indian as a guide. There were no indications he was a guide of sorts; it just seemed natural that he was and appeared right at the point in the conversation that made the most sense.

My friend found it interesting that I would identify his guide as a Southwestern Indian. I was not the first to make this identification. While my friend was in New Mexico the previous year, he ran across some local holy men, shamans, and shamans in training, but he never spoke of the experience with anyone. The shamans informed him that he had taken from their meeting a guide who would like to join him and help him along his way. And that this guide was a Southwestern Indian who would wear gold clothes, much like the ones I described.

Now, this farm, where all these new experiences were occurring, sat on the outskirts of a small college town. As colleges would have, there were many professors who lived about the town. As this was the time in our society when wives seldom worked and instead kept house and minded children, one professor had a wife who was a stay-at-home mom, and her name was Adele.

One day, Adele was at home alone, ironing her husband's shirts. She told me it was then that she heard someone in the other room say to her, "Go into town to the main intersection.

Your son needs you." *Who and what was that?* she wondered. She ceased her ironing and walked into the other room. There was no one there. Astonished and questioning her ears, she returned to her ironing.

Again, she was called from the other room, and again the voice said to go into town to the main intersection. Without further hesitation or even thinking why, she gathered up her purse and keys and drove the three minutes to the main intersection in town.

The main intersection was a four-way stop. Drivers pretty much had the traffic flow at this intersection down pat. But when Adele got to the intersection, she saw what appeared to be a small fender bender. On the side of the road were two cars and their drivers talking and exchanging information while standing over broken headlights. One of the drivers was her son, who was out on one of his first solo driving expeditions.

Adele tended to business at the intersection. Comforted her son and assured the other driver that she'd be responsible for any damage. But later that night, when she was home and it was quiet, she thought about hearing that voice and wondered what it could be.

Adele spent some time in discovering what the origins of the voice could have been. She talked with counselors and therapists. She decided that a prescription for Valium was not the way she wanted to go and decided to look for nontraditional explanations. It was one year after her son's accident when she had her first gathering of a few friends to converse with her about the voice and its origin.

There were five of us friends sitting around Adele at her big dining room table. It was during this first meeting and in the middle of a conversation about the potential origin of the voice when she changed. Her facial features seemed altered. I thought it was the lighting, but no one changed any of the lighting. She had shadows on her face where seconds before there were none. Her voice was different. The tone was deeper. The words spoken slowly and precisely were articulate and flowed smoothly from her mouth to our ears. Adele was very articulate to begin with, but what I was hearing now was different. Basic meanings for various words seemed to be presented differently than what I had come to recognize with Adele. And instead of *me* and *I,* she was saying *we* and *us. OK,* I thought. *This was different.*

We were still on the topic of discussing the possible origin of the voice when we were to learn that the individual speaking was not Adele but self-identified as Captain. *Interesting,* we thought. Further discussion brought another name that seemed to be speaking from Adele's mouth, and that was Amahl.

Death and Taxes

The evening ended, and my roommate and I returned to our farm. We referred to Captain and Amahl as Captain and Tennille, the current rock sensations, as we spoke lightheartedly about the event. We were to return to Adele's dining room table one night a week for the next several months as we enjoyed deeper conversations with Amahl and Captain.

They proclaimed themselves guides for our learning experiences. My conversations with them would hallmark the beginning of a long and lasting relationship with individuals who live in their neighborhood, dimension, and universe. The content of their conversations was uniformly filled with positive and uplifting intellectual and emotional values.

To say it explicitly, our talks were filled with lessons of service, dedication to us and our well-being, harmony with those about us, and an appreciation that the world is a beautiful place filled with wonder and mirth, where the truth is stranger than fiction. We, the little people who populate this world, are loved. Not just by Amahl and Captain, but also from all those they represent. For ourselves, from what I gathered from our talks, we are all here for each other, and it's only through loving one another that we can and eventually will have heaven on earth.

Going West as a Young Man

My adventure with my friends in Pennsylvania came to an end as travel to new lands called me. I left Pennsylvania with my friend and companion, Scott, and settled in Corn Valley, Oregon. Corn Valley was not the real name of the college town where we settled. The real name was Corvallis. Corvallis was a quaint place that hosted Oregon State University and some of the largest caches of grass seed in the world. Taking up residence, I got back into a routine of the metaphysical practices I established on the farm. The local area was settled about one hundred years ago. Prior to settlement, the Native Americans of the region practiced their shamanistic ways without the interference of any known church or religion. The vibe from their recent practice was strong in this part of the country. I picked up on it early on.

Scott has been my friend since adolescence. Soon after arriving in Corn Valley, we parted ways on a residency level. Scott moved to the next town to be closer to his new girlfriend, and I took a place in the center of Corvallis proper. Here, alone in my new place, I would continue the practice of daily meditation as I learned it in Pennsylvania.

Yes, I left the East Coast and moved to Oregon. Oregon was a new world for me, with mountains and the coast close by. I could find myself in either local by travelling west or east for one hour, respectively. I frequently visited the Cascade Range and found the town of Sisters to be my favorite. Passing through Sisters for the first time, I picked up a hand drawing of a Native American girl, took it home, framed it, hung it on the wall, and called it my first piece of purchased art.

Working the night shift in an adult assisted living facility, my afterwork routine consisted of sitting around the apartment, reading, and gazing at the drawing. The girl looked different from the other Native Americans I've seen. Up until that time, the only Native Americans I ever saw were the ones on the silver screen. Knowing that the individuals depicted were Hollywood stereotypes, I never took all that I saw with any real credibility. Even so, the Native Americans depicted in the movies were of the American Southwest. This charcoal drawing of a young woman looked quite different in her dress from the actors in the movies. Wanting to know more, I decided to visit the library to start my research into what I was seeing.

As luck would have it, the library was the university's and full of research material. Who would have known that the Oregonians were in touch with their native roots? Oregon acknowledged its history before colonization. Local history was a requirement for graduation from high school. Not only did I find a wealth of reading material, but I also found many people to engage in well-informed conversation on the topic. And then there were the local tribes as well. Being much less than two hundred years since the first explorer came to Oregon, the previous civilizations were well represented in the present day.

Once I got familiar with the basic concepts of the Native Pacific Northwest culture, my research and idle reading focused on the religious and spiritual practices of the local Pacific Northwest tribes. I was soon adopting some of the customs; I began celebrating first foods. First foods were those local fares harvested for the first time in their corresponding season. To this day, I perform a short personal ceremony when eating my first fresh salmon of the season. Usually in the fall of the year, I secure a whole salmon and, partaking of this bounty, carefully save all bones and return them to the sea. While cutting, cooking, and eating, I sing the praises of the salmon in appreciation for the gift of their lives for our plenty. This silent personal ritual is repeated with every such meal, quite automatically.

Another ritual I practiced was the rite of passage, as was common for all adolescents, becoming responsible contributors to the community. The rites of passage per the custom of the eighteenth century included going into the woods and soaking in a cold pond for hours while scrubbing oneself with branches and leaves. Prior to this soaking, those undergoing the passage ritual would remain awake for forty-eight hours while dancing and chanting. Once the aspirant emerges from the pond, he ventures into the woods and searches for his spirit guide. He hopes and prays that he is accepted, that there is a guide in his future, and he wishes for his guide to come to him that day. All throughout the preparations, shamans instruct and assist the candidates in calling for a guide's acceptance. A Spirit guide takes on the persona and being of an indigenous animal. The guide's character is expressed through the traits and mystique of the animal. Salmon, brown bear, eagle, otter, whale, cougar, and countless other species of local animals imprint their marks on these newly minted adults and contributors. The spirit guide animal stands as the foundation of the totem, while the adult assimilates the spirit. The guide and the spirit of the animal stamp their character onto the life and being of the new contributing community member adult. Guide and seeker are then one in spirit, forever.

Well! I was up for that. I made my plans and started preparing for my personal rite of passage as practiced by the residents before the coming of European society. There were some hitches in the plan, and I had to modify my personal journey into adulthood accordingly. Not being an observer of strict orthodox custom, I decided to undergo the ritual tomorrow. I was to travel up to the mountains and forests to seek my spirit guide tomorrow after my night shift was over. I would not be dancing and chanting for forty-eight consecutive hours. I also did not know which animal's spirit I should align myself with. Nonetheless, I would proceed as best I could.

Working the night shift assisted in my preparation for seeking a guide. Though I could not dance and stay awake chanting for two days, I was able to forgo my morning sleep cycle and drive directly to the Cascade Range. I headed for Sisters. Altering my system schedule and remaining awake after work helped me to become sleep deprived as if I had been at a real rite of passage ritual. Walking and strenuous activity would help replicate the bathing in cold pond water. Scratches from underbrush as I climbed the mountain trails would substitute for the need to scratch myself silly with branches and leaves. While not orthodox, my plan should deliver the same net mind-altering effect as an actual ritual. My plan was passable and doable; I began my undertaking.

Helping along the mind-altering effect, I fasted. I began my fast the minute I committed to the ritual. Arriving at Sisters in the morning, I rejected any thought of having breakfast in my favorite café, as I would usually do about now. Regardless of my resolve to keep my fast, I found that I must take some effort to avoid the place. When I came face-to-face with the

Sisters Café at the main intersection, I made a quick and sudden right turn down a highway I had never traveled, just to get away from there and avoid the temptation. The highway leads me on a series of curves that quickly ascend in altitude. The surroundings were ponderosa pines and light scrub brush ground cover for as far as my eye could see. Traveling farther down the road and higher up in altitude, the trees thinned, and I was able to see the tops and sides of mountains through the openings in the forests. I was traveling down a road that was to become my favorite place: Grants Pass between the Three Sisters and Mount Washington, with Three Fingers Jack behind in plain view.

The road up to the pass gradually sank into the surrounding rock. The road was carved or blasted out of this very strange looking porous black and red rock. The rock had scant vegetation growing on the sides that I could see. The road went deeper into the rock that rose up to five feet in height on either side of my car as I traveled down this new highway. My field of view was limited to what I could see upward at an angle while sitting low in the car, driving. To my left, as I drove up to the pass through the rock, I saw the butting head of a knobby mountaintop. The mountaintop was black, and half of its face caved in or fell away at some time in its history. The side that had caved in was sheer up and down for what looked like a thousand feet.

Arriving at the pass, I parked and visited a two-story high observation tower. The tower was made of the same porous black and red rock I tunneled through on the road up here from Sisters. Inside the observatory, I found that some considerate groups of local businesspeople were kind enough to erect a brass map and guide to the sites from the observatory. Grants Pass, and this observatory of the same name stood directly on the Continental Divide. The porous red rock was leftover lava from the last major eruption one hundred thousand years ago. A large brass map pointed out the mountain peaks with arrows and lines of bearing so that I could clearly identify the peaks. The day was cloudless, clear, and of moderate September temperature. I could easily see and identify the peaks from this vantage point, and I learned that the first mountain I saw to my left while driving up the pass was Black Crater. Brochures in the observatory's lower level showed the trail map up to the top of Black Crater. How marvelously accommodating were those local businesspeople. Before me was the map of my route up to the top of Black Crater where I would find my spirit guide. The events of the last twenty-four hours were all leading me here to the observatory at Grants Pass and this brochure in my hand. I could feel my spirit guide call to me. It was reaching out to me and calling me to the top of Black Crater. It was all clearly laid out before me.

Death and Taxes

The trail was well-maintained, like all trails in this neck of the woods and offered spectacular vistas of the Three Sisters and surrounding mountains. Once breaching the summit of the crater, I could see as far north as Mount Rainier and south to Mount Thielsen. The top of the crater was a different world from the treed forest below. It was like no other place that I had visited on this earth. The top was flat and level with slightly downward, rounded edges around the rimed circumference. The summit consisted of one large, solid, single piece of vegetation-free rock. Above the tree line and higher than the tops of the trees below, the only earth I could see was the tops of other, much higher mountains. The surface area of the summit was equivalent to an acre, perhaps. Off to one side, my right side as I ascended the crest, the mountain fell steeply away into nothing. A perch of rocks rose up from the solid summit. Likely a remnant of lava upwelling from a crevasse solidified into a steep and small knob. This lava outflow was a perfect place to perch myself and take in the fresh mountain air while waiting for my spirit guide to find me.

From where I ascended the summit, I would have to cover some distance to arrive at my perch. Walking over the giant slab of rock, I noticed two large, black birds hovering over me at some altitude while riding the current of wind keeping them aloft. They must have noticed me as they started to descend. The birds were alternately keeping station and descending to a lower plateau, getting lower and closer to me. I wondered, *Are these my spirit guides?* As I was walking over the crater top, the birds were maintaining a constant bearing and decreasing range as if they intended to land on my shoulder or on the top of my head. As the birds were descending, they started looking bigger and bigger. They were close enough for me to identify them. They reminded me of Edgar Allan Poe's raven, but much bigger and not, definitely not, sitting on a perch in his study. I thought that they were ravens, but I never in my life believed they were this big. Their wingspan was wider than I was tall. Being born and raised in the urban East Coast, I never saw ravens, and I never saw any birds this big. And these big birds were coming closer and looking bigger as I was crossing the open summit, walking atop that big slab of a rock to my intended perch. "Are these my spirit guides?" I wondered aloud.

Halfway to my destination and having these two birds keen on my mind, I instinctively turned to take another bearing on them, only to be met with the sight of a pointy beak rapidly approaching and on course with the back of my head. I instinctively and reflexively ducked. The bird passed over me, lifted on the air current, and gained twenty or forty feet of altitude. The bird's retreat was enough for me to straighten up. While keeping a sharp eye on the aggressor, I straightened up only to be confronted by the other bird that had been hovering several air layers above the aggressive partner. The second bird dived. I had no idea what these birds were doing, but this one was coming close enough to strike. I dropped to the ground and flattened myself to the solid, flat, table rock summit.

I lifted my head up to look around and see what these two birds were up to. I saw a third large bird quickly approach, as if out of nowhere. This third large bird flying around this mountaintop was smaller and sleeker than the two ravens that were harassing me. This new visitor to the scene looked more like a bantamweight boxer. Compact, tight, and in great shape with not a gram of unnecessary weight. He had every feather in place, and he looked magnificent as he dived right into the midst of the two hovering, gigantic, threatening birds. Now it was their turn to maneuver to avoid a collision. Had not the two giant, black ravens succeeded in evading their attacker, outstretched talons would have connected. The ravens retreated by lifting up higher yet on the air currents and eventually fled the scene, taking a course northward and away from me. The one who scared them off flew around the mountaintop, making a long, wide circle around the summit and me. One second, this new guy was twenty feet above me and the surface of the mountaintop I was standing on, and the next he was several thousand feet above the treetops below the summit I ascended.

What's going on here? I wondered. I didn't know that ravens attacked humans, especially five-foot-something humans. And why was this other guy attacking the ravens as if he were defending me? Whatever the reason was for this intervening attack, it all worked out to my advantage. As the rescuer completed his one or two circles around the summit, he took off southward toward the peaks of the Three Sisters. I got a good look at him while he was circling. He was white, predominantly so, like a dove. His wings were outlined in blue trim. Indeed, his entire body looked like it was outlined in blue trim. He was a very nice-looking bird, smaller and more muscular than the ravens. He also wore a blue mask across his eyes. He had what looked like a mask of blue that stretched out sideways, covering both eyes and passing to where the ears would be. *Almost like the Lone Ranger,* I thought. *But what kind of bird is white, wearing a blue mask with blue trim around his wings, and has talons like an eagle?* It was a mystery to this city boy. I decided to hold the thought till I returned home to town and would ask Brad to identify the species for me. Brad was in the forestry program at Oregon State University. He knew everything about these forests and woods. Onward to my perch, I walked.

As I walked, I kept looking south to follow this masked white bird with the blue trim. This high up and with the clear sky about me, I was able to keep sight of him for quite some time. He was traveling away from me, but not very quickly.

Every now and then, he would tack around, which seemed odd to me at the time, looking back at me. On his third successive tack, and again looking back at me, I had another instinctive feeling in the back of my head and turned to see that my two raven friends who broke off from the fray and flew off northward were now, in fact, engaged in another dive, beaks leading, aiming right for my head. Reflex took over and I dived as one, then the other, passed what seemed inches above the farthest extension of my backpack as I lay there, once again, on the sunbaked slab rock summit on the top of Black Crater. What had gotten into these two? Instead of climbing and leaving for good, they were alternately riding on the air current, rising in altitude, then diving down again at me and aiming for my person, one then the other. I looked over to the white bird that was again tacking and looking back at me, hugging the rock mountaintop.

"If you are my spirit guide, come back and chase off these two attackers once and for all." Perhaps he heard me and had some sympathy for this city guy lying on his stomach, hugging the solid rock beneath me. Without further ado, he continued through his tack and, arriving on a new course, headed right for my position. Climbing in altitude, he took a posture that was advantageous for his mission. Having the weather gauge, he, as before, dived straight at one of the two attackers. The white bird dived steeply like a bullet and at the last minute pivoted his body and swung around to present his open talons to his target, which was attacking me. This attacker must have had an instinctive feeling of his own, for at the very last second, he broke off his attack on me and violently flipped over and to the right, just avoiding the many sharp talon points of the masked white bird.

The white bird recovered from his dive and swung off in a tight circle again, gaining altitude and positioned himself above the two threatening ravens. The masked white bird dived again, taking aim at the previously unmolested partner who succeeded in avoiding the attack by engaging in an emergency maneuver. At this point, the ravens must have thought that whatever was so interesting in me was not good enough to risk another assault by this sleek, muscular, masked, white bird of prey. The ravens withdrew at speed downwind to the east, turning into little specs and finally disappearing from view.

As the ravens withdrew, the masked white bird with the blue trim circled the mountaintop one last time. It took a minute for the ravens to altogether disappear from view. And as soon as they were clearly gone, the white bird left and continued with its journey to the south, flying off in the direction of the northernmost Sister.

Whew. Getting up from hugging the ground, I again dusted off and finally advanced to the lava outcropping on top of this summit, taking my perch where I tarried for a good portion of the remaining day.

Upon my return to town, it didn't take long for the next social event to take place. In attendance was my forestry friend Brad, who was more than willing to help identify the bird. First off, he tells me, there are no masked, white birds with blue trim residing in the Cascades that attack eagle-like with talons open for the strike. He said I must have been seeing things or was mistaken in identifying the color. That was possible, I thought. I do see things that others do not see, but I clearly saw the colors as I stated.

Brad retreated into his room, where he maintained a well-stocked library of books on forestry that he kept on his makeshift shelving system constructed with cinderblocks and two-by-eights. Opening a book on birds of prey, he turned the pages to arrive at a series of photos and asked me, "Is this the one you saw?" No, no, and no, I answer until he opens the next section of the book, where we come across a bird of prey with the same body type and trim. "Hold it," I tell him. "That's the one." He asks, "Are you sure?" I explain that I am very sure, and after looking at several other birds in this one section, I return to my first selection and proclaim with surety that this is the bird that came to my rescue and drove off the ravens.

Brad scratched his head and then closed and shelved the book. The bird I identified was taken from the section of coastal birds that primarily eat fish. My rescuer was a sea hawk, an osprey. That's it. It's the osprey. The osprey is my spirit guide.

Brad went on to tell me that there are no nesting ospreys at Grants Pass. It's too dry. The area to the east is semiarid, and there are no lakes in the immediate area. He said that it was unlikely that the bird I saw was an osprey, but some other type of hawk. And he could not think of any reason why a passing hawk would stop to attack two threatening ravens. By this time, the party was heating up, and people were pairing up, dancing and conversing. Neither Brad nor I wanted to miss out on any opportunities to meet new people, so we left the discussion for the birds to pursue something more immediate and fun-filled. Brad soon, if not immediately, forgot all about our conversation as he engaged with the party revelers. I stayed and engaged in the fun but could only keep thinking of my adventure.

I completed the ritual of the rite of passage. I deprived myself of food and sleep. I engaged in strenuous activity by climbing a mountaintop. Once there, I was attacked by hostile forces of nature and rescued by my spirit guide. Osprey is my spirit guide and my totem foundation.

Death and Taxes

Out of Balance

Perhaps it was the adjustment to living alone and on my own, with everything being unfamiliar. The friends I had were all from Oregon, good ones and all new, but this would be the first time that I was completely separated from any connection to my home region and the people I knew for the span of my short life. Or perhaps living alone and engaging in metaphysical pursuits nightly got me too separated from my earthly connection, causing me to "float about above the ground" for long periods of time ungrounded. And I could certainly call it floating about. As my workdays ended, I returned to an empty home only to penetrate deeper through the veil into the other dimensions. Shamanism, lore from the medieval romances, or music of my making, enhanced the vibrational rates of my meditation. These were my nightly activities and the way I occupied my time away from friends, people, and any connection with my roots.

Where could I go from here? I would ponder. *How high could I get in meditation and ritual?* Then one day, with no warning, everything just stopped. Music no longer interested me. Making music stopped. Meditation was a frame of mind I could no longer achieve. Meditation stopped. Reading the medieval romances stopped. I couldn't find any more books in the university library that interested me on the topic. Reading the romances just stopped. Shamanistic studies and ritual stopped. I no longer had the desire to formulate a complete thought or projection. All that I saw now of the animal, spirit, and energetic representations was a lunatic's vision of monsters crawling on the roof, not wanting to come in but wanting me to think they wanted in. My connection with a spiritual and life force was severed. I closed my eyes and listened for it. I felt for it around my cranium, expecting the connection, a connection that I had felt twenty-four/seven since I was a small child; it was absent. It just disappeared. Gone. Severed. I was no longer plugged in.

I cursed the gods. This distinction was absent from my life. The different that I was, no longer existed. It was taken from me. The joke was on me. This is where such distinction was to end, I thought, with a feeling of intense isolation and disassociation from the budding me I only just now was seeing for the first time and experiencing some level of comfortable success with this identity. Gone. No more. No desire. No initiative. No connection.

Now I was like everyone else. Life then became a series of small jobs and over-the-top social celebrations. I moved from Oregon to Washington. I took on work cooking for some interesting restaurants and learned a little about commercial cooking. It was plentiful work, and I had a knack for it, but it wasn't for me.

From this early age, I experienced the effect of too quickly ceasing energy work and flow. I did not know what caused the energy to stop flowing, and as it ceased abruptly, I found myself on the rocks with my bottom ripped out. My initial impulse was that the sudden crash was from flying too closely to the sun, like Icarus of mythology, bringing me the distress of melted wings. Possibly, there was something in my practice that I was missing altogether. Investigating I continually looked to the metaphysical and ignored the possible physical stimuli or implications associated with the pendulum swing. What did I know? The crash effects caused immediate changes in my world, changes in mood and personality that would challenge the stoutest character.

I would peer through the veil from time to time over the next two years, but for the most part, it was just a small glimpse to satisfy curiosity or to test the waters, ensuring that I still got the touch and gift. The gift never really left. But the time for developing the gift at the hectic pace I knew was ended for the two years following the initial blockage and loss. On the strictly physical and social levels, I was growing dissatisfied with the status quo. I decided to do something out of the ordinary, and with no notice to anyone, I left Washington State to return to the East Coast family home. Within a week, I was signed up for the Navy and would be leaving right after the holidays.

What caused the sudden stoppage? The gifts were there, but the desire and ability to exercise them in earnest were at an apparent end. As life progressed at that time, I would observe several hills and valleys in my metaphysical development and closeness to the heavenly host. I would learn that I am human, of the physical. And that the higher I got on the bliss of development, the more anchored to the here and now I must be for me to maintain a satisfactory level of comfort in my emotional and mental stability. The physical me must balance the intensity of the energy I manifested, or chaos ensued. But at the time, I had no idea that any relationship between physical and metaphysical existed or if one affected the other.

Life and my spiritual, metaphysical living style would persist through the ensuing decades at various levels of passion, or not. I experienced moderate waves of development while sampling one spiritual community or another. I was able to maintain a level of balance that would positively impact my physical being and environment throughout the moderate peaks and valleys of my development. My health was always good. My ability to generate income was stable. My immersion into the world of spirit and the heavenly host was measured throughout the interceding years. I am so not a measured soul when it comes to the metaphysical. So not measured. More than three and a half decades would pass before I was to again have the opportunity and experience of total immersion into spirit and willfully blowing the balancing act out the window.

Spirit Guides and Angels

Chapter 3: Self-Taught

A Short Life at Sea

I didn't have much time to think about the cause and effect of losing my physical/metaphysical equilibrium at this early stage. Navy boot camp would be occupying my mind for the next nine weeks, then it was off to training in navigation. An earthly duty started calling, and I was to become an integral member of a ship's crew. There were to be no differences in the hues of my uniform or in the lean in my posture standing at attention for morning quarters. Worldly integration and grounding would be unavoidable.

I picked the Navy over the Coast Guard so that I could see the world. I was assigned to a frigate. I went to sea and stood watches piloting and navigating the ship from one point to the next. One night, right after my watch ended, I decided to get some air on deck. It was the middle of the night, and I was just relieved from the midwatch. My watch ended just before 4:00 a.m., and I had morning muster at 8:00. I knew I should get some rest before the workday started, but I was not ready for sleep yet.

The night was the darkest you could imagine. The moon set hours ago, and all was quiet. We were maintaining station two hundred nautical miles due south of Pearl Harbor and ambling around aimlessly while passively looking for submarines. I went behind the bridge to lie down on my back to look up at the stars. The trade winds were blowing softly upon the ocean and me. The swells rocked me gently.

Sailing on a US man-o-war, you would not want to strike a full lotus position and bliss out. You could, but if the older hands and lifers got a gander, you'd never hear the end of it. Eventually, if it happened more than once, it would paint your reputation and character aboard the ship. For good or bad, that's the way it works, and you live with it. Having already a label of being "weird but a pretty darn good quartermaster," I didn't want to push it. So, when I would repose and go inward, out on the deck at night, I would recline and lie upon my back to gaze out at the stars.

This one illuminating night was a little out of the ordinary. There was a certain atmosphere about me that I could not say whether it was produced by the weather and sea conditions or by my own spirit. We were sailing two hundred miles from the nearest population center, and moonset was several hours ago. The stars and planets were the only sources of light. The clarity that night was magnificent.

It happened without warning. I didn't gradually slip into another frame of awareness and consciousness. There was no preparation on my part. Indeed, my only intention that night was to just gaze upon the stars and get some fresh air before retiring for some sleep. One half of a second, I was fully aware of the steel deck I was lying on and the architecture of the stars' light and the second half of that second, I was dawn in among the stars. The only visual anomaly I can relate to a similar physical experience would be dipping my head into a shimmering pond and, eyes wide open, breathing and being sustained while seeing and visiting a different world. In such a case, the barrier or separation between the water world of the pond and me, an air breather, was removed. On the steel deck late that night, in an instance, there was no separation or distinctive barrier between me and the stars in the heavens above. I was now a part of that world.

Every light had a song, a song in harmony with the others. And for that instance, I knew each individual song and story of the chorus. For me and for now, what was wanted was to explore the extent of this emerging personal discovery and cover as much ground as possible. The lights, stars, and planets were related. They breathed a single breath. They were life individually and in common. They were bonded through an unseen collective life force to an unseen core and center. This pond I was immersed in was egg-shaped yet finite, such that I could comprehend and relate in my present state of development.

Death and Taxes

My thoughts at the time were not god centric. I was not focused on the concepts of a one source and center of this and all universes. At the time, my interests lay in nature's essence within all living things. The stars were alive, and part of nature's universe, and I would celebrate their beings. My lessons and impressions given to me by these stars were best expressed as astrological in nature. I wasn't given my horoscope or a lesson in laying out a chart. What came was seeing the workings of these stars, constellations, planets, and all that was beyond. I felt the movement of their light as it traveled from there to here and beyond forever, unstopping. My life on that frigate was somewhere on that traveling light for the instant that I was there. The traveling of the light, the binding together of all the lights' travel, the laws and applications of their movements physically and in concept, all in consort with one another, a syncopated dance and turning that was now flowing through me with no clear self-definition of who or where I am in this onward flowing tide. I was to discover that I was present on one point of light; I also existed on all points of light in the same moment.

I was on a stream of light, and at any given point—past, present, or future—I existed in the moment. The movements of the stars and planets and the trailing light as it traveled throughout the known universe reminded me of the maypole ceremony where the ribbons were braided and intertwined to form a colorful tapestry, neat, in order, and happily done.

When this awareness shift came on, it formed an immediate image in my mind, an image of the transformational process from me on the deck of a frigate to me with my head immersed in heaven's pond. The translation can best be compared to how the stars look right before Star Trek or Star Wars space vehicles' transition into light speed. The points of light elongate and shoot past my field of vision. Well, it hit me something like that. What came along with the impression of entering warp speed was the presence of Someone. Seeing this Someone, I was struck by the sight of his staff. The staff reminded me of the one carried by Charlton Heston as he played Moses. The Someone looked a little like Heston's rendition of Moses, but Heston had a better tan, was visibly younger, wore makeup, and had been working out at the gym. The Someone was lithe in stature, his long beard was stunningly trimmed and formed, and while he was personable and kindly in essence, he had a sternness associated with him that would combine the attributes of a headmaster, drill sergeant, and loving grandfather all into one. Throughout the experience, he remained in the back of my mind, not at all interacting or attempting to converse. He was just there, pointing and holding his curved, headed staff.

Then, in an instance, I became fully aware of lying on the steel deck of a frigate swaying with the waves. There was no fanfare that I was now returning to my physical and occupational level of consciousness. On the contrary, I was quite surprised to find myself back. And in coming back, I felt as though I landed with a thud, dropped from my pond as though a bucket upending tossed me upon the deck for swabbing down. I may have muttered or shouted, "No!" I didn't want to leave where I was or had been. Not only were the lessons such a joy, but also the experience of existing within the stars was something I had never felt and did not want to let go. I was a note of a chord in perfect harmony. I was a hue of light that was combined with others to form a color. A drop of the rushing yet unhurried tide. I became a surveyor of the light that lived and traveled from beginning to end, and a protégé or associate of one who traveled with me holding a staff of power.

I immediately tried to get back into that state of mind and consciousness. I may have chanced crossing my legs and going into a lotus position. I don't remember. I was not to succeed. Just as the experience had taken me up and wrapped me in movement with no forewarning, it had placed me back down into my own bag of bones and denim just as abruptly.

It was time to hit the rack. Zero eight hundred would come quickly, and I had a full day of work and watches ahead of me.

Place a Finger into the Stream

The frigate to which I was assigned was homeported in Pearl Harbor, Hawaii. The ship was eventually to undergo a one-year refit in the local navy shipyard. While laid up, Mel, a shipmate, and I rented a two-bedroom apartment in Honolulu. Oahu Island was a happy playground mixing the world's traditions. Residing in a civilian apartment complex away from the shipyard and naval base brought one clairvoyant experience after another. The crowd that I ran with was a mishmash of Huna, Wiccan, and Spiritual practitioners of the most pleasant order. They were all, to the core, innocent and true in their pursuits of finding what is really behind the curtain. Once found, they made fast their gifts and continued their everyday lives as seekers and seers.

One lazy Saturday night, a bunch of us were sitting around our apartment wondering what we would do for entertainment. All of us were dabbling in one or many of the diverse intuitive and long-standing cerebral, supernatural, mystical, metaphysical, and spiritual disciplines we found among the island's diverse population. What's a bunch of clairvoyants to do on a Saturday night for entertainment? What else but give readings, past-life regressions, and dabble with tarot cards and Celtic runes.

We started our entertainment that evening by giving one of our gathered mystics a past-life regression. First up was a palm-reader friend from Chicago. We had him lie on the floor with his head on a comfortable pillow. The other five of us sat on the floor around him in a circle. We all prepared for our flight in our own individual way. None made a fuss. If you were to watch from the sidelines, you would see five people quietly taking their position while sitting, some of us cross-legged, in a circle around an ethnic-looking Chicagoan. Some of us closed our eyes for a moment. Others did not. When you walk daily in two worlds as these good people did, seeing was never a difficult undertaking. The visions came quickly once the individual tuned the dial to the correct frequency.

Once all were comfortable and the subject was reclined and in a relaxed state, a past-life reader spoke up. My roommate Mel took the baton. Mel described to the group what he was seeing or picking up from our subject's, Gresham's, immediate vicinity. Our friend Gresham, in another life, was what appeared to be a Bedouin. On this occasion, he was hanging around the oasis with his friends, family, and tribe. One of the fair maidens was his betrothed. He and she stole away behind one of the dunes for a brief interlude.

It was at that instance I realized that I was able to see the scene Mel was describing. As Mel spoke and relayed his message, Gresham started blushing. Gresham also saw the scene of the night he lay with his betrothed among the dunes. By this time, Gresham was in a light hypnotic state. He may have picked up on the image of Mel's story. Or he may have traveled with Mel back to that time and place where the life occurred. Gresham may also have imagined the visions playing around in his head and mixed them up with some recent personal escapades. It's never certain. This is so not a science.

My attention was caught not by the retelling of the story or by Gresham's blushing but by the vivid images I was picking up in this past-life regression and the fact that I was seeing the scene in the dunes unfold before they were revealed in Mel's presentation.

I couldn't help but escape into a meditative and investigative state of mind. In the back of my mind was the soft-spoken drone as Mel delivered his rendition of Gresham of Arabia. As I was listening to Mel's drone, my mind was filling with the scene of tender embraces that came at me in real-time sequencing replete with the sensations of lying on the still warm desert sand as the last of the day's light faded. At some point in the telling, I no longer heard Mel's even drone.

I remember looking up to his last known position to see if he was still speaking. His lips were moving. As I lost my focus on physical structure and faded back into a deeper meditative state, I saw the whirlpool. The narrow end of the funnel terminated at Mel's crown. Zooming in to take a closer look, my attention was drawn to the connection between Mel's crown and the narrow end of an inverted whirlpool cornucopia. Through this connection flowed what appeared as crystal clear water passing through a faucet-like opening. The flow of this waterlike material was perfectly laminar, even, and smooth with no sign of turbulence. The flow entered the mind of Mel, was digested, and thrust out as mists emanating from his upper torso and cranial area.

Odd though it may be to see what represents itself to me as water flowing through a faucet at the end of a whirlpool and into the head of my roommate, only to be misted out to those seated and listening. Yet the image was effective in describing to me the manner with which we take in inspiration and heaven's pearls of wisdom and relay them to those who sit and listen. As the data stream transited the energetic presence of Mel's physical body, portions of that stream were absorbed, morphed, rearranged, and conditioned by Mel and all that he is per his life experiences. The telling of the tale was that data that remained, passed through to us, or allowed through to us by the speaker.

I found the behind-the-scenes images and activity scribing the interchange of information interesting, more interesting, in fact, than the tale of the past-life regression. I was no longer paying attention to the individuals in the room or the telling of Gresham's several past lives. It was good entertainment, but I tend to gravitate toward what's behind that curtain. I looked closer at this dynamic between the whirlpool and Mel and surmised that this was the transmission process for intuitive reception and the resulting dialogue. It struck me odd that I was also seeing and directly receiving the information flow that Mel was pulling intuitively from the ether, his intuitive sources.

Investigating deeper, I extended myself outward to caress the flowing faucet water coming out of the whirlpool cornucopia by extending the tendrils of my thoughts. At first, I observed this phenomenon from afar, wary of upsetting its elegance. But it was inviting me closer. And closer I went as I extended forth from my mind a finger to test the water and feel the beehive-like intensity that filled the area about Mel. Just for a second, I thought. And with that touching came a clear, vibrant, and undistorted, living 3D image of the Bedouin and his betrothed behind the sand dunes as if I were standing right next to them. I quickly withdrew.

The strength of the image propelled my voice to act as if it had a mind of its own. As the speaker was presenting his tale and the product of his intuition, I started speaking along with him, synchronized and in stereo. I was completing his sentences. Mel and I frequently completed each other's sentences when at home hanging about on our own. However, now we were hosting guests, my disruption drew the consternation of those assembled as they shot me glances with eyebrows eschewed. I ceased my blurting and settled down to rejoin them in the here and now.

But I couldn't stay away from that vibrant transmission and display that was going on before me. The story that Mel was pulling down from the heights of heaven sang to me. It spilled its notes all around me. As I continued to think about what I was looking at and placed my attention on the story, the information flow reached out to me directly and spoke. I was receiving from the celestial the intuitive feed that Mel possessed and called upon himself. Interesting, I thought. It's a bit like eavesdropping.

The past-life reading baton passed to the next seer, a Hawaiian priest, a Kahuna named Aulani. She spoke of another time and a past life for our friend Gresham. This time, he resided in Italy as a laborer. As she spoke, I paid the utmost attention to what she was saying but could not help again slipping into a meditative state and extending my vision to the unseen. Aulani had something about her that appeared as swirling light. Gone was the whirlwind funnel terminating at the crown as with Mel. Gone was the residue of the data feed payload as it first appeared to me—mists sent outward from the speaker's torso, chest, throat, and forehead. Here, now, was an information flow that looked like light rays in nature. The rays were moving in two directions. One light ray flow was tight, bright, and compacted, coming from above and into Aulani. The other flow was outward from her and diffused, yet while the outward flowing rays were diffused, they were still mirror images of the rays going into the speaker, a match in color, frequency, and rhythm. All rays were of varying shades and textures. The inflow textures and hues were changing rapidly through the spectrum.

When Mel was drinking from the fountain of intuition, I saw a funneled whirlpool terminating at the crown region of his head. This time, with Aulani speaking, there was light, unassailable light. All I needed to do was amplify the light I received and drink from the direct feed effortlessly. With light filling the atmosphere, there was an immediate and direct flow of information into my mind. Effortlessly, the transfer of information to me was motivated or placed into motion by no single conscious thought on my part, only by my recognizing the light display and allowing myself to receive its influence. My experience with Mel took some effort on my part to pull the information inward. The contents of Aulani's story and the corresponding information flow now came to me in vivid detail with no effort at all. I anticipated each future sentence and, once again, I was blurting out the speaker's completed sentences that were given in testament to this version of Gresham's past lives. And yes, as before, my colleagues were not entertained.

The evening ended, and we all went on our separate ways and onto our daily lives. The vision of the information flow was to stay with me during the workweek. And during the week, about me frequently, I would see wisps of emanating light that were to become quite distracting. I tried not to notice but to focus on the occupational work at hand instead.

The full episode happened again, in honesty, at a nontraditional church service where my colleagues, fellow clairvoyants, and I were in attendance. We were accompanying a friend who asked us to participate in a service at her church. The pastor assumed the podium and started speaking. The display of light returned. I gave the phenomenon my full attention. This time, there was something different going on.

As I had previously witnessed with Aulani, a ray of projected light from above made a direct line toward the speaker. This light flowed evenly, unrushed, and laminar in all respects. The light ray going into the speaker was focused, tight, and compacted. With the pastor, as with Aulani the week before, diffused light rays also emitted outward from her. I expected the diffused, outward-flowing light rays to again match the inward flow in rhythm, vibration, and color patterns. The outward flow of the emitted light traveled toward those seated in front of the pastor and beyond. However, this time, with this pastor, the emitted light distorted from time to time throughout her oration. When distorted, the light became uneven in gradient, but again, not always. Portions of the directed light were as nourishing and radiant as that which arrived directly from above, the source of all intuition, but other portions were twisted and conflicted. I could not decipher the reason for the distortion. Where the emanated light matched the speaker's inflow light, I was able to interpret the pastor's intuitive information feed, bypassing the filter established by the speaker's life experiences. When the emitted light became distorted, I sat perplexed at an uneven feeling I had in the middle of my mind. I was well grounded at the time and relaxed, at ease generally. But during the distortion, for some unknown reason, I was tensing, ever so slightly. And my eyes involuntarily squinted. The information coming out from the pastor did not match the intuitive intelligence that she was receiving, but again, not always.

I was no longer paying appropriate and respectful attention to the words the pastor was speaking; the confusion over the lights distracted me. Some of her words I absorbed and processed. Others seemed to slip into an unknown void and simply passed from my attention. I investigated this dissonance I was experiencing. The inflow and outflow streams did not match. The information given was corrupted from what was received. I visually perceived the entire dynamic, and I was uncomfortable with what I was seeing. I brushed off my personal experience as my limited proficiency with this new phenomenon.

The pastor's oration generally triggered not only thoughts and images but also feelings of heartfelt sincerity and love. She was eliciting an emotional response with her oration. That was skillful on her part. She was a skilled orator and a longtime pastor in this church. But something was off, and I felt it intuitively. I then noticed a correlation between my intuitive unease and the dissonance between the inward and outflowing light rays. Whenever my intuition and emotions were askew, the outward flowing light conflicted with the inward flowing light in rhythm, syncopation, frequency, and color patterns; the outward flowing light did not match the inward flowing. While throughout the pastor's oration, words sounded ever so sweetly and produced the most heartfelt of emotions for the listeners, the dissonance caused discord within me.

Why would that be? I wondered. Why would the oration not match the intelligence of the source light? I looked again at the dissonant light being emitted from her being and contrasted it with the light from the source again. And then I understood. The pastor's words did not match the intelligence and inspiration that she was receiving by an act of intention. The emitted light was conflicted, jumbled, and out of kilter, and my intuition was issuing me a caution.

The service ended with all participants holding hands in a circle and singing a song of love, health, and well-being. My friends and I gave our appreciations to our hosts and took our leave after having finished our parting conversations.

As we all walked back to our homes to continue with our day, I overheard Ruthie conversing with Aulani. Ruthie casually mentioned that she enjoyed the service and the reception in the church's kitchen afterward. The members of the church were pleasant, considering the circumstances. She mentioned that the church's board of directors was having challenges and that they were questioning the direction and methods of their current pastor. The pastor spoke of the challenges during her oration on the podium and suggested some personal actions for each of the board members to undertake. The actions, she said, were coming to her as inspiration from the divine mind of a single universal fountain of truth. And that she would, heretofore, lead in the board's disposition of her interpretation and implement the word of

God within her church as she received it and spoke of it that day.

Well, I thought. This is interesting. There is something deeper here to investigate. But alas, I never returned to the church again to hear the pastor speak of her accomplishments and capacity. My path just didn't bring me there again, but I continued to see the emanating, diffused light at the inception of any inspiration that comes to anyone in my proximity. It could be quite distracting at times. To gauge the accuracy of the speaker's interpretation of inspiration from heaven, I simply look at the inflow of light and note any discord in the outflow. It helps me know what's really going on when leaders or speakers deliver instructions to assembled groups.

As if some unseen directors were interpreting my squirming over all these distracting lights that I was seeing, the everyday visions subsided. From that time onward, the hairs on the back of my neck stand to attention, and I occasionally shiver when I am in the presence of true interpretation of intuition and inspiration. And when that interpretation from above is perverted and transformed by the receiver before being given to the audience, I intuitively know that something is being intentionally misinterpreted. If need be, I can simply fill my vision with light and witness the entire transaction directly, at the root level. And that is always a good thing.

Dreaming Again

My ship's yard period came to an end. Mel and I gave up our apartment and returned to shipboard living. I soon found myself underway and floating around the South China Sea on board that United States frigate. It was another day of effort and stress, and when it came time to sleep, I happily collapsed onto my rack and fell into a deep sleep.

I was so tired that once asleep and in no time at all, I was pouring out of my body down to the foot of my bed and heading for the floor below. I was dreaming. As I saw myself in the dream, I separated from the mass that lay on the mattress and floated about in the dreaming bliss of exhaustion. For while my body was snoozing away, unmoving, there, for that time, I saw of myself as a double image that floated, slowly and evenly, out from my physical body. I was seeing what I considered to be my shadowy body. That part of me that is an exactly me was hovering about, but instead of skin, bones, and brain, this image of me was of shadow, light, and mind.

I was so exhausted that night that even my soul-self seemed in need of rest and took me into the most relaxed state. In this state of consciousness, I drifted off out of my body and poured out from the foot of the middle rack. Instead of falling to the tiled steel deck, I floated aimlessly as if on a mattress of air currents going nowhere. This floating, detached state caught my attention, for although I was dreaming, a portion of my conscious waking self was engaged, and I was thinking rationally as if I were awake and pondering a problem. It was as though my waking self was directing the activities and focus of my sleeping, dream state self. I decided to float higher.

I was to find that consciously bringing my mind into a more relaxed state by going through the motions I use to reach a deeper meditative state, lifted my floating soul-self higher in this dream. Yes. I was consciously able to direct my activities in my dream. I directed my dream self to reach a deeper meditative state. As I raised my vibration to dive deeper into meditation, the image of me in my soul-self rose higher. I finally expanded my consciousness to its limit by merging with the world about me and beyond. Upon merging I blacked out.

Once merged with the world and reaching a higher vibrational rate, I emerged from my blackout. I was aware again of the activities of my dream. I noted still that I was able to direct my activities. I found myself standing on a trestle bridge. The bridge was under construction. It was a rather short suspension bridge, not very long but very sturdy. The bridge was traversing a canyon. The bridge span was completed, but the track was yet to be fully laid. There were boxes, vehicles, and tools about the bridge. Men were working.

I surveyed the work scene. I noted the boxes and their contents and walked about the vehicles parked on the completed portions of the bridge. The workmen were going about their business paying me no heed. I started to walk across the bridge, over the canyon to the other side, and came across a crew sitting in a circle having lunch. I attempted to lift a lunch box to see what was inside but was unsuccessful in influencing the lunch box's physical position. The lunch box, like the workmen here or those working over there, ignored me. I was watching them interact and talk with one another unnoticed. And that was the last I remembered of that dream.

I awoke after four hours of sleep, ready for the next at-sea activity. The evening's dream remained in my mind and memory throughout the day. The dream was in my head, in the middle of my mind with a life of its own. As I moved my head, mind, and consciousness to and fro during the day's activity, the dream remained in the center of my mind like a gyroscope spinning, remaining centered, and resistant to any sudden physical movements or changes in consciousness without making its gyroscopic properties known and felt.

The day's activities came to an end for a predictable amount of time, allowing me to get some rack time, sleep. Again, I collapsed on my bunk, exhausted and spent. I immediately went into a deep unmoving sleep. I soon entered the dream state and felt the now familiar sensation of pouring out of my body and floating on air currents away. Again, I saw the image of me in my soul-self, this exact replica of my physical-self. Again, my consciousness floated off to destinations unknown, dreaming.

By this time, I was familiar enough with the controls of my dream state. Here with my soul image, to enter deeper meditation was to rise, float higher. To merge with the earth and air brought a blackout that propelled my shadowy body away from my physical location. When I came out of this blackout, I discovered I was again at the bridge I had visited the previous night.

While in my previous visit to the bridge construction site, I was ignored. This visit I was still to be ignored but was able to hear voices and read thoughts. Both forms of communication came to me as thoughts placed directly into my mind. What I came to understand is this: There was an event at the bridge. A worker lost his life. Some of the boxes were being lifted by crane to the top of the pier and once so placed they fell, landing on a hapless soul. The workday progressed from that point onward, much like any other day for the construction crew. But for me, I was getting to know the workers by the thoughts they were putting into my mind.

I picked up a general sense of sadness and grief. The man they lost was a dear friend to many. I wished there were something I could do to help to ease their sorrow. Walking about on the bridge, I examined the boxes that had fallen. I pushed on one box, and it again ignored me. It didn't move. I wasn't in its world or dimension and the box knew it. I was not able to alter any of its physical properties. At that point, the dream ended.

Shortly after this brief visit to the bridge, I awoke for another sixteen-hour activity. And for this day, just like the last, this dream would remain solidly in my mind influencing my thoughts and emotions with a gyroscope-like property keeping my mind affixed on the dream and my experiences within.

The day dragged on and turned out to be a little longer than the last. Thinking that sleep would be coming soon, I recalled the dream and directed myself to participate again whenever I was lucky enough to get some sleep. I thought about the falling boxes and the death of the respected friend. I wanted to return to this dream to investigate and possibly participate in some form of remedy.

I finally got some time to hit the rack and fell off quickly. When I awoke, I was quite surprised to learn that I retained the memories of a vivid dream but could not immediately remember the details or my participation. It took an amount of time for the dream's memory to unfold into my daytime consciousness. Once able to recall the dream, I knew I had visited the bridge for a third night in a row. It was very uncommon for me to have repeating dreams. I have had only one other in my life up to that point. Before I fell off to sleep last night, something inside me knew that I would be back at the bridge. And as the fog of waking lifted, I remembered that that is exactly what happened. I dreamed I was separated from my body and that I traveled to the bridge again for the third night in a row.

That third night it felt like the dream arrived the instant I fell asleep. The warning signs were the same this night as with the two others. First, I experienced the now familiar separation of me into two beings, one physically rational and the other soul metaphysical. Then I was floating about calmly and peaceably. I recalled the acceleration my soul body underwent as I raised my meditative state. I again lost all recall upon merging with the life universal. And when the blackout ended, I was again at the bridge.

The scene of the bridge was all around me. The workmen were at their trades as before. There was progress made in the construction of the rails. The trestle was taking form and definition. And again, as I now find to be typical, I was completely ignored by all that was in this physical world represented by the scene of my dream. How was I ever going to influence anything here at this bridge?

I surveyed the area. There is nothing I could do here to bring back the respected friend. If I knew about the accident in advance I would hope to warn him. But how could I warn him? Push him aside? Or perhaps I could move the box. Or at the least stop the box from falling by holding it. But my previous attempts at moving objects at the bridge failed. Nothing would be moved. I was not on the same physical plane and frequency as the bridge in the real, waking world. I could not affect the movement of the boxes to stop them from falling again. And I was in the present. The accident happened in the past. I would have to do something about the time issue.

Recalling this last dream, my memory grew clearer by the second. I remembered that something about my participation in this dream was strikingly different from the others. In this last and current dream, my soul-body was not at the bridge as it had been during the previous dreams. On my previous visits to the bridge, I walked about in my soul body, and all observations and experiences were from a single focal point as seen from the eyes of my shadowy body. However, for this last visit, my vision and presence claimed no center or focal point of perception. For this visit, I recall being everywhere at once throughout the bridge site. I, as a being, had no central point and focus. For this trip instead of me visiting the bridge as a shadowy body, the bridge and the actors appeared as if they were inside of my mind, and I was the universe around them.

Once I realized that I was the world around them I started to again raise my vibrations to achieve the next level of consciousness just to see where I would end up. I remembered the electrical sensation in the atmosphere as my spirit grew in strength.

Per my memory I addressed the issues I had with the accident and focused on influencing the physical properties by thereby altering the history of the respected friend. Previously, I desired to move the errand box from one location to the other, but now I found that movement was no longer necessary. For in this state of consciousness, I saw that the box was where I originally desired it, the exact location I desired, and that was safely placed where it belonged. I came to realize that in this version of my dream, the workmen securely placed the box on the pier in its proper place the first time around. Being so placed, the box never fell. The respected friend was never crushed. It was just another regular workday. The accident never happened.

My next memory found me awakened, eyes wide-open, and ever mindful of the quiet and the rolling of the ship as I lay in my rack knowing that I dreamed but with no immediate memory of what I dreamed about.

I was able to get some sleep again sometime within the next twenty-four hours. I did not dream that night. And then another night I slept and again did not dream. I was not to dream again for several days no matter what my intentions. When I did finally dream, there was no awareness of separating my physical and soul bodies. No traveling to a bridge construction site somewhere in the mountainous regions of Asia.

The days wore on peacefully. Past were the combat-like exercises, and a more subdued pace commanded the captain and crew. I had a late lunch and was lucky to get any food at all that afternoon. They closed the chow line right after I entered the mess deck, and I sat eating in an empty dining area.

Somewhere between finishing the meal and sitting quietly staring at my after-lunch coffee, it hit me. Just for a flash I saw an image of the bridge construction site. There, in the middle of what was to be a rail line, was the box that had not fallen on the respected friend. Here, the box was placed where it safely belonged all along. Gone were the thoughts entering into my mind of sadness and of loss. Gone was the emptiness that follows the loss of a respected friend.

I will never know if that bridge ever really existed in the physical world. At the time we were sailing some distance off the coast of the Korean Peninsula. The scene of the bridge could be from any of the mountain passes or canyons and ravines in the north. The workmen could have been from any of the cities I visited on shore leave in South Korea. But on the latest dream state visit to the bridge, the past changed and brought about a new present and future. And in this new rendition of the present, at that bridge construction site at any rate, a respected friend lived to go home to his family after his long day at work.

Witches of Scotland and the Spanish Armada

I met two women while stationed in Hawaii who still hold a place in my heart and mind. They lived together. Their cohabitation was a matter of convenience and friendship. They were both from different backgrounds yet had much in common. Both, in their early sixties, were practitioners of the healing and spiritual arts.

Alexa came to Hawaii from Texas. She owned the house on the side of the Koolau Mountain Range in Palolo looking out over the sea where the two ladies lived. She talked with a slow Texas drawl. When I visited, she would tell me of the husbands she had. She had three of them. All oilmen and all of them from Texas. The first husband was an oilman and worked as a drill leader. He was the best darn drill lead out of Odessa, Texas. He was a real workingman and stronger than you could imagine. Her second husband owned a small oil import company. With the second husband in the late 1940s, she lived in Saudi Arabia for four years. She observed the local dress code and didn't care to drive anyway. What else was the driver for? She came to Hawaii with her third husband when he retired. He passed away a little over five years ago.

Ruthie, the other woman, was from Scotland. She was the frailer of the two. She walked hunched and had to sit often. Her most striking feature was her smooth, wrinkleless skin. For someone who lived in the blazing sun of Hawaii, especially someone from the weatherly Scottish northern coasts, she possessed the preverbal porcelain skin of a doll made of china. She was a living contradiction as she walked and shuffled, bent over slightly at the waist with her forward curving back. She would tilt her head over in your direction when walking and flash you the most perfect and mischievous smile. She looked like she was going fast with her short steps and her arms swinging with purpose when she walked. And while taking in this scene, I would notice she was wrapped in the smoothest alabaster skin with not a wrinkle on her face—not even a single laugh line.

Death and Taxes

Ruthie was from a long line of Pictish holy women, healers who honored Nature with words, rituals, practice of her craft, and teaching those who were so inclined as to work with Nature and Spirit. Not knowing the traditions of the British Isles, I would respond to her claims of lineage by asking her to clarify. Up to that time I had only heard of the Druids. I would ask her, "Are Picts Druids?" She would explain to me that the Picts came over to the British Isles long before there were Druids. They were a people that were short in stature with darker skin and long, thin noses. The Picts commanded the forces of nature and were the basis of the leprechaun legends spoken of in Ireland. "No, Cesaro," she would say. She always called me by my last name and always pronounced it in the colloquial Sicilian. "The Druids were priests and worshiped Nature in an offhanded manner as compared to the Picts. The Picts were the true masters of magic. They work with the nature of the British Isles. Their ways were very old and originated long ago before the ice age and the thaw. Their small stature never stopped them from accomplishing whatever task they, individual or societal, needed to get done. If they did not have the strength to build or modify, they would simply use their skills to take care of the need."

Ruthie was a born and trained Wiccan. She learned her craft from her mother who, in turn, learned it from her mother. And so, the skills of healing and working with the forces of

Spirit and Nature were passed down to Ruthie from previous generations, skills that were first discovered before there was history. She could never tell me how far back her family tradition spanned the years, but she was sure that it had been so for many centuries or more.

One lazy Sunday afternoon Ruthie, several friends, and I were all hanging around the backyard telling tales, drinking iced tea, and enjoying each other's company. She then told us a story of her lineage in the craft of Nature work.

The British Isles were an isolated lot. There were many areas in the isles, Scotland for one, that were never conquered. And so, they were never assimilated into the civilization of the day. At one point in history, the Romans erected a wall to keep the untamed barbarians at bay. This edifice is referred to as Hadrian's Wall. The wall was erected as a barrier and line of defense protecting the Roman legions from the Scottish devils. Up to this point in time, Rome was yet to be defeated. The Roman legions strode their way through most of the known world. They easily conquered the Gauls, barbarians of France, and the Teutons of Germany. Both peoples being of Celtic ancestry, they shared common traditions, beliefs, and customs with the Picts and their descendants who were to become Scotland.

Death and Taxes

Back in the day of the Roman Empire, the advance of modern civilization on the continent of Europe did not completely eradiate the ancient traditions, beliefs, and practices of the Celts. With the Picts, or Scottish if we were speaking of modern times, their fierce defense and corresponding success kept the Romans at bay well enough to keep the Celtic culture of the north safe and unmolested throughout the ensuing generations.

Meanwhile, back on the continent, civilization grew, and their Celtic brethren were confronted with an ever-strengthening Roman Catholic Church, society, and empire. The belief systems clashed. The Christians had the power of monarchy and the church, both all-powerful in their abilities to pursue their agenda and to decimate any belief systems contrary to their teachings, along with the people who practice the contrary beliefs.

When we asked her to what extent the Celtic traditions were eradicated, she drew upon modern New World history by reminding us of what the Spanish conquistadors accomplished in Central America. In the New World, most pre-Columbian traditions, places of worship, and ancient writing were destroyed. Most traces of the Incan and Mayan histories were purged and lost forever.

Spirit Guides and Angels

On the continent, those Celts who escaped the Roman conquests and socialization were no match for the Inquisition. To survive, the Celtic practitioners of ancient arts and sciences amalgamated into the Christian churches that controlled some level of political and policy-making authority. It was the only way the Celtic beliefs and traditions could survive, to enter the belly of the beast and be as one. However, the age-old arts lived on to some extent as they were passed from generation to generation, albeit in a more subdued and hidden manner than before civilization's rise. Yet the origins of the arts were lost. The traditions remained only between mother and daughter. They were rarely shared beyond the immediate family members.

In the isolated British Isles, the inquisitor was held at bay in much the same manner as the barbarians held off the Romans. The Romans erected their wall. The wall kept the Romans safe and the Picts isolated and unmolested. In the day of the first Queen Elizabeth, there were the English Channel and Britain's wall of wooden ships saving the Picts from suffering the same fate as their brethren on the continent. But still, back in the day of Queen Elizabeth and the sixteenth-century political geosphere, there was severe concern among Ruthie's ancestors. The Armada was coming.

Death and Taxes

The reign of Queen Elizabeth was a long, stable, and relatively peaceful one. And regardless of the ups and downs caused by the various waves of religious persecution, Ruthie's Wiccan ancestors lived unmolested as they had for centuries before. During this era and only for a short time, Queen Mary ruled the British Isles. Mary Tudor was Roman Catholic and having married Philip of Spain, she was determined to set all things on the island right in the eyes of the Catholic Church and God. Philip of Spain and Mary allied in efforts to make England Roman Catholic and return to the fold. It was a time in history for Ruthie's ancestors to be quiet and still until the passing of this one ruler.

Mary was eventually overthrown, and Elizabeth reigned. Though Elizabeth had her own form of state-sponsored religion and requirements of practice throughout the land, the threat to the Pict progeny abated and all were safe to live as they always had, once again. Practicing and living by the beliefs of the ancient traditions were commonplace among the families that were birthed in the northern reaches of Scotland. The ancestors mingled little with strangers. They felt safe with those locals who knew them and were able to practice their art in the open among themselves. The local vicars gave their practices the nod. It was the thing to do. One could not change the nature of people who grew up with the land and all of nature's blessings. It was the way they lived for hundreds of years. So long as outward appearances were maintained and the truth hidden from strangers and visitors from the crown, all was well, and the traditions continued.

The countries that lay on the continent were also once steeped deeply in the traditions of Nature and Wiccan practitioners. The inquisition and proximity to the ever-watchful eyes of the Church's minions successfully severed the lines of Celtic or Wiccan lineage on the continent. Practicing the arts and honoring life, nature, and spirit, even at a speakeasy level, was simply too dangerous. Many practitioners were to lose their lives. Matriarchs and sages went underground. The teachings from parent to child were interrupted, and many skills were lost forever. Open communications between families ceased. The last thing the Wiccans of Scotland wanted to experience was an English version of the Spanish Inquisition.

Yet the threat of war with Spain amplified the worries of the Wiccan Pictish elders. Spain was raising a mighty fleet to conquer the small ships of the British Navy. Once the English fleet was destroyed, the Spanish would land a force on the English soil and march on London. The Spanish king was determined to return England to the one true and apostolic Church. The Wiccans knew that losing the conflict would destroy their culture; their traditions would become lost forever just as they were lost on the continent. They had to do something to protect their country and ensure their customs.

England amassed a small navy to battle the coming Spanish Armada. After a series of running battles up the English Channel, the Armada was finally served up a tactical defeat on July 28, 1588, anno Domini, at the Battle of Graveline that prevented the Spanish from landing soldiers on British soil. For the next month, the ships of the Armada were to maintain their positions off the coast of the Low Countries from Dunkirk northward. But the Armada's presence in northern waters, with still over one hundred ships containing many soldiers, posed a simmering threat to England.

It was during the month of August, while the Spanish continued to threaten the coast of England, that the witches of Scotland determined to act. This was a time for all inhabitants of the British Isles to protect their homes and culture from the invaders. Ruthie's ancestors were not able to wield sword and musket, but they were able to command nature to do their bidding. The witches of northern Scotland convened a council, calling all elders to Callanish, located on the Atlantic Coast of the Isle of Lewis in the Outer Hebrides, where stands a prominent stone circle and many other stone monuments assembled by visitors throughout the eons.

The council's decision was to turn air, fire, water, and earth against the Armada. An edict was issued for all Picts to gather at the stone circles of Callanish and Stenness. Stenness was the site of the Ring of Brodgar on the largest of the Orkney Islands and close to where the Armada would eventually pass. Callanish, on the largest of the Western Isles, was home to other stone circles and places of nature worship. Work at Callanish would protect the western coasts of Scotland.

As September approached, the Armada began their transit back to Spain. While this latest attempt to defeat the English queen and to purge England of any sign of any dogma or practice that was in contradiction to the Roman Church failed, the Spanish still had their ships and soldiers. They would return to Spain, refit, and try again next year. The Spanish admiral, the Duke of Medina Sidonia, issued the command to commence the passage to Spain. The Armada would sail north, close to Orkney Island and the Ring of Brodgar, and round the northern tip of Scotland. After sailing west, the Armada would stand out to sea and well off the rocky coast of Ireland. Once safely positioned, they would turn southward to Spain.

As the full moon approached on September 4, 1588, the witches sprang into action. Assembling at the two stone circles, they first called the element fire. At Callanish the witches assembled in the center of the stone circle. Their apprentices and servants surrounded them with a ring of fire. This circle of fire they were to tend till the next full moon in October. The witches were to remain in the circle till the threat was gone and they would have one full moon cycle to accomplish their work. On Orkney at the Ring of Brodgar, the fire was placed in the center of the circle. The witches danced around the fire. Their dance lasted till the next full moon in October. Many of the witches participating in this Nature work perished as they expended their life forces and cast their spirits to the four elements. It was their will, passion, and life force that commanded the elements and created the storm that was to torment the Spanish Armada.

The witches commanded the element of water, and the sea responded. The sea changed the course of its currents and bent the Gulf Stream closer to land. When the Spanish ships weathered the northern points of Scotland and set course to the south and Spain, they were pushed north and east, back and dangerously closer to the coast of Ireland than they had planned.

The witches then called the element of air. The element responded by blowing fierce out of the west. For weeks the gales battered the battle-damaged ships and pushed them ever closer to the rocky Irish coast.

The witches then called on the element of earth, and in response, the earth drew up its teeth to clutch and chew the hapless ships as they were blown against the rocky shores.

One hundred and sixty ships formed the Spanish Armada. All 160 ships left their Spanish ports on their mission to conquer the English, remove the English queen, and return her subjects to the Roman Church under Spanish discipline. They were first defeated by the stout English ships and prevented from landing their Spanish troops. The English sailors destroyed ten of the Armada's fleet. The Spanish ships dispersed. One hundred and ten Spanish ships remained together as a single fleet and sailed north from the English Channel into the North Sea and around the tip of Scotland to return to Spain. Twenty-four ships and five thousand men were lost on the Irish coast having been driven there by wind and sea. The Armada was not to recover for years. For those ships that escaped the rocky shores were so battered, their crews made so ill from typhus, that the hopes of Spanish conquest were set aside till another time when the memory of defeat would grow faint.

Some of the Spanish survivors of the twenty-four ships driven onto the Irish coast were lucky. Some were given safety and security by the Irish. Most were not so lucky and lost their lives or their freedom taken into slavery. The Armada was to rear its head twice again within the next ten years but was again driven off by storms. Storms generated by the same witches who were now alert and on watch for their freedom. But for the time being in 1588, England was safe, and the Picts of Scotland were secure to practice their traditions, to worship as they chose, and to pass their ancient arts on to their children.

To this day, yet there are those in Scotland who are direct descendants of the witches of Scotland who helped defeat the Armada. Ruthie is one such descendant. There are many still who learn the ancient craft from their mothers and grandmothers and pay daily homage to those who saved the traditions long ago in Elizabethan times.

Spirit Guides and Angels

Chapter 4: Living Is Dicey

Rules

It's said that perception is everything. Unfortunately, it matters little what something is as opposed to what it is perceived to be by a significant majority. So, we have the issue of the public's perception of what spiritual life and clairvoyance are as opposed to what I experience it to be.

I see a resurgence of traditional religion and a growing wave of evangelical devotional practices. I notice spirituality, as well as religion in general, also becoming more noticeable. The newspapers report on religion and devotional activities daily, much to my chagrin, as political discourse. I validate this claim by randomly looking at the morning paper. Today I see in the Seattle Post-Intelligencer a conservative evangelical group opposes the Supreme Court nominee. I see in the Seattle Times a failed firebombing probed at Shoreline Catholic Church. I note that these examples do not center about religious devotion, but then I turn the page and read Billy Graham's daily column in the spiritual writings section. Should these tidbits be examples of how our society interacts with religion and devotion? If that is the case, then the statement claiming America is paying close attention to religion and devotion would be a correct one in that we see a news story or philosophical statement visible in mainstream media every day.

I contrast the visibility of traditional religion with my rise in the paranormal cosmic consciousness over the last few decades. I seem to approach my spirituality from a different focal point and notice that many others also have growing interest and involvement in the metaphysical discipline and spiritual train of thought as opposed to the practice of formal religion.

With the current atmosphere of politics and religion, many eyes are turning toward spirituality as a path away from the new, emerging norm of marrying politics and religion. People may not necessarily seek out a spiritual mode of living, but within the current atmosphere of religion in the news, many people seem to feel that religion in general is not for them. Many people I have conversed with are seeing the benefits of spiritual practices decoupled from religion as they participate in purely spiritual pursuits for the first time in their lives.

Those I know who found interest in spirituality had one of two possible interactions with the lifestyle: they took a passing glance at spirituality after having a childhood steeped in traditional Christian religion and found it interesting and applicable to their lifestyle or they took a focused and purposeful look as they were inspired and intentionally considered living a spiritual life in advance of establishing the practice. The perceptions of living spiritually are seen through the prism of the beholder's value system and life experiences. The perceptions are also the measures of the personality's foundation and comfort level having some potential conflict with the original traditional belief system as practiced through childhood.

Spiritualism, as opposed to spirituality, is an organized and recognized religion. Many do not generally understand Spiritualism. Perhaps the impression of the activities and attributes of the lifestyle may be based upon the old-time stories of mediums. Mediums were the original ambassadors of the Spiritualist movement and religion. They were considered the living, earthly delegates of the spirit world to the general population.

Mediums were once associated with fraud. People did not understand the talents of the mediums. They labeled mediums as master illusionists and the facilitated communication from spirit as parlor tricks. Instead of mediums being considered a portal or channel to the mystical world and providing context for the continuity of life, mediums were associated with a negative representation of the mystical communication by the general population and the mainstream media. The act of communion with Spirit opens many opportunities for misconception. Clairvoyants pass messages and impressions from the world of Spirit to individuals. Consider this communication from a religious traditionalist's point of view. Some traditionalists with whom I have interacted, the evangelicals, share the perception that messages from spirit as delivered by mediums and clairvoyants may be from evil entities or the devil himself. The act of spiritual healing is another area where perception may come into play. The activities and motions associated with healings are also foreign to many. I see many opportunities for misguided perceptions.

The deck may then be stacked against acceptance of spiritual living by mainstream traditionalists. I, personally, chose to be discrete in my beliefs and to refrain from displaying and vocalizing my practices to the general public. How then shall I purport myself considering the prevailing perceptions?

Aside from the obvious, I conduct myself with personal integrity to remain beyond reproach. There are, however, overt precautions that I observe when practicing the art and activities of spiritual living. When engaged in spiritual and energetic healing, I keep hand movements to a minimum, thus, maintaining decorum. I work on a spiritual level with my thoughts and intentions. When I speak in lecture, give classes, or in general conversation, I keep on topic and stay away from topics that are too far out of the realm of the traditional belief systems, lest I open a can of worms. When or if I am confronted by the beliefs of others or their interpretation of the heavenly hierarchy, I stay positive and hold my tongue. Using my intuition in the work-a-day world, I keep highly personal topics for individuals till after an explicit invitation is given to speak of such items. When I am participating within a spiritual community and conducting circles, group gatherings, or when requested by others to speak of my spiritual observations, values, and beliefs, I ensure that the participants are sincere before I open and use my metaphysical gifts.

Right or wrong, people will perceive what they will. Thus, I maintain subdued politic viewpoints and outward appearances, remaining somewhat cautious and refraining from outlandish behavior to allow for a good first impression. I do not want an incorrect or unwarranted perception to muddle the true nature of any of my relationships whether they are of a personal, professional, or social nature.

Maintaining the status quo is human nature. It is not a conspiracy of persons in power to remain in power as much as it is the nature of humans to remain in power once achieved. They do so by maintaining the status quo. My thoughts free me from playing into the influences of the status quo.

Locally, I have personal experiences that are carried over, passed on, to others. The personal view is that I am boundless and unique. I praise and appreciate myself. I praise others and appreciate their uniqueness.

Thought is a vibration and a wave that radiates out from the center—a radio wave that broadcasts out. It reproduces itself whenever and wherever it can. Similar thoughts arouse themselves in the receiver's mind. The effectiveness of the penetrations or impact depends on the strength and clarity of the original, transmitted thought.

Effecting the reception is speech, attention, and the receiver's ability to understand the content. Yet the conveyance of the thought is more associated with its intent and heart driven quality than of the details. Spiritual thoughts initiate the types of vibrations that tend to stimulate a similar level of thought in others but also influence personal values within the given sphere of authority. We are surrounded by a sea of energy that responds to thoughts making every thought an impulse cloaked in a vehicle of vitalized matter. Every person tracks though life enclosed in a cage of forms created by their thoughts and desires. We live in a world of illusion where we make our own reality. Our thoughts are reproduced in the physical world as actions, events, or physical things. Thoughts are silent and invisible to most and this creates the illusion they are ineffective and not important. Yet thoughts should be chosen as carefully as words and not allowed to ramble aimlessly for thoughts create reality. My daily life is my reality. My thoughts determine the quality of my daily life. I am responsible for my own life and how I live. I recognize this aspect of thoughts as being proactive in practice.

Creation comes first from my mind in the form of thoughts then manifest into the physical world. I am constantly creating. I choose my creation by guiding thoughts and then I go out and create.

I cultivate self-discipline. This ain't easy for me, and it takes some work. I start by picking the best for all persons. Not my way or the highway or your way but the better way. I know the better way by first listening and seeking to understand. Then afterward, I seek to be understood. I try to take time to gain new skills and thought pools by reading and learning as the eternal student.

I try to inspire others and uplift those around me. If this is all I accomplish in my life, my life will have meaning. My success in this life will be realizing my potential and progressing in both mind and spirit. My obligation to progress does not end with knowledge. I must learn to apply whatever I learn to every part of my life.

Encouragement for All

There are many spiritual prisoners out there. Churches and spiritual organizations free spiritual prisoners. I support the organizations and those individuals that work them by giving my time or resources. It is at times difficult to give money. But if I've got it, what more noble cause than to support a not-for-profit spiritual organization? If I don't "got it," then I just participate in the service or activities that are provided.

I know that seeing new smiling faces adding to the number of people at a service provided by a teacher, preacher, priest, rabbi, or monk is an uplifting sight. I know that those keeping the spiritual organizations alive with their time and efforts are now in need of encouragement. I recognize that my participation in their services helps uplift the organization's members.

Sometimes I take in a service or session in a philosophy or religion that is entirely new to me. And at times, I recommit anew to the venues with which I am more familiar. With the current economy revenues from charitable donations are hitting all-time lows, those individuals buttressing spiritual places or servicing community-based organizations are in real need of some proof that what they are doing means something, somewhere. My participation and interest contribute to their sense of worth.

Spirit Guides and Angels

Many light workers are writing books, selling spiritual wares, and offering classes. Times are slow and revenues are hard to come by. Some light workers are losing heart and questioning their worth and value to the cause of freeing spiritual prisoners. A little nudge and notice go a long way. I try to participate in events, give my time, or just show an interest. That's all it takes.

I had a call from a friend who is also a light worker. I consider her a shaman. She intuitively receives information about the creative aspects of the universe and then publishes the text. On this call, her sales were down. She was despondent and unable to meet some of her financial responsibilities.

Shouldn't it be assumed that one who is so well versed in manifesting positive events and creating a dynamic life would be well-off? Unfortunately, as I am learning though experience, manifesting abundance requires keeping the thought of creation for months, staying focused, and remaining in the frequency that produces events that could potentially bring about the objective. One detracting thought or despondent word seems to negate all the work previously derived to create the happy results.

For me, that one detracting thought comes from my subconscious. I think it, and so it is, because the conditions within my subconscious are ripe for a negative thought or two.

Death and Taxes

I am learning that the key to manifesting anything is to approach the job with a completely positive attitude. That positive attitude is reflexive once it becomes part of my nature. Building myself a positive attitude requires me to always consciously look for the good in life and keep my focus fixed on the big picture. My positive attitude trains my subconscious. I experience setbacks training my subconscious. Setbacks are expected. But when I allow myself to succumb to the setbacks by becoming despairing, I reinforce the obstacles already present and place additional hindrances in my pathway. Dealing with my subconscious takes much time and effort to train this part of myself. There is no mode or method to directly train my subconscious that I know of. It can only be trained through attitude and time.

Cultivating attitude and training, my subconscious requires that I connect with the philosophies I learned when studying business in community college: "the Four Stages of Competence Model." The "Four Stages of Competence Model" originated with management trainer Martin M. Broadwell in the 1960s, who first described it as "the four levels of teaching." The model was popularized and subjected to further development. The model lent itself handily when undertaking a course of study in the sword, the Samurai sword.

The phases as applied to sword play are thus:

1. Unconscious incompetence: I don't know what to do with this sword, and I don't know that I don't know what to do.

2. Conscious incompetence: I don't know what to do for a given situation and I know that I don't know what I'm doing.

3. Conscious competence: I know what to do but I must think about it first and pay much attention to directing my bodily motion.

4. Unconscious competence: I know what to do and I don't even think about it. It's a reflex and muscle memory, and the skill is a part of who I am. It is a part of my being.

If I must think about what I am doing to parry a thrust, it's usually too late. The response must come without thinking and as a matter of instinct. Swordplay directly represents aspects of attitude and the connection with self—the core of my being—and how I process life using the typical practices of the day when addressing life's bumps in the road. Competency in the perspective of samurai swordplay directly corresponds to the attainment of correct subconscious responses in everyday life. Attitude improvement directly corresponds to the hours of training undertaken to become competent when wielding the sword once confidence is achieved.

The real-life application of the mentioned-above axiom would go something like this:

Death and Taxes

1. I travel my road reacting to whatever comes my way, never controlling my thoughts or cultivating my attitude and approach to life. I just respond to events madly and insanely at the mercy of the affair. I don't comprehend the connection between my thoughts and the influence those thoughts have on manifesting external events, events that draw uncontrolled reaction from me. I don't understand or consider that my life's a mess and I don't know what to do about it because I simply don't see or know that there's a problem.

2. I grow in maturity. My next step in development has me feeling that something is amiss in my life and I'm tired of being stressed out and at the mercy of all those external events that hit me at the wrong time. I think of this in terms of when I graduated high school and having no direction. I didn't have a clue of what I was to do next. I never gave living in the world any real thought. After wandering aimlessly, I started thinking that there has got to be more to life than working mundane jobs and partying at night. So, I reflect, think, plan, and focus because something in life is not right, and I know that because I'm not happy. Still, I don't know what to do, and if I did, I likely did not have the skill to do it.

3. Opening my eyes, I discover the relationship between my thoughts and the events that surround me, invading my space and peace of mind. I start to plot a strategy, a focus, and

I determine not be so reactive to external stimuli. To, in effect, control my mind and emotions when confronted with something out of the ordinary. I chill. I calm down and work in a direction of success. And when I slip and stray from my path by becoming emotionally upset or overreacting to something that I had absolutely no control over, I stop and take a breath. Yes. I know I'm overreacting and driving myself into a tizzy even though I'm lost in the moment and momentum, and I try to use the skills I have gained to calm myself and act constructively. That's progress.

4. After a time, I develop an attitude of success. My natural reaction to adverse events is to remain calm and focused. I do not fly off the handle but look on the brighter side. What follows, regardless of the trauma to which I am subjected, is natural and I ride out any storm in calm serenity. On the physical side, it may be that I work well in an emergency or am able to comfort a family member in time of need, guide a child, and become an example to follow.

Now hook this up with the discovery of the self in association with the spirit of life that resides within.

Every encounter I've had with the center of my being leaves me overflowing with positive, loving, and constructive energy and information. I go within and listen. I cannot believe my "ears," the information is that good. I receive a wealth of acceptance, peace, tolerance, and love of self. At first this information about myself was alien in nature. I've never been exposed to such good things about myself. Sure, I love people and some unconditionally but that part about loving myself comes with a bit more difficulty. Call it conditioning from this world and the life about me. Call it what you will, but when I do communicate with my spirit within or seek the spark of creation, I encounter positive acceptance and the call to love myself.

Once self-love and a relationship with the quiet, inner core of me solidified, I have never again been alone. People see a light about me or have some comfortable feeling when I'm around. Close friends and family comment on my relaxed look. They say that I have color in my cheeks and look healthy. The relationship with that spark within can be called many things. But whatever they call it, I've discovered it by developing a habit of calm, quiet meditation and by seeking the silence of the self. Seeking the silence is what I know as to be the first step in becoming conscious and conditioning myself to be who I want to be.

Quiet calmness can come to me at any time. It's a trip outside to grab a few minutes of solitude. At times it's a quiet, hot bath with the bathroom door closed. Maybe I light a few candles or maybe not. Others may take yoga or meditation classes. Some sit in quiet prayer. Whatever it takes.

I have conditioned myself to seek the quiet solitude within and be calm. I desire to have a relationship with my self and center and to recognize that spark, the creative center, that once unfurled signifies the universe. When I arrive, I feel the presence of angels about me and the peace of that universe.

With practice it gets easier. Eventually I don't even have to think about it, the going within. I've attained the unconscious competence and can approach life with a winning, confident attitude. Then whatever events come into my life, they will just be events. Nothing more. And I will be calling the shots as to how I respond—emotionally, physically, and financially.

Truth for Me

The world is a very colorful place. Many say that it's gray for our current situation. And it is at that. But at times, it is also colorful in its bounty and graces.

I don't have the luxury of having it all pass before me as one extreme or the other. I don't have it that easy. I can't just say that's all there is to it. I cannot ignore what is going on around me. And things are not that easy for me as I struggle with my life's challenges. The world is not all black and white—or red or blue or any two colors or trains of thought for me. It's not that easy for me to decipher. For I live in the current times. I recall this Chinese proverb or curse: "May you live in interesting times." Well. Interesting times these are.

I can't escape the times, but they don't have to define me. I must define myself in these times I live in and carve out my place. What is going on around me must not define me. What is going on around me must not impact me unless I allow it. I choose to be blessed by not having to suffer political or financial strife. I must go about my life making very local decisions that affect me in this life. I must live by philosophies and life's personal principles that enable me to live my life on my terms.

Living on my own terms is freeing. It is accepting. Accepting of self. Doing so provides me with pleasant memories. Good or evil throughout the world doesn't matter to me anymore. Only I and the immediate, local world around me matter.

And what gives me license to feel so? What allows me to ignore the times and to look at something from an eternal perspective? The law that my spirit and my soul are mated as one enables me to transit life with the perspective of my choosing. For this perspective is the manifestation of my connection to the infinite wisdom. I am a soul and within me

I carry the spark of eternal love and creation. I am of the divine and the infinite. And my soul is eternal.

All who live in these times are souls. We could feel it if we but tried. A soul is who I am: an eternal being. The immutable spark of life is within me, and it is an expression of a spirit. And my soul is my spiritual shadow that keeps measure of my progression through eternity.

I live my life as a soul. I know my times, but I choose to know myself better. I will state my views. I will speak my feelings and truths. Refine them. Define them, in words for all to hear so that I can place voice for others to witness the passing of my life. The words I utter will implant upon my soul like a shadow of an eternal record and I will become the master of who I am and how I shall live. I shall be courageous and fearless. Am I not eternal? Will I not live forever?

Reincarnation and Karma

I chose to become a soul and to enter the earthly life cycle. This cycle can last for many years—millions of years. The choice tends to bind me to a planet and the destiny therein. The choice is mine from the start. My intentions are to learn, and to identify with those to whom I provide service. I take a turn, put shoulder to the wheel, and join in with all souls to Godhead and Source. Again, it is all my choice.

Death and Taxes

Before my choice was made, I entered the mentorship of others who have been to this place before me or with those who are higher heavenly beings than I am in the eternal hierarchy.

I and other celestially generated beings that carry the spark of creation choose to undertake the worldly learning cycle, the life cycle of the humanly souls. I determined my milestones and defined what it is I sought from this life cycle. I made my choices while at the seat of all knowledge. My undertaking is not an expression from the perspective of a single life. It is an expression from an eternal outlook as I am an eternal being. As I previously opined, I chose to undertake the cycle, and I understand that the cycle can take millions of years to arrive at my chosen goals.

Karma is not a matter of concern. It is not the determining factor in reentry into a single new life. Karma is expunged through intent and expression. Karma is a balancing act, or better said, a balancing measure to assist in selecting the follow-up needed to keep on the path to stated objectives. I, in this life, any life, or while in between lives, can take my destructive thoughts and deeds or those shared with others' and clear them through thought, expressions of love and forgiveness, to understand the relationship between my thoughts and my actions. My goal is to learn and then to move onward. I can take my karmic debts and settle them in this life, the next, or while in between.

Yet the term "karmic debt" is a misnomer. There is no debt. Not ever. There is just a measure to be used in learning processes, and the measure helps to navigate toward destiny and goals.

During this life appearance, I place destructive thoughts and expressions into the violet flame to transmute the resulting manifestation into grace. While in between lives, I come to terms with the effects of my previous life's thoughts and actions and regain my equilibrium. All that is needed is my acknowledgment and understanding to create the cleansing, loving fire with which to burn and transmute the thoughts into love. With living in this manner, there never can be a debt accumulated from one life to the next.

Karma, therefore, is not a penalty. It is not a heaviness of materialization that has so encumbered me that I am forever bound to repeat another life on the earth. It is not an eye for an eye. It is merely a measure that marks the understanding of a journey within the soul cycle no matter what the environment and circumstance of the life past.

One's actions in the current life are not effects of causes occurring in another. Take for example a violent act and how that would pertain to karma. Is the violent action the originating cause setting effects into motion, or is the violent action a settling of a karmic debt from another life? Is the violent act initiated as a learning opportunity? A victim's remaining family members may then gain the opportunity to learn forgiveness. Does the originating act of violence require a payment in return? And is the payment required if the survivors forgive the perpetrator? The Hawaiians in their Huna discipline believe that sins are those actions executed by one person who tramples or hurts another. The hurt does not have to be physical in nature. The sin is forgiven or cleared as the perpetrator settles through communication and honesty with the one violated. The one so violated forgives. The sin is forgiven. The civil debt is nullified and becomes but a lesson for a soul. The lessons to be learned in this example are to understand the consequence and effects of actions or words, to learn empathy, to communicate with others, and to forgive and to accept forgiveness. The individuals involved eventually come closer and better understand that they both carry the same spark of life.

There are many ways and methods that I balance out my thoughts, words, deeds, and actions. As such, karma is not the determining factor that guides my entry into another life on this world, this illusion. Karma is not what binds me to the repeating, individual life cycle.

Spirit Guides and Angels

As I transition from one life to another, I do so in pursuit of my goals. Goals formed long ago in my life—my eternal life. Not all choose to enter the cycle, and of those that do, not all choose to reenter into another single life at any given time. The choice is ours to make at every instance, and I make that choice while sitting in my eternal peace among my heavenly brothers and cocreations. I do not have to reincarnate. I choose to reincarnate.

As I enter one life after another, I do not necessarily advance in my physical circumstance, understanding, and development. One life I can be a head of state with the greatest knowledge and spiritual understanding of my times. The next I could be a broken wretch. It's all relative to my development goals and the potential outcomes. The determinations of my entry into life and the circumstances I choose are made when residing in my eternal place and in counsel with my mentors.

What are my individual goals for each reincarnation in the first place? These goals vary for each life but are originally motivated through wisdom and experience gained after living the previous physical life. Why do I reincarnate into the next life or the next one after that? I do so because I want to. Is it because I have a debt to pay? No. Debts have nothing to do with it, for all debts are settled as I am forgiven by the one true source. Forgiveness is given at the instance of my discretion.

Death and Taxes

Do I reincarnate to learn? Yes. Do I reincarnate to help others? Yes. Do I incarnate to help myself? Yes, at times. To help myself learn a specific life experience or a characteristic attribute of a person, or a soul, that can only be learned by living through the earthly physical experience—to experience something that can only be experienced in this crazy, demented, and dysfunctional life we live on this crazy, demented, and dysfunctional world.

Who then am I that I should choose to reincarnate and enter the cycle of life of this planet? I am an eternal being. I am the direct offshoot of the One Source, the Thought, and Creation. I am the act of Creation. I am a child that carries the essence of my Parent. I am the child of the Father and the Mother and of the duality of the Thought. It is not my sole intention to finally and eventually express the God within while on this earth in human form, as that expression already exists within my being. It is my intention to better identify with the human soul's condition so that I may serve to a higher degree. My goal is to gain empathy for this species and those others that inhabit this planet.

Many of us spend countless years, lives, and eons running from the true expression of the God self within while transiting the material illusion called life. Some have lost their way in the density of the material illusion. Many have forcibly remained blind during life. They cultivate attitudes and beliefs that are carried to their eternal life after their journey though the single, last life. Their emulsion into the depths of materialization becomes their folly. Yet while in the afterlife, such souls still choose to return and to live again on this earth. Why? They do so because it is within their nature and the cycle of reincarnation is just one avenue to remain in the game and to conquer the challenges of the physical, material illusion.

While living, I am much like the salmon that return to the spawning river. The salmon can't tell you why; they only know that they must travel to where life is renewed. And so, I seek the spiritual path. When this physical body is shed, I will return to the source to renew and to again join with creation as the eternal and heavenly being that I am at my core. The entry into the incarnation cycle is a method for me to learn, but it is also a method for me to teach others, to help others. The intention to be realized through each single reincarnation and each life cycle is the raising of vibrations for all created worldly souls in the hope that all will fully attain Oneness with the Creation. Whether I choose to reincarnate or not, I am tethered, bonded, and bound to the destiny of my charges and to their eventual triumph and glory.

How I Do It

My spiritual perspective is comparable to science and philosophy, based upon the demonstrated experience I have in communication with a life force that lives within me, otherwise known as spirit. My spiritual perspective makes fast the relationship between my spirit, soul, mind, and body. A universal spirit or infinite intelligence animates my experience. My spiritual outlook brings about a living, active, and working belief in the continuity of life and knowledge that I am not alone and that the truth is stranger than fiction.

My spiritual perspective brings about spirit-minded experiences as I strive to understand and to comply with the physical, mental, and spiritual laws of nature as I observe and understand them. My spiritual outlook brings about an appreciation for natural law. Natural law is the orderly, progressive, and evolutionary process of a life spirit manifesting in every aspect of nature and time, seen or unseen.

My interaction with Spirit is real, and the celestial beings I interact with are like human beings stripped of their outer garments of flesh but still possessing a substantial body called soul and an animated mind called spirit. As I experience these spiritual phenomena, I investigate, analyze, and classify the facts and manifestations of my experiences. My interaction with the celestial is real.

Spirit Guides and Angels

There is a difference between science and spiritual. My spiritual thought recognizes and accepts the existence of spiritual substances and interactions through my personal experiences. My thoughts assume the existence of a nonphysical reality that is as great as the reality of the physical or material world and life as I see this illusion. Science is neither able nor willing to accept such a premise because the phenomena are not currently concrete and provable in the world of proof and demonstration. Science requires predictability and repeatability where set procedures are established and conducted. My spiritual experiences are not always so predictable and measurable.

Living my spiritual life promotes my observance of the golden rule. All cultures recognize a golden rule. The reoccurring theme is that one should treat others as they themselves would want to be treated. The common thread is to project a respect for self and for others equally and to love others as one loves the self. I tend to remember to love others and to express that love, but I forget to love myself and to outwardly express some form of this love. For me to live a true spiritual life, I must first love myself. Then love others as I love myself. Then treat others as I would want to be treated.

My spiritual living promotes a need to be in service to others. It is through service that I can cultivate the actions necessary to live the Golden Rule. Service is good for my soul as it is an outlet for generosity. It is also good for society as it mingles all people and classes. It uplifts others and, in so doing, raises the consciousness of the environment and those about and around me.

Service brings me appreciation and gratitude for my offered gifts and awareness for the conditions of others. My duty to others is thus through service, and through this service comes the path to higher spiritual living and to finding the heaven within. It is activity and action that bring me down this golden path. Sitting in quiet contemplation brings answers to my questions, but it is action that propels my thoughts into created physical representations and expressions, the direct advantage of contemplation.

Through service to others, I raise my life to higher levels. If not directly, then indirectly, as the others about me rise in consciousness and awareness. Then, as they are raised up, they can buoy and assist me. It is a circle, yes?

As a spiritual practitioner, I am a student of nature's law, knowing that the truth is planted in every heart. I realize that there are different stages and planes to consciousness. The law of life reaches into my flesh as well as into my spirit. I am spirit now as much as I shall ever be in this physical life. My thoughts and senses of being are the things of the spirit. The laws pertain to that continuity and duality of life. These are the foundations of my spiritual living.

Death and Taxes

Chapter 5: Living Is Constantly Learning

Always Angelic Intervention

We were living together for just over two months, my future dear spouse and me. We lived in a nice rental owned by the mother of an acquaintance. We were to eventually get married, but for now, we chose to live together in a rental and enjoy what life had to bring us.

She had a Honda Civic. It was the first brand-new car she ever bought. It was her baby. She referred to it as "her." I was getting to take "her" out solo to run errands and spend some time with "her" on my own. It was a first.

The street we lived on was not busy but popular. We were smack in the middle of a road grid system of main arterials. Our house was one block off a main arterial and five blocks south of a second perpendicular arterial that had a traffic light. I would go straight north on our street, five blocks through the traffic light, and bypass the arterials and traffic. At Eighty-Fifth Street I stopped at a red light and waited for the green light and for the cross traffic on the main arterial to clear. As I waited at the red light, cars approached the intersection from the opposite side of Eighty-Fifth Street and queued up facing me, also waiting for the light to change. The car across the street facing me was signaling to make a left, intending to cross in my wake to head east on Eighty-Fifth while I traveled north on my road. The cross traffic cleared the intersection, and the traffic light turned green. As I was going straight, I had the right of way over the other car in front of me turning to his left. The car across from me, a BMW carrying a mom, dad, and kid, waited for me to proceed straight through the intersection and take my right of way. I got a nod from the driver. It was understood that I was cleared to go.

I pressed the accelerator. I tried to press the accelerator. At first, I thought a bottle or object rolled under the pedal. There was none. I glanced at the other driver. I was proceeding. I'm going. I'm going. He was waiting. I pressed the accelerator again. I tried to press the accelerator again. My thought and intent were to press the accelerator. I gave the mental and reflexive command to press the accelerator and for all assumptions, intents, and purposes, I was pressing the accelerator. But the pedal did not depress. My foot never pressed it, and my ankle joint never bent to the task. Somewhere between my mind, brain, and foot, the electrical stimulus and command to press just didn't get through. I glanced up at the other driver. It was clear that someone had to proceed now. He honked his horn and took a hesitating jerk forward to cross in front of me. He must have assumed I yielded the right of way. But to proceed on an assumption and to collide with me would bring liability to him so he hesitated just for an instance as I looked up at him dumbfounded. My body was poised to move the car forward, and I was sure this time that I would succeed in entering the intersection.

The driver of the tank had long, scraggly hair. Not too long but down to his shoulders. He wasn't a hippie. His hair was not a fashion statement. It matched his beard: long, unkempt, and scraggly. He was driving a twenty-five-year-old Dodge station wagon tank. You know the type. Heavy, steel construction that stops at nothing and suffers nary a dent to the fender or a scratch to the paint job upon impact, leaving the car it collided with bent and mangled. Bronze in color and needing a carwash, it blurred in front of me and across my path as it flew through the red light from right to left, into the intersection and through.

As the bronze station wagon tank cleared the intersection, I once again pressed down on the gas pedal and proceeded straight across and through the intersection. The driver in the BMW glanced at me with a look of surprise and visible relief. I shot him a smile and a salute from the brim of my ball cap and proceeded across and through the intersection on my daily errands while driving "her" solo for the very first of many occasions.

Spirit Guides and Angels

My First Shaman Journey

Upon our marriage, my dear spouse and I purchased a house. This house was our home in every sense. A nice old-fashioned Tudor, it had the perfect layout and floor plan. At one time, this house sat on the outskirts of Seattle: the very last northern street. That was in the days when Seattle reached up to Eightieth Street. The city would eventually expand to 145th Street and beyond. But back in the day, this old Tudor house of ours was on the very outskirts of town. The house was originally built as a custom home. How do I know? The second floor had oak hardwood floors instead of the typical fir found on second floors. And the mahogany throughout was 1920s straight grain. It was a grand old house and quite comfortable if not noisy from being placed on the last main road in the Seattle city limits. That last main road in Seattle turned into a heavily used arterial. The house sported a postage stamp backyard with some very old foliage and fruit trees.

There is a dead cherry tree stump in the backyard. It stands about six feet tall. I call it Mother. It looks like it's holding a child in swaddling clothes, and the child looks like a smaller version of herself.

At night, when the outside light is turned on, you can see her face in the shadows. And sometimes during the day, you can see, too. The last springtime she was alone. This springtime, arriving early, and I can see that she is no longer alone. At first, her face was the only face I saw in the shadows, but this spring, now, others joined her. I started seeing several different faces when I looked by the light of the lantern, faces that were not there when I first met her.

I call her Mother because she is the mother of all that you can't see in this region. The "all" are the fairies and elves, and the lives of unseen nature. They were once known, recognized, and honored by all the inhabitants that lived in the region till this civilization came. With all the homes now owned and run by average citizens, Mother and her kin go unrecognized, lost, and faded from our imagination and memory. Yet I recognized her and her children. They are alive to me. The other faces I see with her are the etheric residents of the neighborhood who have come to visit with her and me.

The others are not here now, at this moment. Their visit lasted for a couple of months. Now it is again just Mother whom I see.

Motivated by my studies in shamanism, I took a journey to the underworld. One reaches the underworld through a hole in the ground. My visit to the underworld was accomplished through the holes in Mother's trunk. There are two holes in the Mother stump. Either one can take you into the underworld. I use the one at her crown. It is by traveling down into the holes and into the earth that we arrive at the underworld, where shamans visit.

My first trip to the underworld was to look for spirit helpers. The first introduction I had to spirit helpers was in 1973. After studying the ways of the Northwest natives, I traveled to the Oregon Cascades to find my spirit helper. The animal that was then shown to me was the osprey.

For this journey, I traveled down to the underworld through the hole in the stump placed at Mother's crown. It was very small and led to a tunnel that channeled springs of fresh water. As I proceeded down into the ground, I traveled upon these springs. At times, I floated on the springs. At times, I flattened myself or turned into a mercury-like pancake to travel between the layers of rock.

I soon came into a cave. I could see light at the far end of the cave. It looked like there was an exit on the other end. The area I was approaching appeared to be an antechamber, a room. I gained entrance into the antechamber through a narrow tunnel with light at the other end. That light soon displayed the faraway images of scenery, although I could not tell from the entry point if it were sea or mountains or forests. At that moment, and immediately before me, appeared a spider with teeth and fangs. As I got closer to the spider, it grew in size. The closer I came, the larger it got, eventually taking up the entire breadth of the tunnel. Blocking my path, I was not able to walk around it.

Unable to proceed, I looked for help. From the fissures of the passageway that I traveled came animals to fight the spider. First, a squirrel came. Then a rabbit came, followed by an otter and then a rat. None were able to combat the spider because the spider remained so large. These animals were also not natural predators of spiders.

But then came the crows. One crow led the rest. He said to me, "I'll do this for you." He and his associates began attacking the spider. Yet once the crows arrived, the spider was no longer large; it returned to a natural size. The one crow that spoke to me ate the spider. That was all that was needed to free my path to the other end of the tunnel into the antechamber.

With the spider gone, my path to the underworld was clear. I proceeded. After entering and then exiting the antechamber, I discovered that the cave opened in all its grandeur. I could now see the exit ahead and the source of light clearly. Instead of proceeding onward out of the cave, I took a perch on a ledge that stood immediately before the opposite opening. The ledge was more like a balcony in a theater, a perfect place to survey the landscape and scenery that lay on the other side of the tunnel and cave I traveled in my journey. Upon the balcony, I surveyed the landscape before me. This, I surmised, was the underworld.

Immediately beyond the balcony were gentle sloping hills. The underworld, overall, looked like the Cotswolds in England. To the left were rolling hills without vegetation except for field grasses and an occasional tree or hedgerow. To the right, again, were rolling hills that transitioned to a steep and rocky slope with a mountain range beyond the slope. I instinctively knew that on the other side of the mountain range, the topology before me was repeated but in reverse.

I left my perch and continued my journey, exiting the cave and choosing the path to the right, to the mountain range. The terrain gradually increased in hilliness and vegetation. First came underbrush, then hedges, then trees, till near the foot of the first mountain, there were forests. Thick forests.

This first mountain was not like a Northwest volcano that comes to a peak, but more like a segment of the Endless Chain Ridge in Canada. As far as my eye could see to the right and left of this initial mountain was the giant slab of uprooted ground forming a mountain chain, with this initial outcrop the highest point.

I walked to the section of the hills leading up to the mountain that had the sparsest number of trees. I sat and rested in a clearing overlooking the Cotswold below. I called for spirit guides, and several came. First came the small animals of the forest, soon followed by a bear, a wolf, and a coyote. Then came a horse, small birds, crows, eagles, and a hawk. I asked which one was my spirit guide, and they answered that they all were. They said that I would not have one single guide for this visit but all the animals in the underworld are to be my guides. They all would help and assist me. They told me to go to the mountaintop. They did not want me to walk so I should take the horse. The rest would follow and see me later when I arrived at my destination.

I mounted the horse and the horse started along the path. Once started, the horse took a jump and left the ground to begin flying. This horse did not have Pegasus wings and fly in that manner. It just spread its front and rear legs ahead and behind and flew looking like a cross between Superman and Rocket J. Squirrel. There appeared webs between the legs as the horse glided and rode the air currents up to the mountaintop.

Once on the summit, I could see all the land below me: the land I had flown over and the land beyond. Far off in the distance, I saw the walls of the underworld. The walls had many cavern openings and within these openings, many balconies. The ground of the underworld in general and below the mountain looked like the landscape I mentioned, the

Cotswolds. The underworld in total seemed to be an extremely large cavern, but between the ceiling of this giant cavern and me were clouds and a light source. The roof of the cavern was not lighted, but a light source was situated somewhere between the roof and me.

As I alighted onto the mountaintop, there were others to greet me. There were the leopard and the bear and small birds that were playing on a flat and grassy outcrop. The mountain goat, eagles, and condors then arrived. Then others arrived. These others were the animals I first saw at the lower hills. All the animals were walking on hind legs except for the cats; yes, there were cats also. Last arriving were two others: an old man with a book or papyrus and a child man wearing white. I asked who my spirit guide would be and for the reason of this gathering.

The old man spoke. He conveyed to me that all the animals of the underworld would be my guides, as previously mentioned. He said this was out of respect to me. The respect came to me from these underworld inhabitants because I believed in them and because I believed in and spoke with the elves and fairies of the outer world. They honored me as I lived my life with knowledge and recognition of their existence and because I often paid them nobility and homage. It was because of this they would lovingly repay the honor by offering me their services as a bond through love, not through obligation.

The child told me that I would come here often for meetings with others of my kind and then told me to look to the other side of the mountainside, the side I had yet to view. I did as I was instructed, and I found that the other side of the mountain was just like the side I came from—just as my intuition informed me when I first saw the mountain range.

All gathered then started to dance. The animals danced on hind legs and the birds did acrobatics in the air. The eagle danced on his talons while walking on the ground. Soon after this celebration started, I said that it was now time for me to return to the physical world.

I raised my hands and stretched. My hands and arms grew longer, eventually reaching the roof of the underworld. I entered the fissures in the roof, turned into water and mercury, and traveled up through the fissures till reaching my physical self and took my place sitting in my backyard lawn chair.

So ended my first intentional trip to the underworld.

Shape-Shifting

When shape-shifting, I don't actually change shapes. I feel the wind under my wings. I feel the air when moving through the changing layers. I feel the muscular exertion as I flap my wings. I look down while my eyes are closed in meditation and my vision sees from great heights. I look at my body, and I see that it looks like the animal I have become. I feel strength, the pounding of wings, or the beating of the hooves.

I may make sounds. The sounds may not be those exactly of the animal. But I feel that they are. If I had the vocal mechanisms of the animal the sounds would be exactly those of the animal. My Homo sapiens vocal cords do not well reproduce the call of an owl or a horse.

And when the shifting is over and I open my eyes, the very first thought is one of surprise. Surprise to be sitting where I am and in the body I am in. Surprise. Even though my conscious mind knows who I am, there is a moment of surprise and shock. The animal spirit is still with me. I recognize it and catch it by surprise and unawares before it goes away by slipping slowly out of my frontal consciousness. My conscious mind and the animal spirit mingle just for that singular moment when one returning as the other leaves. As they rub shoulders, I see both sides of the mirror at once.

What is there afterward? What am I left with? Knowledge that it has happened, and I did take flight, if only in my mind at first. I know that a shift in my consciousness has occurred. The more I fly, the more I retain the experience and ability to slip into flight at will. Eventually to carry the experience on to the awakened state and to walk about, drive a car, and talk with a coworker all at the same time as I fly high above the hills looking down from my height having the sense of an eagle. Multitasking.

The more I practice my flight, the easier to call it at will. Instead of being recessed deep within my being and felt as a vague memory, the capacity to place myself into the spirit of an eagle experiencing flight, vision, and understanding; will become more of a way of life for me with every session and occurrence. The knowledge of the freedom will never really be recessed, deep within my psyche again, but will always be there, ready to take flight the moment the window is opened.

Thus, I develop a tool to look down from heights while bonding across the species. Or perhaps a tool to bring the feeling of freedom and escaping the doldrums of work and occupation.

Into a Mound Covered with Hides

My self-induced exercise was to visit a temple. Any temple. For once I reached a meditative state with my intention of entering a temple, one would appear. I've done this exercise often enough to know that there will be an appropriate temple when and where I needed it to be.

This time, and for my first time, the temple I had before me was not the traditional structure that had doors and columns. This time the temple was a mound covered with skins. It was shoulder high above ground as it was partially dug into the ground. Before and in front of the opening were two Native Americans. The one on the right was from the Arizona area. Hopi, I believe. He wore an eagle headdress. The one on the left was of the northern hills and mountains. He was Crow or Blackfoot. He wore a buffalo headdress. His headdress, once I recognized it as a buffalo, changed to the coyote mask. Then it changed back to the buffalo. This switching continued throughout my visit.

This mound hut or temple was covered with hides. The hides were tan, white, and brown. They looked like an Appaloosa horse. There were other coverings. There were no large furs like bear but small ones of the beaver and the dog. The domesticated animals and beasts of burden had connections to the owners at one time during their physical lives. The animal hides placed upon the mound were in memory of the service the animal provided during their span of life. As the animals met their natural demises, the human partners preserved and retained their hides honoring the earthly experience they had in common.

The Indian to the right, the Hopi, wore clothing top and bottom. He was red like the red rocks of Sedona. I've heard that the eagle feather is given only to those who have conquered and mastered hardships, to those who were brave. My right side represents my physical aspect in this physical life.

My left side represents the spirit or spiritual aspect of my physical life on earth. The Indian to my left, the Crow or Blackfoot, stood before me bare chested. His persona alternated between the buffalo and the coyote. The buffalo roams the open fields of nature and is hooved. It is the four-footed creature of strength and stamina bringing prosperity to the tribe, community, and nation. The merry trickster, the coyote, is full of fun and jokes. The coyote also represents innocence. Something about these two representatives of Native American tribes reminded me of myself while also signaling that these two were showing me aspects of my physical and spiritual beings.

Into the temple we went. The inside, the walls and ceiling of the mound that I stood within, was lined with crystals of various shapes and sizes joined as one solid piece. The various sections of quartz crystal looked both rough and polished, some weathered and others not. None of them were in a man-made shape but all looked as if they naturally spawned there within the mound, growing from infancy to maturity upon the walls and ceiling.

The crystals about me represented and emanated their typical gemstone properties. This would go without saying. Rose quartz emanated a loving vibration and heightened my corresponding emotional state. The amethyst cleared me of any out-of-sort skittish feelings I may have had at the time. And the clear quartz just amplified the properties of the stones nearest to their proximity. The presence of the gemstones I had before me in vision radiated and provided me a practical and beneficial physical impact that I physically felt as I sat in a meditative state on my comfortable living room chair. I was to discover that this meditative visit and vision would leave lasting physical impacts, beneficial to my body and state of mind throughout the following month.

Inside the temple were also a bed, chairs, and tables upon the floor. There were various tools placed throughout the inside of the mound. I did not take the time to identify each tool or its use. There were items lying on the table. The mound had a lived-in look about it.

After some period, my guides and I left the hut temple. We proceeded to yet another temple. Our procession was in the company of others. Several members of the procession carried a platform. The platform was one that would carry the dead to a final resting place, to be then placed, buried or cremated. I was raised up to lie on this platform of the dead, and once situated, the processional continued onward.

The processional halted at the next temple, the temple of death and rebirth. As we remained in place and I still was lying on the platform of the dead, a host spoke praises of trust, appreciation, and love. A choir sang melodies of peace and rest. "Having carried the battle and the life thus far, rest and have peace," they bid me as one by their words and song chanting a repeating chorus. "I was free. Free of earthly limitations and I was reborn of the body and the identity. The soul that first animated my body was now another. The soul that started with my physical life at natal birth some fifty years ago left and now was another. Now another received the baton to carry on for the remaining span of years. And now comes another, stronger and of greater brightness, new energy, and strength."

My Living Room Chair

The living room of the old, custom-built, Tudor house had a comfortable winged back chair in the far corner. This spot was the perfect place to seek the quiet and silence within my spirit. The chair was the most comfortable I had known up to that time.

Spirit Guides and Angels

I sit in my nice comfortable chair and close my eyes. It doesn't matter that there is noise outside. There's always noise outside from traffic on this heavily traveled road we live on. What is important is my physical comfort in the chair. The chair must fit. This chair fits perfectly. The noise about me, background noise from the neighborhood, doesn't distract me and it wouldn't distract you either.

My eyes close and I take a deep breath, and it's off I go. My immediate sensation is the growing of roots from my hands and feet into the ground. The roots extend into the earth and take hold. Roots, tendrils—however you would refer to the phenomenon. But for me, I feel an immediate, though unrushed, discharge from my body and mind into the earth. This discharge affects my muscular system. I become quite relaxed and tension free. The release is so noticeable that even my ears tone down their constant ringing.

The earth reciprocates my reaching out and comes up to meet me. Not as though I am being buried by an upwelling of earth where it will take me over and cover me up but like a scene from time lapsed animation, I slowly turn to rock. First my feet and legs turn to rock, then completing the sculpting, the top of my crown and everything in between morphs into solid rock. Just for a moment at any rate, or so it may seem as the image flashes before my mind. If I were to interpret what

I looked like in this situation, I would be the sculpting of a Babylonian patriarch or merchant sitting in a high-backed chair, arms on the rest and frozen in granite taking on the hue of New Hampshire's Man in the Mountain. As I sit in a chair, there is no discernible boundary between the earth and granite me. I can feel down to the bedrock and the tensions and pressures of the local geology as the seismic plates rub shoulders and torque against one another. As I identify with the land, I soon feel the push of water against me.

First, I feel the land and its natural pressure and tension, then extending my awareness, I feel the weight of the water in the sound pushing against me. I find that there is no boundary standing in the way of my identifying with the salt water and the life therein. Puget Sound is sprawling with life and the constant pull of currents, always moving and always breathing in some form. Retreating glaciers carved the sound. The waters are deep with the land dropping off sharply, immediately plunging to the very depths of the sound. Eventually, and in some places, the depth of the water reaches 1,250 feet with the land forming almost vertical walls, descending to the bottom of the sea.

As the volume of the water pushes against the wall of land, I feel this pressure against my cheek as if a hand is gently cupping my face. The water draws away any lasting tensions in my body, and I lose myself into that sea world. No longer aware of my skin or any worldly fears, worries and apprehensions for this physical life I live in, I am now ready to reach out into the heavens by going deep within my being.

Next, I feel a sparkle. I feel or see a small and quick, penetrating flash as if I am seeing the setting sun reflecting off a distant window on an opposite shore. This spark is tickling my forehead, and I am ever mindful of the physical sensation. The tickle settles, leaving the lingering remains of a delicate finger touch or of a soft and tender kiss upon my brow.

Next, I notice a low, humming vibration and a circling of sparks taking place at the base of my spine. Some would say that this was the area of my first chakra, the base chakra. Identifying this area of my body as the first chakra is an adequate way to identify or classify the point where the body's physical anatomy interacts directly with the celestial counterpart. These chakras are tools. They bring attention to the workings of my localized body and the energetic characteristic associated with the corresponding facets of my being. In all, the dynamic helps me focus my interaction between heaven (chakra) and earth (body), with me (mind) in the middle. Mentally focusing on and physically pointing to a chakra at a particular point on my physical body helps me relate to these relative energies, dynamics, and interactions I may not fully understand. For my purposes this is a method I use to build my personal relationship with each chakra and the mode of communication between physical and mystical.

The base, first or root, charka is associated with my connection to the earth and provides me a mechanism for grounding. I say that the first chakra is the center of earthly manifestation. Influencing change in my material environment, business ventures or material possessions, the energy to succeed in this world will come from the first chakra. This is not at all a comprehensive interpretation or explanation of the first chakra's domain.

The internet is crawling with data on relationships with the chakras. Generally, the data is good. The object, however, of my focus is my personal relationship with my chakras' representations of subjective energy, interaction with that energy, and the intersection of that energy between the physical and the mystical. The flux and flow of my emotional and physical bodies are defined and influenced based upon my personal intimacy and familiarity with each chakra focal point. My goal is to regulate the relative aspect of my energies as defined for each of the seven chakras and to bring them all in balance. This brings my mystical being in balance with my physical existence. The meaning or technical definition of each chakra might be generally accepted principles agreed upon by all. However, the intricacies as to how I relate to the energies and principles are unique to me. I tend to stay away from harvesting metaphysical information from the internet or any spiritual teacher. For me, keeping my own counsel and allowing my intuition to teach the technical lesson works best.

At this point in my session, I see the area of the first chakra begin to spin in response to my initiation. The spinning looks like a fireworks display, but instead of sparks, the emitted lights look like the trails of shooting stars. Silently they radiate out from the spinning wheel's axis. The spinning wheel is turning clockwise. I initiate a second spinning wheel superimposed upon the first. This second wheel is spinning counterclockwise and trailing off shooting stars. I create a third wheel, also. This third wheel remains stationary and is in the shape of an orb. The combined activities of the three separate and distinct representations cleanse and vitalize my corresponding physical area, my connections to the physical earth, and my work-a-day present-day emotional state. By the time I am finished giving attention to this first chakra, it's a vibrant and unblemished red in color.

My awareness rises from the area of the first chakra on my body, up to my belly. My belly is the location of a second chakra. This point of focus influences my creativity, intuition, and my self-worth. Friendliness, harmonic emotions, and confidence in my own creativity and my ability to relate to others in an open and friendly way are characteristics that all emanate from this chakra. As I engage in creative or friendly pursuits in social settings, I get a warm and comfortable feeling in my belly. When my belly feels balanced, my emotions flow freely, and I reach out to others more willingly. I've heard that a man's heart can be reached through his belly. Perhaps this is where that ditty comes from, but for now, as I sit here, my mind wanders through the visions of family eliciting a warming reaction in the navel of my belly.

Here too the spinning wheels are active. As with the area of my first chakra, the counter rotating spinning wheels with a third stationary, in place, orb emit the shooting spark of falling stars. The color I see here is orange. A clear and unblemished orange that I wrap around myself as a smile slowly appears on my face.

The sensation or imagination I have of energy centers sprouting from my spine and core is now advancing up my spine of its own accord. Where at one moment I felt that my mind or thoughts had to stimulate the spinning of wheels and brightening of the colors, I am now letting some unseen momentum take over and the spinning wheels appeared again and again effortlessly and thoughtlessly, once for each chakra region.

I can't tell you how long this process lasts or how long it takes for my awareness and attention to climb the ladder of the seven chakras. There were times when I would sit and, immediately after exhaling my first breath, the light show would commence and end before my second breath began.

At other times I would pause at each focal point and inspect the prevailing conditions. I would energize the light and contribute to the intensity of the spinning shooting stars. Or I would polish and buff the orblike representation of the chakra. Perhaps I would peer into the center. My mind's eye would follow a tunnel focus as it tangles, turns, and intertwines with my being. Arriving at the emotion, organ, or state of being represented by the chakra. I would then objectively project harmony and calmness into the region symbolized by the defined chakra.

My physical body is directly impacted by my attention and harmonic influence when I work with my chakras. After I cease my session, my body shows no outward signs of change. My emotional state as it relates to the seven aspects of the individual chakras, however, is peaceful and in harmony with the physical me. In addition, the relationship between my celestial self and my physical me gets closer and somewhat in alignment, balanced, and agreeable toward one another.

Moving my center of attention from one center to the other also has its effects. The momentum of my attention's movement from one chakra to the other clears away any debris in the middle. The clearing connects one vital point to the other and enhances the exchange of information between energy points. This enhanced exchange keeps the chakras in alignment with one another, like a straight spine and excellent posture, benefiting the infrastructure of my being, physically, emotionally, and intellectually. I categorize and group my seven chakras into three domains: the physical (first, second, third), the personal spiritual (fourth, fifth), and the universal celestial (sixth, seventh). A good transiting and energizing of my chakra tree harmonize the three categories with one another to a noticeable degree. This harmony beneficially influences my physical well-being and my interactions with others.

The momentum of my focus eventually drives my awareness beyond my crown and to a point above me but within easy reach. This focal point of consciousness brings to me an aspect of that part of me that resides in another dimension or consciousness. Perhaps the sages call this aspect the "higher self." I call this a meeting of the minds and a reminder that while I walk the earth there is still a part of me residing in the celestial dimension. A good rapport with the celestial representation of me is a friendship that I value and find to be quite handy when interacting within the celestial realm.

Rising still I enter the spirit of our world. I feel connectivity to our earth, an attraction, and dedication all at one time. I wouldn't say that in my mind I see an image of a spinning sphere as seen from the moon or a space station in orbit. The representation of the relationship between the earth and me is energetic in nature. The feel is that of a static electric charge with the intimacy that speaks to my electron and cellular levels.

The next upward energy point brings me to something that I can only describe as astrologic in nature. Where the environment of my previous personal center of energy was earthly in nature this new center is on a galactic scale. I become familiar with the heavenly bodies, their movement and significance with each heavenly body sending me its personal greeting and signature. They speak to me.

I continue lifting my conscious awareness and arrive at another energy stopping point. This point is universal in nature. Dimensions mean nothing here. How many dimensions are there? Three? Four? Or forty? Who knows? Dimensional partitions, in this area of focus, are irrelevant.

I then advance upward to the ultimate center of my personal energies for this energy point can only be explained as the God center. This center, this chakra, is the living source and center of all universes and dimensions. There is nothing to be aware of here at this God center. The God center is not about awareness but of being in the moment and the present. And in this energy center, I am.

The Seven About Me

There are seven that help me along the way. They are celestial. They sit or stand in their places about me, always. They each have their jobs to do. I don't know their names. I never asked. I would forget the names the next day if I had asked.

The seven are most noticeable when I am relaxing on my living room chair. I sit on a dais at the end of a carpet, or so it seems to be when I am really sitting in my comfortable chair in the corner of the living room. To my left is the old man sitting and at times standing. He wears the white robes of Rome. When he speaks, he is wise. He speaks directly into my ear. Obviously being of the intellect, he is a teacher of many things.

Next to him, again on my left and farther away along the side of the carpet, is the scribe. He sits and he writes. He writes for history or for record. He researches and consults records. He wears the robes of Athens.

The one next and farther down the carpet is the doer. He is the handyman. He does not wear robes but tradesman's clothes of the Bronze Age or Iron Age. He is not always present within this company when we sit together as he is often out doing things.

Then there is one to my immediate right and close in. He does not sit down, never. He stands. He is a young child. He wears robes also. But I often cannot see him as he is often moving about like children do. He has nothing to do. He does whatever he fancies. At times he jokes. At times he runs about. And at other times he brings ideas that no one else would ever think.

They don't interact with each other but directly with me, except one. There is one who does interact with all that are in attendance. This one stands behind me and to the left. He is the Indian. He is from the Indian subcontinent. He watches over my shoulder and sees that everything is ready. He interacts with the others. He is the number one. He speaks to me and represents the others and himself. Clairvoyant and sensitive people most often see him when they look to see what spirits or celestial beings are within my presence. He brings me the most important messages. While the old man on my immediate left passes only his individual wisdom directly to me, the Indian behind me passes communications that are the results of the groups' combined wisdom and collaboration.

There are two that do not sit at the carpet as members of my original celestial company. These two were drawn to me at some time during my life. One was drawn to me through my thoughts that I created and the other was sent to me from on high. These two came and decided to stay; they have the option to leave at any time. These two interact directly with the physical world on my behalf. I pass them instructions frequently. My instructions to them address the physical needs of this life experience. These two will change in appearance frequently while the others always look the same remaining within the same character, function, and personality. These two are dynamic as they are more closely associated with the physical aspects of this changing physical world, what I do, and who I am. The members of the unchanging original company are bound to the celestial and do their work on metaphysical and emotional levels.

One of the two is the osprey created from my thoughts, actions, and intentions. He seeks opportunity for me. Once when I was learning of the Pacific Northwest Native Americans, I sought out and found my spirit guide as the local tradition instructed. I have carried the expression of the osprey with me ever since. I instruct this one to go out and pass to me news of the world's prospects. He has grown lately. He is now much larger than when I first met or thought him. He tells me that the reason is because I believe in him, and I interact with him often. He used to be able to perch on my hand. I would stroke his feathers. Now he is too large.

The second is an angel who wears Roman armor and carries weapons. He is my protector. This angel was sent to me from the love of god, from those of god. I pass the angel instructions to protect all family members and me. He guards the parameter of the property and my well-being. He guards the house and the entrances and all the cars while driving or parked. He protects my employment and livelihood. He looks different from time to time. I think there are many angels taking turns keeping watch over me. But I only see one angel in my presence at a time, or at least when I look.

When I call this angel, he responds and salutes me. It would be at this time, during the greeting, that I notice he looks different and may be one of the others that keep their watch over me. Sometimes he has a staff or a spear. Or he carries a shield and a sword. Sometimes he salutes with a touch of his heart or with a dipping of his weapon. On a few occasions he dances martial dances or engages in martial drills and feats of swordsmanship. Usually, he is just there reporting his presence.

They all engulf me in their radiance. As I sit in my chair within their presence, my chest, throat, and temples vibrate and emit heat. Then at some point, the phone rings. I answer and speak while leaving the chair and abruptly ending the audience.

Attending a Development Circle

Many times, my dear spouse and I joined with fellow clairvoyants for entertaining evenings of metaphysical practices. Many couples of our age and station would take in a show or a movie. Some would go bowling. My spouse and I would join metaphysical practitioners gathering in a meditation circle to see what we could see and to learn as much as we may from the heavenly host about and within us.

We formed a circle one Saturday night. Once seated, we joined our energies together through the chant of om. Within the center of the circle were formed the four cardinal points represented as pillars. The pillars were celestial beings. Guardians. But the word guardian paints a contrary picture. Guardians might be thought to stand between here and a place. They may be thought to represent protection and thus having means or accoutrements to protect. One might feel intimated or threatened by a "guardian" type. There was no such worry here with these radiant wonders we manifested from the etheric. Seeing their beauty and residing within their countenance and influence, I wanted to join them by becoming one with them accepting the peace, calm, and joy of enlightenment they projected.

Sitting at the feet of the guardians were four seated beings in lotus positions. These four seemed to be green or red skinned. These four were aligned with the four cardinal points of the compass.

There were other celestial beings alighting here and there. These other beings were not the main attraction but more like the background assembly. Naturally flitting about like a flock of birds or mayflies buzzing around a sun-drenched pasture, they naturally belonged in the picture. They too were occupants of the center of our circle.

Many clairvoyants participating in this development circle saw the guardians, the sitters at their feet, and the multitude of celestial beings. One radiant representative drew the notice of a circle participant as being particularly unique. I also noticed the uniqueness of this celestial representative and engaged in communication with him. As I gave greeting in recognition of the celestial being, he responded in mutual recognition by emoting joy, elation, and pride in me being able to recognize and communicate with him. It seemed as if he was pleasantly surprised that we could see and connect. Other circle participants witnessed the communion between this unique celestial being and me.

During this circle, there also appeared one particular angel of note. Immediately prior to the announcement of the angel's presence, I was looking at the lotus-positioned, seated beings. Another of the participants brought this particular angel's presence to everyone's attention. A second before the participant declared the angel's arrival in the center of the room, I saw the feet and legs of the same. I then brought my attention upward to the full figure. The angel was fading in and out of vision as if it was a little bit off from the required materialization frequency. For me to see the angel clearly and solidly, it was necessary to direct my focused attention to the purpose of seeing the angel alone, dropping my view of the guardians and their retinue. The guardians and the lotus sitters faded from my view. The angel came in clearly and brilliantly.

The particular angel of note and the guardians resided in diverse frequencies and energies. They were in different levels of the celestial metaphysical plane from one another. I saw the guardians by matching their frequency and energy level. I shifted my energy and increased my frequency so that I could see the angel of note. My lesson for this development circle then became a matter of vibrational and energetic foci. Others who had the gift of sight confirmed the presence of the celestial beings. They also noted the need to raise their vibrations to behold the angelic presence that blessed our development circle.

A Rock Apport

An apport is a gift from Spirit, heaven, provided via a paranormal transference of the article from one place to another. Apportation is basically the materialization of an object from thin air. A medium or facilitator channels a connection with the heavenly host attaining a high level of etheric energy and corresponding vibrational rate. The heavenly being is said to gift the item, the apport. The medium acts as the conduit. Apports are also known to materialize from thin air with no initiated activity by a medium or anyone else, for that matter. There is no conduit in such cases. The apportation is a direct bestowal from some heavenly being to the person who finds the item. The items are just found in unlikely places. An example would be a daughter's discovery of her long-deceased father's lost wedding ring. The ring just appeared in a drawer the daughter rummaged through a dozen times in the past, only now to find the ring in plain sight.

When I receive gifts of an apportation, I typically place the items casually about the house in places that I consider appropriate. I like to keep the apports I've received close at hand. Each apport radiates energy of one type or another, specific and matched to me, the current possessor.

I was once given three apports from the heavenly host in a single day through the facilitation of a medium acting as a conduit. The first apport was a clay bobble that I put on a string around my neck. I wore it daily for some time. To look at it, I could clearly see it was a representation of the mother earth, a woman with breasts and a belly.

When I turned the apport over, it looked like the ears of a wolf. Turning it over again, it was back to the mother earth, and then turning it upside down, it looked like a rabbit. I laid the apport on its side, and it looked like a dog or a hippo.

The spirit who gave this apport to me called himself Golden Eagle. Golden Eagle said it was a wolf. Then he said in a humorous tone that it would also look like a rabbit. And that if you looked at it in many ways, it would look like many other animals. And so, it does.

The second apport I was given that day came from a spirit doctor whose name I forgot. The doctor gave me kai nuts. They look like almonds. They are reputed to have been common items found in the pyramids at Giza. Kai nuts are for healing. Recipients who ate them in the past have been cured of AIDS and cancer. Several other metaphysical seers were with me the day I received the kai nuts. We each were given three to eat. The rest were to go to someone who had leukemia.

The kai nuts appeared in a brass bowl. The room was pitch-dark. I was sitting right next to the medium at the time of the appearance—materialization, if you will. When the kai nuts materialized, they did so with no warning. I heard no rustling noise before the materialization. The only sound to break the silence was the nuts hitting the brass bowl as if dropped from several feet above. They landed in two waves. Splash and splash again.

A spirit called Silver Feather gave the third apport to me. He said that he was with me when I was a young child, when people doubted me. He said he would be with me again in my adult years. I don't think that he was ever channeled by this medium before. The apport he gave me was a rock. The rock was from the garden of Gethsemane. As the Christ walked in the garden of Gethsemane, his foot touched this rock.

Before receiving the apport, the medium asked me to stand and approach his seated position. I stood and approached when I was called. Silver Feather spoke through the medium and told me how he knew me. He called me brother. He said I was going to get a big present, a gift. He told me to cup my hands and ready myself for something relatively heavy. Silver

Feather's voice came to me from a speaking trumpet. When first voiced, the volume startled those in attendance.

As I approached the medium, the speaking trumpet extended in my direction. I cupped my hands under the wide opening at the business end of the trumpet. The apport came into my hands after sliding down the inside of the trumpet. Again, as before with the kai nuts, I heard no rustling, just the sound of the rock sliding down from the inside of the trumpet. The rock apport took on physical form within the trumpet and completed its materialization at the terminus and fell into my waiting hands. When it landed, it was warm to the touch. The apport was a palm-sized rock. The rock had a notch in it. Some of those present would afterward say that the rock had the tracings of a dog upon its side.

As I held the rock in my hand, it vibrated and spoke to me. It passed me a wave of impressions about the future, about where I was now in time and space and about the people with whom I associated. The messages came into my mind through an opening between my heart and my throat. Or so that seemed to be the pathway I felt as the message transited from the rock to my mind. When the vibrations ended, I was drained of energy and could no longer concentrate or focus upon any one topic.

When the circle ended and the lights illuminated, we looked at the rock and the trumpet. The opening diameter of the trumpet, the small end, was large enough to get my thumb through but not large enough to get the rock through.

During my quiet time when I sit in silence lost in thought, I see me sitting on the top of a hill with others. There are people below me. I get the feeling that I am to tend to these people. And there are many, many people to tend to. I longingly want to be of service to them, I do not refuse the honor. But I am overwhelmed.

This impression of this hill started coming on the day after I was given the rock. The rock now sits on my nightstand next to me when I am sleeping. I seem to remember a story that some two thousand years ago there was a Crystal One who did just that—sat on a hill and provided comforting messages and services to those about who came to listen to his stories.

From the catechism classes of my youth, I recall that they referred to the event as the Sermon on the Mount. From this event came the first recital of the Lord's Prayer and the Beatitudes. You know those Beatitudes. They focus on love and humility rather than force and exaction. They echo the highest ideals of the teachings of the Christ as he espoused mercy, spirituality, and compassion.

Death and Taxes

A rock appears. It brings to my mind a vision of a people gathering on a hill to hear the beloved Jesus, our Enlightened One, speak. I get the feeling of being associated with this event to the point of being a participant. Feeling that I was a participant brings me a closeness to one known as the Son of Man and with the life he led here. I walked about every day for a month with this vision playing out in my mind, repeatedly. Basking in the light of what seemed to be a core remembrance of being at the mount and participating in the event. Was it memory? Perhaps it was a long-lost memory of my soul, or maybe just my imagination. But the experience of participating at the event where we heard this Master speak of compassion, mercy, and spiritual ideals remained in my heart and mind for a month and guided my daily deliberations with others. And for that month, I walked in the energy and mindset of one who witnessed the Sermon on the Mount and participated in service to all those who listened. All this brought about by the appearance of a rock that was presented to me during a meditation and development circle.

The gifts kept coming. One fine spring afternoon, I tended my yard. Mowing lawn and clearing the brush were my chores for that day. During the preceding month, I was thinking about my late grandmother. Perhaps it was an earlier conversation with my mother and aunt that got me thinking about Ma. I called her Ma. She raised me.

The sidewalk, cleared by me with broom and brush, was as close to immaculate as could be. I then placed my yard waste bucket upon the newly cleared and swept sidewalk. There was plenty of parking strip lawn clippings needing to be picked up and placed into the bucket and made ready for the sanitation truck that would be picking up the neighborhood's yard waste tomorrow morning. With the yard waste bucket now full to the brim, I set myself to moving it back to the sanitation truck pickup area. On the freshly cleared sidewalk where the bucket recently stood lay a small, silver medal, worn and slightly tarnished. Interesting, I thought. The medal was not there on the freshly swept sidewalk five minutes ago when I placed the yard waste bucket in that very same spot.

Upon examining the small silver medal, I see that it's got an impression of the Blessed Virgin and constructed in such a way as to be worn about the neck on a chain. Some research on the internet tells me that it was called a Miraculous Medal. I placed the medal into my wallet in the transparent compartment that held my driver's license.

The month passed and it was again time for my routine phone call to chat up my mother. The conversation bends toward my grandmother; Mom was reminiscing. Grandma, Ma to me, would always buy me watches to wear as a young man and to look the professional part. Young I was. Ma got me the watches throughout grammar school. My mother and I remembered that no watch ever lasted me more than a month before I broke it. Still, Grandma would just get me another watch.

Grandma also got me medals to wear about the neck. I think she gave up on the watches. My mother was keen on getting me St. Christopher medals as she wanted me protected when I traveled, walking the city, then riding my bike, and finally driving as a teenager. Grandma, she reminded me, was keen on getting me medals of the Blessed Virgin type. She recalled one medal in particular, a Miraculous Medal, that I always wore till it was ripped from my neck, chain and all, when I was playing football with my mates. Mom always loved that medal. She described it as a small silver remembrance of the BVM, that's Mary, standing atop the world with light rays emitting from Mary's outreached hands. My grandmother was also named Mary.

The Miraculous Medal my mother described matched the medal sitting close to my driver's license in my wallet. Since that conversation I have always associated the found medal with my grandmother. I thank my ma regularly for the present.

Spirit Guides and Angels

Rest, Relaxation, and a Reading List

I ended one facet of my career on a pleasant summer afternoon in July. The past year under this employ was a challenging one for me and drained away all energy, rationality, and mental edge from whatever uniqueness I had within my character. I wanted to leave this situation for all the past five years but was never able to solve the income and healthcare ratio riddle at any given time. So, I stayed. And I was miserable.

Perpetuating a self-fulfilling prophecy, I was eventually let go with an enjoyable severance package. My immediate goal after leaving the employment of this company was to relax and get my mind straight. I planned on doing nothing more than sitting in the sun and catch up on my reading for the remainder of the summer. The house my dear spouse and I purchased the previous year sat atop a bluff with commanding views of the Puget Sound shipping lanes and the Olympic Mountain range. The sunsets were magnificent. The original settlers named Sunset Park appropriately after them. Sunset Park was up the street. Here was my first opportunity in decades to escape into reading, enjoy the view, sit in the shining sun, and gain new insights study time on my hands would bring. My summer reading list: Masters of the Far East.

Reading of the channeled mysteries and the exploits of ascended masters on earth soon elevated my mind to a state that was extremely receptive to the cosmic reality. For the remaining summer months, my daily routine consisted of reading during the day and observing the sunset in the quiet of the evening. Capping the day of reading mysteries and exploits, my mind was well conditioned for the rest and solitude I would have at the day's end. Many evenings, sitting while watching the sun sink behind the mountains, I would investigate the glow of the setting sun as the rays would illuminate and separate the clouds. There in the glow I would see the host, the opening to another world, and I would extend my mind, free my heart, jump through the door, and join the divine company.

The sun setting behind the Olympic Mountains is a colorful sight. The light from the low sun hits the opposite side of the mountain range backlighting it with a canvas of a sometimes-unearthly glow. As the sun sinks and approaches the mountain line, sunrays break through or scatter among the clouds casting a bright shining burst. The mixing of the yellow sun and white clouds makes for a great backdrop when resting my feet on the table in between. The light diffuses into the almost ever-present intermittent cloud coverage. As the sun rotates through its orbit, traveling lower in arc, light rays point upward illuminating the undersides of the cumulus clouds and radiate in all directions forth from an eye-squinting center. The lower the sun sinks, the more angle to the light as each separate ray engages in their travel through the visible spectrum, all emanating from a central glow that slides slowly into the horizon. The rays, long known to sailors as "God's stays," bend upward and strike the underbellies of the surrounding clouds, reflecting colors through the red to blue continuum till all that remains is the remnant light outlining the mountains between us while the night invades the sky from the east.

It is within the core of this display that I see the host. The light of the setting sun encases me; colors above me, before me, on both sides, and behind me surround me. Within this exhibition I see the opening to heaven, and I surrender to its song. At the onset my heart, by now warm throughout, opens to an influx of calming, stable, secure acceptance. I feel a physical reaction. From inside, my chest is vibrating. Yet as I touch my chest with my hand, it is still. My full attention draws to my heart and my heart reciprocates. Joined, mind and heart both fly off together toward the opening in the curtain that I see off in the distance. My breathing, stable and very shallow, fades from my internal recollection and sets itself to operate on its own with no further effort or concern on my part.

I then find myself in a hall. Not the hallway from the bedroom to the bathroom but a large, circular hall with a high ceiling. No ceiling could I discern, though, as I was not looking in that direction. I could remember seeing windows, but again, I was not paying attention to the architecture of the hall. The windows, mere openings in the wall, displayed no landmarks, only sky. There were many gathered about in the hall. They lined the walled circumference, single file, in a circle forming a ring. And here I was within this ring shoulder-to-shoulder with the ones beside me. They raised their arms above them and proclaimed as one, "Hail, brother."

I could not describe now to you what these colleagues and brethren looked like. Now after time has passed and I write these memoirs, I have ultimately interjected some conscious and self-needed definitions to this vision and experience. Looking back, I remember that at the time, I was getting the information that they were a host of angels, members of the angelic choir. They had no wings that I could remember. No banners or signatures to define them. They were about me, they were brilliant, and they were calling me brother. I reveled in the camaraderie, and I felt at home. But how could that be? It flew in the face of all that I had learned through catechism and other religious instructions. Angels. Humans. Even souls that are human. Both very different entities and origins? Yes? Well, what did I really know anyway? I know the feeling I had as we all bonded together as one. I know what they were signaling to me in their hail and beholding. It felt natural at the time so I'd go with it and see where this meeting would take me.

Finally, I thought, I am here among my kind. Those who are about me know me. I know this intellectually and emotionally. Something pulled me to that single conclusion; I am here among my kind in the world of life everlasting and the purpose within. And while my conclusion flew in the face of all that I was taught regarding the heavenly hierarchy and the angelic choir, I simply accepted the notion as it was presented.

There were no messages passed to me at this meeting of those assembled. There were no lessons of livelihood and circumstance or of spirit and growth. Our encounter was of reunion, of again being one with solitary purpose, turning the cosmic wheel. There was nothing more I wanted or hoped for than to reside always with these who called me brother. Our greeting lingered for what I perceived as some slice of time. While engaged in this communion, other aspects of my consciousness gathered data and readings from a constant and overwhelming information flow. I kept up with considerable effort and wanted to take in all that I could. The more I expended effort to fully experience everything I could, the more I restricted the reception. I then relaxed and surrendered to an unseen guiding hand. From that point onward, I existed only in that moment. Then suddenly and for no inexplicable reason, those of the hall silenced their communion and joined together, closer, and raised our consciousness as a group in that one moment. From my observation point, the room responded, taking the glow of the setting sun as I see it from my patio.

Within the golden orb of sun-drenched clouds, others emerged. The brilliance and sheer radiance of our new company blinded what would have been all sense of sight I had within me, were I in the physical world. Soon the radiance in the hall draws me in like a magnet. As if by outreaching arms, I am hugged close within the bosom of a newly discovered presence.

Residing within this brilliance took every bit of me. I lost myself. It was all I could do to keep up with the constant flow of peace and serenity overcoming me as provided by this hugging joy before me. The new occupants in the center of the hall were three in number. Their beings generated frequencies of energy that were somewhat varied from my brethren about me. While finer aspects of the frequencies were subtle, we all shared a foundation, that spark of life that united us as one. My attention drew to the center spark and my emotions responded lovingly, compassionately.

What do we hold as our greatest recognition? I was accepted, welcomed, and appreciated. Never have I felt this sense of security and contentment or been in the company of such kindness. But here it was, here in front of me, engulfing me. I glared into the glow and discerned or imagined the deepest blue eyes intently seeking my gaze. This was the spirit of the Christ before me as I stood shoulder-to-shoulder with my brothers.

There were two others with this Crystal One, both emitting the same intensive sparkle, but with these other two shining personalities I could decipher form as well as eyes as they stood there in greeting. To me they extended their hands and took mine in welcome. To the right of the Christ stood the one I called Beloved Lady Nada. She wore a shirt of white and yellow and had about her an aura of blue. It was to her I had surrendered the keep of my heart. To the left was the Count St. Germaine carrying gifts that I could not identify. I stood before him his bastard son giving him greetings and appreciation of his love for me and for all inhabitants of this earth.

As I again stared into the eyes of the Christ, I could faintly make out the appearance of a face. But the full identification I was never able to decipher. I couldn't get past the radiance and glow. The exposure to this radiance sucked me in to a world of bliss and contentment. If I were to equate the communion to something physical in feeling, I can only describe it as floating on a cloud. If one were to float on a cloud, the body would feel the utmost in comfort, I imagine. Here, my being and mind were in the utmost comfort. Indeed, my very core was at peace and in harmony with all things seen and otherwise so much so that that was all I knew or ever knew. I was like a bird that joined the flock or a fish joining his school, both getting that customary sense of belonging, balance, and freedom. Anything I've regretted, and for any transgression against another and myself, forgiven. I had the peace of forgiving myself and the tranquility of knowing all was at balance.

It was only natural to interject something from my conscious mind at this point. Always in my travels and no matter how deep beyond the curtain I pass, I always maintained the sliver of physical consciousness about me. And for this instance, my connection was my patio of the here and now. I extended myself and connected with the core of all this bliss and addressed the Christ by his given name, Yeshua. I said, "Give my dear spouse physical well-being." I didn't know what that necessarily meant or what healing could entail. No one would know, including my spouse. I reached out focusing on the connection I had with those wonderful blue eyes and sent a heartfelt entreaty. I remember, while sitting on my patio, speaking softly, whispering as if to myself, and asking Jeshua to intercede on her behalf.

My request being submitted, I opened my eyes to see the sun set behind the mountains, glow of the sunlight dissipate with the underbellies of the clouds turning a relaxing mauve. I remained in my seat till the last vestiges of light left the western sky then returned to my comfortable living room, where I lay down to rest and took an evening nap.

The next day my wife and I awoke early. It was Sunday and we were going to visit a spiritualist church. Appearing at the church that day was a medium that we heard a good deal about. We arrived at the church in time for the service and took our seats. The service proceeded as per their spiritualist routine consisting of a greeting and announcements followed by guided meditation.

Upon completion of the guided meditation, the medium gave an inspiring oration. The service ended shortly after the ensuing dialogue. We all gathered in the kitchen on the floor below for introductions, conversations, and beverages.

The medium traveled with an assistant who maintained his schedule and attended to business affairs. This medium was a good one and was known for his gifts in physical phenomenon and trance. When introduced to my spouse and right before taking her hand in greeting, he immediately stopped his motion and took a step backward. Retreating from those gathered, he pulled his assistant aside to chat with her for a short minute.

Upon completion of this quick confidential side conversation, the assistant approached us. The assistant told us the medium received a message from Jesus. And that Jesus expressed an interest in working with my spouse through the medium in trance. The assistant went on to further inform us that Jesus would like to provide my wife with some healing energy and asked if he may do so by acting through the person of the medium. The medium would enter trance and allow the spirit of the Christ to work through him. My wife accepted the offer. I accompanied her into the antechamber, and we began.

The medium, his assistant, my wife, and I entered the room and took our seats. We quickly reached meditative states. The medium stood and began speaking in soft, even, and gentle terms the words expected from a knowledgeable, caring, and compassionate individual.

As I sat in the room, all was calm and restful. Though this room was but an antechamber in a dated building, I was no longer within the confines of that enclosure. The structures and people beside me were but props and faded away. What remained were sparks of life riding on bands of light swimming in a sea of brilliance. The room filled with a multicolored misty rain, and I shuttered in the consciously perceived closeness to my body. I observed the proceedings and marveled at all else I was experiencing.

The channeled trance lasted about thirty minutes in total. When the healing event ended, my wife and I thanked the medium and his assistant and took our leave to return home. Although it was the afternoon, my spouse was very tired, so she lay down to take a nap. She slept for the remainder of the day, evening, and night.

We'll never know what the channeled Jesus Christ healed. We'll never know the result of the healing. Was something growing within her body and thus removed from existence? Was the healing for physical remedies and circumstance? Or was this a healing of the spirit?

After awakening from her sixteen-hour nap, my wife spent the day walking through the local woods with her dog and then returned home to cook an amazing dinner served to several friends she invited over on the spur of the moment. It's been a long time since she had the energy to walk for several miles then comes home to create a feast entertaining the night away. It was nice having my old friend back again. I continued with my summer reading on the patio of my house.

Welcoming a Celestial Lady

The room was absent of all light sources. It was dark. Not a single speck of light was anywhere to be had. Before entering, we removed our watches and left our electronic devices in a drawer in the kitchen. The facilitator placed a rolled carpet at the bottom crack of the entry door sealing off any possibility of external light appearing in the room. All other possible light leaks in this old structure were long ago covered, rendering a completely darkened room.

Sixteen of us sat in folding chairs lined around the walls to eventually form a semicircle. At the apex of the circle sat a curtain suspended on a frame made of plastic piping. The curtain was purple in color and violet in hue. Looking at the frame, I could see the hanging curtain folded around on either extremity eventually forming an enclosure, a room, inside of this room where we assembled. Inside that enclosure sat a medium separated from those in the room by this framed curtain. He sat alone in what is known as the cabinet.

We were gathered here today to meet one of the ascended masters. The event was referred to as a séance or a circle. We gather and remove from our minds all that block the spirit from her interplay with the material life we live in. We float together calling on divine blessings of the Holy Trinity and the angelic choir. We surround the room with an impenetrable wall of light that only the truest and best may pass in the name of Jesus the Christ. The room fills with the spirit of creation and of the one source, the God dynamism. Increasing our meditative frequency and consolidating our collective consciousness, we chant the word om and merge among the vibrations originating in our throats. Escaping our temporal bounds, we trail off to discovery. Over and over, we sing the word om. The vibration of the sound fills all so gathered with a uniform presence and just the right amount of energy to open the gateway to the divine. Our minds vibrate to the harmonic of the word om, and we become one in mission with the celestial.

The medium hosts the presence of the celestial wonder. The Beloved Wonder speaks through a trumpet to all those gathered. The trumpet, long ago used by sea captains to bark commands to sailors in windy seas, amplifies the voice of our celestial guest as she offers us the blessing of the most holy of holies and the spark of life that resides within us. The spirit of the celestial presence solidifies and takes form walking through the room, offering loving touches to those gathered, and speaks her lesson through the trumpet protruding through a separation in the curtain, anchored inside the cabinet that stands as the focus of the gateway.

She speaks. Her words are of the divine love offered to us from those who reside on the other side of the curtain. She tells of the angelic host and their ever-vigilant caring for our well-being. They are the messengers of God and their duty to life is ever among us. We are cherished. We have much in common with the divine celestial brethren, much more than can be readily apparent. We are all cut from the same mold.

We all carry within us the same spark of life. Together in this spark we are one, united in the love that binds our universe. Though she may have once received the title of ascended master, she tells us that she is no different from us and we are no different from her. All she did was master some skills and come to appreciate living with a certain point of view and perspective. Love guided all her actions, and it was this love for all things that lead to her mastering the riddle of life and ascending to service everlasting. And now, she was here for us. To carry on her work and to bring any level of that love she lives to us in lesson and experiential form. She came for the betterment of humankind, offering all that was her facility.

As she spoke, her words wrapped around my heart and brought forth the union with my mind. To me, she was speaking directly to me. I could have sat in private audience and received the answers to my long-held questions no better than I received them then and there. She spoke to the essential thread that binds my temporal center to that of my eternal self, living and yearning for that nirvana that only the very lucky attain. The nirvana that comes with knowing the answers to the mystery and living in accordance with the divine will while moving creation's wheel. Of connecting and living within and throughout from that higher self above us that we hear so much about and are lucky enough to grasp the occasional glimpse, the higher self of whom we eternally are cast. She filled the void of unanswered questions and cemented one thread after the other, leading to that elusive harmony between the earthly and the universal. Thus, she spoke to me, alone, or so it seemed. Yet her voice filled the room for all to hear, for while she was speaking to me, she also spoke to all in this same fashion. This one conversation touched all hearts as if each person was the single focus of the encounter.

The event ended after about one hour. The lights were slowly turned up so that we could again see. My eyes adjusted to the light, and I was able to see those about me. All remained seated in silence, scanning the room and making inquisitive eye contact with one another. The atmosphere was quite serene. We were all rather contemplative at that point after that one-hour past in total darkness with the smooth-flowing voice of an ascended teacher to assist us in our spiritual development. Surrendering to the moment, it took all assembled some small amount of time to ground themselves to the here and now about them.

The teacher spoke. She provided us clues to living that spiritual life we survey during our deepest meditation. We can have it all. We can live by those tenants of love every day. We can live those precepts and realities that we discover in our prayers and in the lingering wonderings of a sunny afternoon. Here, in the flesh, now or very soon. Knowledge and self-discovery will free us. Proceed lightly and in the love that bathes us. The attitude we cultivate will dictate our actions. Our perspective will provide us options. When making life's choices on a day-to-day basis, do so with love for yourself and for those in your life.

Those in attendance gained a cosmic perspective that evening, a perspective that powers the will advancing the personal human condition. By focusing on the relevant, choosing our path and actions, we can transcend the fates and define our own destiny. And so, we departed our meeting place to carry on with our daily routines and held close the lesson in love and potential.

Throughout the following week, my mind was focused not on the words of the lesson and the suggested options when exercising free will but of the closeness I shared with the celestial source of cosmic light. I felt that the door was open, and the invitation lent to me by that introduction the night at the séance. Her spirit followed me about through the day's activities. And then, as I sat in my perch to observe the sunset behind the mountains and the passing of the day's toil, the closeness of that darkened room returned to me, and I was no longer alone. She was there in the sunset. Standing brightly in all her magnificence while touching the very strings of my heart, she gave her greeting, to which my heart replied. Bowing my head, I saluted her, "Beloved Lady Nada."

The presence of her spirit returned the following night and again the portal opened. My heart fused with the divine host, and my mind guided my dialogue and communion with my celestial company. We were not speaking in words but shared a common connection through our hearts. My chest pulsed and vibrated, and my breathing became measured and deliberate. I felt her in the sunset, before me and within me. My thoughts were hers as I surrendered and lost myself within her radiance. I did formulate propositions and entireties, expressing gratitude and blessing her for her holy work. Each evening as I sat on my patio watching the setting sun, I drew closer to the one I would know as Beloved Lady Nada.

The séance event of the other night offered by the local spiritualist community repeated, occurring again but to a wider audience. Here the lady was scheduled to speak at a larger center that could not only accommodate the large number of participants gathered but also the requirement for a total absence of light. The audience numbered in the scores, and all was ready.

The room was darkened. The protective and energizing chants were sung or said, and the lesson proceeded. The love of humankind equals our love of the one source of all, and we honor the spark of this source that resides within each of us. In service, love, and in appreciation of our journey, her words filled the room for all to hear. Her glow bursting throughout the meeting hall filled the air with her electricity for all hearts to be so touched as mine. The radiance of the opening between heaven and earth consumed all there assembled that afternoon. One cannot long stand within the flow of a heavenly herald and the source of all knowledge and not be carried away with the rushing tide. And the spirit is carried away in the tide as we enter the gates between this life and all life.

The lesson concluded and it was time for our goodbyes and fare-thee-wells as we expressed our gratitude and appreciation to our gracious mentor. Sitting near the cabinet and directly to the facilitating trumpet, I spoke, "Thank you, Beloved Lady Nada."

Her laugh and giggle were immediate. "Tee-hee. You flatter me. You're flirting with me," she said to me, encapsulating the statement with another of her lighthearted giggles. I held myself. I wanted to say so much more, to burst upon the scene my years of questions and wonderings about me and my celestial origin. Who really was I? I wanted to know. I held back, thinking that I had one quick shot at it. I had only one opportunity to hear an answer with my ears and confirm the answers I received in my heart.

"Was that you?"

"Tee-hee, yes. In the sunset."

Death and Taxes

Chapter 6: Impressions of Past Lives

Who Knew?

I have a horse named Spike. Spike is my buddy. He is also my first horse. When I was a little kid, I got my first dog. My uncle unexpectedly brought home my first dog for me one night after he was out and about with his friends. The dog mysteriously disappeared two nights later. I happened to be looking out my bedroom window and saw a man walking down the street with three dogs, my dog being one of them. When I ran across my grandfather in the kitchen the next morning, or that evening, I couldn't remember, I told him of the man walking outside with my dog. He said, "Really?" I never got that first dog back.

Imagine a little boy with his first dog, a dog that was a stellar fellow loved by all and so cute that he was a natural match for his people. Spike is that first dog that I never really experienced, and I am that little boy. Spike is my first horse. He is a well-loved member of the family. My dear spouse got me Spike as a birthday present. We had just moved into our home on Whidbey. The place was perfect for horses. It had a newer barn, field, fences, and all the equestrian trappings. My dear spouse always loved horses and had herself an old mare. She felt that we needed a horse for me.

Becoming proficient with horses and riding requires lessons and a level of dedication to establish the cross-species relationship. Never having a horse, I was a bit unsure of how this would all work out. I figured the horse would end up hanging around in the field, eating hay, and needing the veterinarian at the most inopportune times. I'd go on a ride or two occasionally and thought that was about the limit of how horse ownership would likely turn out for me. But my dear spouse and all her friends had other ideas. I soon found myself enrolled in riding classes. Dressage classes riding on an English saddle would be my new pastime.

Discussing the realities of the coming adventure with my dear spouse, I expressed my apprehension with committing to owning and tending Spike as well as taking regularly scheduled riding classes. This being my first horse, there were questions as to how I could manage and if this was a match for my temperance and abilities. I confessed the fears associated with my frail, old body sitting five feet off the ground atop a moving, mind-of-his own, half-ton animal. My dear spouse's immediate response surprised me in its offhandedness. Her immediate response was to laugh a small chuckle. Seeing my obviously hurt face in reaction, she went on to explain. She reminded me that horses have been around for quite some time and have interacted with men for eons. She would be surprised had I not lived many lives with horses under my saddle. She assumed that I had previously, during many of my lives, established strong ties with horses at a very personal and professional level. All I needed to do is to spend some time with Spike and get to know him. My soul's muscle memory would do the rest.

True to her words, Spike and I bonded and became best of friends. I have a special relationship with Spike. I've never had a horse in my life, so the theme of this interspecies bond is new to me; I've no other horse relationships to compare. Yet I am not the only one to attest to the intimacy of my relationship with Spike. The instructors, associates, and others who are experienced horse people constantly remark that Spike is special on a grand scale and that he most assuredly is my horse.

Many a time and many a life, I transited the species divide and rode as one through memories that left lasting impressions on the record of my soul. I, at my core, remember horses, and horses acknowledge the bond between us and respect the memories we share deep within. This familiarity plays out in the day-to-day aspect of dressage. In no time at all, Spike and I became the stars of the class, climbing much beyond our expected skill level. It just goes to show what a little past-life channeling can do to bring skills and familiarity to efforts presently at hand. I remember horses, and they remember me.

Rekindling my relationship with horses took no conscientious effort on my part. I did no incantations or rituals. No sitting in meditation, recalling the spirit of the horse, and asking for cooperation based on all that we had shared together throughout the cycle of my soul's life. My horsemanship skills came naturally, and my bonding with Spike came about without a conscious thought, untaught by others. We just bonded. Hello, old friend. It's me again. Here, have a carrot.

Joining the navy when I did seemed to be a natural decision when the time for the decision was right. I wanted to cast off everything about my world and immerse myself in something completely out of the confines of my social, economic clique. The navy. No one I knew joined the navy. I felt, for me, it was a natural progression and requirement for the life that I could not see before me. The navy offered me a chance to see the world. There would be structure, a structure reinforced by centuries of tradition and culture. I was to be on the bottom rung of the hierarchy like any other know-nothing recruit. I had no experience with boats. I've never even been on one. The neighborhood I came from had no maritime tradition. There were no sailors among the neighborhood residents. Yet the navy would be my choice for stripping away all that I had become encumbered upon and forcing change in my life.

Death and Taxes

Advancing from the initial stages of recruitment and training, I soon found myself shipboard assigned to a frigate. A frigate. I knew what frigates were. My naval interest as a child and young adult focused upon wooden ships and iron men, the sailing battle ships of the Napoleonic era. While here on the USS Brewton, I had no knowledge of anti-submarine warfare, high-pressure steam turbine engines, or modern fleet maneuvers. I did have a wealth of knowledge about ships of the line. Yes. I knew the names and functions of every standing and running rigging, every stay and shroud. I could speak at length about Nelson's strategies in battle throughout his illustrious career. Want to discuss the differences between American and British frigates of the War of 1812? Grab some coffee and sit a spell. You're in for an education.

The flow of navy life came quickly to me. I stood watches on the bridge as a quartermaster. The navy quartermasters steer the ship in tight places, keep track of the ship's position, navigate the high seas, and when of high enough rank and experience, command the conn issuing orders to helm and engine. My advancement was swift. Entering the navy as a recruit, I was an enlisted man of a pay grade called E-1. I would leave the navy after five and a half years to continue with a maritime career as a licensed deck officer, eventually rising to the position of captain. "Licensed Master Upon Oceans" is the endorsement on the license. My rank leaving the navy after that five-and-a-half-year stint was E-6, noncommissioned officer, first-class petty officer.

My work on ships continued throughout much of the next decade as I drove freighters, research and passenger vessels, tugs, and training ships. In my mid-thirties, a new global order of international commerce came into existence, and they called it outsourcing. My company outsourced the entire marine department. The company sold the ships to a foreign firm, and citizens of the owning country replaced the American officers and crew. I took the hint. Life at sea as a wandering minstrel was growing heavy on me. I felt a need to set roots and become part of the living world. The catastrophe of a lost occupation came as an opportunity for growth and satisfied my need to plant roots. Having no job and being in a declining American industry, I entered college. My focus was electronic engineering technology.

But the salt sea would not that easily retreat from my veins, and I picked up some teaching jobs on the side at the local maritime academy. Seamanship for yachtsmen grew to navigation and ship-handling programs. The academy's administration, impressed with my subject matter expertise and rapport with the students, elevated me to an immediate position within the local public school system as the instructor and manager of a high school maritime program for at-risk youths if I wanted it. They were in immediate need. The current instructor flew the coop with his wife back to the East Coast under government orders, and with this being the first month of the school year and the program having full enrollment, they were in a bind. I accepted the position and became a maritime instructor of high school students, effectively placing my nascent IT engineering career on hold.

And an interesting lot of high school students they were. I had several students who had a choice between this program and flying straight or residency at the state penitentiary. I had several students who occupied drug and rehab programs in the recent past and one who, at sixteen, was a new mother. There were some college-bound students as well as those who had no clue as to what they were to do with themselves. Together we explored the value and methods of a career in the maritime. The work was hands-on. We met for three hours a day and used our time to wander about the local industry fixing historic vessels, refurbishing lifeboats, and improving our campus grounds. Classroom lectures focused on the job skills needed to succeed and the culture of plying the seven seas. The program was a success in that it provided options for kids who previously had none. It provided hard skills and indoctrinated a work ethic that found its origin with the seafaring Phoenicians, Romans, British, and Americans. Some students excelled and took advantage of their new skills.

Spirit Guides and Angels

The salt sea was always strong within my blood. The mechanics of seamanship, ship handling, and navigation came naturally to me. The structured life and hierarchy of shipboard life gave me comfort and security. I didn't have to concern myself with what path I'd choose at every turn. I simply had to take the next exam and advance through the ranks. Exams were easy. They were typically technical to my rating of quartermaster and later of deck officer. I never studied for an exam but would laze about, get up, and go to the exam room to eventually score in the upper five percent. Teaching also came naturally. I knew my technical topic well enough and had the experience in my field as a worker and a leader. I knew what the industry needed in the workforce and was well able to lead the students onto mastering the skills. Teaching students, especially at-risk students, had its challenges, and while I was new at being a high school teacher, or a teacher of any kind, I excelled at getting my ideas across and mentoring the initiates.

Something about all this maritime life was so very familiar to me. I felt it natural to be at sea on a frigate or any other ship, shooting evening stars and plotting our position. How many times have I, as a soul, stood upon a pitching deck with sextant in hand and scribed the arc of a prominent star? The skill and proficiency came easily to me. The sextant fell naturally into my hands, and my eye quickly grew accustomed to arcing the points of light upon the rolling horizon. In the classroom, students took to my instruction readily. Our familiarity and bonds were instantaneous. My biggest compliment received my fourth-year teaching was delivered by a special needs student when he, in front of the class for all to hear, declared me a natural teacher. How many times have I, as a soul, stood at the front of a class filled with eager neophytes and taught the ways of life and living, occupation and skills? Countless. Countless times on the decks of rolling ships did I teach the midshipmen use of sextant and stars to navigate. And countless times I will be there again.

This Band of Brothers

The impression didn't last long. It lasted just an instant. Yet in that instant, so much information came that I was overwhelmed and in vertigo, teary-eyed, with attending heavy breathing.

I always found interest in sailing ships. When young I had every model sailing ship available on the market: the HMS Victory, Old Ironsides, the USS Constitution (the twelve-inch as well as the three-foot version), Santa Maria, Flying Cloud, and on it went. Having access to libraries, I gravitated to the history section and books on the Napoleonic-era sailing ships and focused on the ships of Lord Nelson. I think it safe to say that this infatuation with ships highly influenced my signing up to join the navy, sail the seas, and see the world.

For an instance I was on a rolling deck. A slight breeze was coming from the port quarter. As we were reaching with the wind, I would only feel a brief wisp and flutter. The sails were filled, and an occasional flap of a pennant cracked like a muffled whip. My shoes were a little tight. That corn or callous on the right foot was causing the tightness. I must have the surgeon tend to it tomorrow. I took a step. The wooden deck under my foot was sturdy. Well-built ship this one was.

I looked about me, and there were others standing. They were about me in calm, stoic silence, with a serious look about their faces but lacking any visible signs of tension. Several were officers in the British Navy. They commanded the high seas and kept England safe from invaders. Others were there also. The others were masters, mates, and common seamen. I was standing away from the helm, the great ship's wheel. Two were tending the wheel. Their heads were in constant motion, looking up at the sails, then the sea, the horizon, the officers about them, and lastly at the compass binnacle.

Who? That was my immediate impression in question form. Who? I stood next to the rail with the wind over my shoulder. I stood on the deck of a large, wooden warship. There was preparation in motion by many men while many others sat crouched at their guns as far down the open deck as I could see. Interspersed throughout the ordered chaos were officers in uniforms, calmly issuing instructions and checking on details. All those standing about me would glance forward from time to time. There was something to see forward that caught everyone's interest. Still the question came to me. Who?

I looked about me with pride, with fatherly warmth in my heart. I knew that this and they were my charges, and I was to serve them and they me. Authority and responsibility weighed on my shoulders. Who then was I on that ship? For I say, "was I" as my vision was through the eyes of the observer. This was not a sight from above looking down on the scene at hand but images as seen through eyes as I see from my eyes now at the scene about me, typing on this keyboard, feeling the time of the day, and the anticipation of the day's list of chores, warm of heart knowing that all is well on the ranch with family and animals. Who then was the owner of the eyes I looked through and the emotions I felt?

Was it the sailing master? Sailing masters on British wooden warships were wise and skilled and had responsibilities and a sense of ownership. Sailing masters were respected and had the authority of the ship's movement within their roles. But as I looked at my uncomfortable right foot, the shoe I was wearing was not that of a rating but of fine leather and polished to a bright gleam. I could never polish a shoe so brightly. Someone else perhaps did so for me. Within the shoe, my foot was encased in white, silk stocking. Spotless. I looked up and again surveyed where I stood. I was on the quarterdeck of a large, wooden warship closest to the railing on the windward side. While there was room between the rail and me, no others stood in that void out of courtesy. During the Napoleonic era, the place to windward was reserved for the senior officer on the quarterdeck. The ship appeared to be at quarters, battle stations. With all hands on deck, the senior officer would be the captain of the ship. Very well then, I thought. I was looking through the eyes of the captain of a large, wooden British warship.

I brought my eyes up and looked ahead. Mine was the third ship in this line with two other large, wooden, ship-rigged sailing vessels ahead of me. Continuing my line of sight forward, I see the sides of ships in line, two to three cable lengths distant. We—I and the ships ahead of me—were sailing perpendicular to the line of battle ships ahead, blocking our path. I look to the left, upwind, and there is open sea. I look to the right to leeward and see in the close distance a line of ships sailing parallel to me. Ten or fifteen ships perhaps I saw. I didn't pause to count each one, but the number seemed to add up with what I knew of the leeward squadron. Behind me were other ships following in a tight line aft of my stern. I, and the ships ahead and behind, were in line. This was a line of battle and the ships ahead in the distance, showing their sides to me, were our destination. The first ship in my line flew an admiral's pennant. Signal flags were now running up the flagship's halyards. Slightly forward of me on my quarterdeck an officer and a seaman were scribing on paper looking through a small booklet. The officer repeatedly glanced up at me, then the book, then to the seaman. Placing his pencil in his pocket, he started to approach. My attention is then immediately forced forward as I hear the rolling thunder of cannon only to see well-developed puffs of white smoke emitting from the sides of the enemy line ahead. I heard one. Then another. Then multiple low booms and felt the disturbance of air as the sound's shock wave reached me. Yes, I thought. This is it. We are under fire. Bless us for which we are about to receive.

With a shudder and a start, I looked about me and saw the living room of my house. The off-white love seat with the antique chest placed opposite the winged back chair that I would sit upon were familiar sights, a world away from the deck of a ship at sea. I was in my living room. My heart was racing. My breathing quickened and tears welled up and steamed from my eyes. I must have dozed off for a minute. I remember that at that time my intentions were to get a few quick minutes of relaxing meditation before I started off on my day. I must have slipped into a deep state and lost all special and temporal awareness. I didn't expect that. Well, I'll think about this later.

Later in the day I did some research. I knew from my earlier studies that this was a battle at sea, and the ships were of the Napoleonic era. The types of ships I was in company with were first rates, ships of the line. The formations of the fleets testified that this could only have been one battle of that era: Trafalgar. The giveaway was the approach of my ship and those of my countrymen. For we sailed in two squadrons, lines of battle, parallel to each other, aiming directly and perpendicular to the enemy line of battle. The idea was to cut the enemy line in half and force the enemy into decisive ship-to-ship battle while the hostile squadrons forward and up wind of our entry point continued to sail on. It would take considerable time to bring the lead ships about to engage us in battle. This tactic would immediately, upon first contact, isolate a considerable portion of the enemy fleet, allowing us to have numeric superiority over the remaining squadrons.

Numeric superiority aside, we were British seamen, the best the world has ever seen. We excel at close battle. Our goal with this maneuver and approach would not only isolate the forward elements of the enemy fleet but also disrupt the enemy line, forcing each opposing ship into close contact with our superior seamanship and gunnery. "Disrupt the line" was the call. "Engage in close combat and bring about the decisive defeat of the allied fleet." Our tactical objectives supported our strategic goal: to make England safe from the French emperor, keeping England free.

OK, I thought. I have the battle down. That part was easy. What student of nautical history doesn't know the battle of Trafalgar when he sees it? What was the ship I was standing upon? For that answer, I had to do a little research, which would be easy enough. Within my personal library there were—you guessed it—several books on Nelson, his ships, and his battles. There on the page of the Trafalgar order of battle was the list of ships and there, the third in Nelson's line in the windward squadron, was the Neptune, a first rate of ninety-eight guns captained by Thomas Fremantle. Interesting. I was looking out from the eyes of Captain Thomas Fremantle of the HMS Neptune while approaching the French and Spanish line at the battle of Trafalgar. But why him? I thought.

As the days passed, I kept this vision, this experience, in my mind. It would not leave. This occurred in the earliest days of the internet. Research in those days was not as easily done as now with the volumes of diverse and detailed information we now have readily at hand. To look further into this topic, I had to visit a library. No ordinary library would do. I had to research one person in all of history, Thomas Fremantle. The library at our local university was the only choice. It would be days till the weekend when I'd have the time to get down there. The research would have to wait. But the vision of that scene would haunt me throughout the week.

Arriving at the library, I found that it was easy enough to locate the section containing information on Thomas Fremantle. He was married to Bess. One of his sons was an officer in the British Navy and has the town of Fremantle, Australia, named after him. Thomas was the ambassador to Naples later in his life. And there was his portrait. Interesting. Same weak chin as mine. Same round head and face. He had the same wisp of hair with lightness in the front and combed it the same as I had combed mine in the morning.

I got up from my seat and walked to the information desk. "Hi. Can I help you?"

"Yes. A different type of question than you're used to perhaps, but can you look at this portrait and tell me if you see any resemblance between him and me?"

The student employee looked at the picture of the portrait of Thomas Fremantle then looked up at me. Again at Thomas, and again he looked at me. For this look, he took his time and closely studied my face. One last look at Thomas, and he gave his verdict. "Yep. Dead ringer."

Death and Taxes

Several years passed from that date when my milestone birthday approached. My wife's present to me was a vacation for us anywhere in the world I wanted to go. Having never been to Europe, I chose England. She knew I'd choose England.

While there we visited Portsmouth to see the HMS Victory in dry dock. It was comfortable visiting the ship. Nothing particularly struck me while there. The ship had been on display in dry dock for years. We were able to tour the vessel. The cannons were all replaced with fiberglass models as the weight of the guns would be too heavy of a load for the ship in dry dock. I saw the spot where Nelson died that day at Trafalgar. It was a solemn place. We then toured Nelson's quarters. I saw the great room that contained the giant table. This was to be the table where Nelson's Band of Brothers met, dined, laughed, and played cards. Most importantly, this was the table where Nelson told us of his strategy to break the enemy line and force the fleet into close contact where English gunnery and seamanship would win the day. This was the conference table where it all happened. Or it was supposed to be the table where it all happened. Something was not right for me. I had no feelings about this place and that was very odd to me. For by this time, I was closely identifying with Thomas Fremantle and Nelson's Band of Brothers. I thought that in such a meaningful place I would have some feeling of attachment, but that was not to happen.

The following week, my wife and I were in London. While there we traveled by boat to Greenwich to visit the National Maritime Museum. Walking through the museum, we came upon an exhibit of the Nelson era. And there, behind glass walls, in a controlled atmosphere, for all to see and for history to keep, were the conference table, chairs, and furniture that once stood in Nelson's great cabin on the HMS Victory. Before I read the placard explaining this factoid, my heart started to quicken. My breathing became deep and slow and there started within my chest warmth and a glow while shedding a single tear. For a second, I felt like a puppy whose master was at the door ready to walk in. This was Nelson's table. The table and furniture at the dry-docked Victory were reproductions. That's why I felt no connection. I was connected to the wood of this furniture like a rabbit is tied to his hole. My atoms, the atoms of Thomas Fremantle, were intermingled with the atoms of these wooden chairs and table. This was where our Nelson told us of his audacious plan, the "Nelson Touch." A complete departure from the rules of battle that would bring about the final defeat of the French and Spanish allied fleet. But sadly, it also brought about the end of Nelson himself, for he was not to survive that battle. And Thomas Fremantle was to live on.

North Africa and the Twenty-First Panzer Division

I played army when I was a child. Always. I always played army. As I advanced in age and dexterity, I started to build plastic models from kits. We had two major model manufacturers back in those days, Revel and Morgan. I liked the scale of Revel better and the figures were more applicable to my use.

Advancing in age along with the advent of technology and game development, I first came across war game bookshelf sets. The D-Day operation, Overlord, as well as those taking place on the World War II Russian front or in the North African desert were the theaters that drew my attention most. I spent countless hours over a decade and more with these types of board games. Some were gigantic and some were not so much so. With the advent of the personal computer came the strategy and tactics games of World War II combat. I wasn't into the first-person shooter types of games. What interested me most, and what consumed many hours of the days, of what could be valuable time spent otherwise, were those games that featured tactical armored combat of a single battle through campaign scale.

What particularly drew my attention was the armor combat of the WWII era. My interest was consuming in time and treasure. My library contained hundreds of books on the Allies and Axis orders of battle, armor tactics, armor fighting vehicles and on the specific battles of the era. I knew every American, English, Russian, and German tank down to the modification, armament, road speed, and thickness of armor, strengths, and weaknesses. I knew where the vehicles were deployed. The effect they had on the advance across Europe and Northern Africa as well as the back-and-forth maneuvering on the Russian front. My library and book collection told the tale. If there was anything you wanted to know about WWII-armored warfare, I could pull out the correct book and show you the details right down to the insignia on the tankers' uniforms.

In other areas of my life, I became aware of reincarnation and past lives. I knew from experience and study that if I had an abnormal or intense interest in one area of history or another, there would likely be a reason. And that reason would likely be connected to another existence or incarnation that I had experienced in my soul's journey. The thought then struck me that I might as well put this intense curiosity to bed and find the life I was looking for.

I turned to my library and upon the floor laid out all my books depicting WWII-armored warfare. I didn't have enough floor space. I had to stack several books that were similar in theater and battle. I hovered above the books and used my hands as divining rods anticipating some type of harmonic revelation that would give me a clue into this past-life mystery when close. I really didn't know what I was looking for or how I would know if I found it. I only knew that somewhere within these books laid before me resided a piece of the puzzle. And once the puzzle was constructed, I would know the story of possibly my last incarnation on this earth.

It took about five minutes. Three books lay open to what appeared random pages. I took the three and retreated to the kitchen table, leaving all other books spewed about the floor space. The three I then placed upon the kitchen table were the following: Panzers in the Sand: The History of Panzer-Regiment 5 1942–1945 Volume 2, Inside the Afrika Korps: The Crusader Battles, 1941–1942, and German Tanks of World War 2.

Taking another half hour to read the pages that were open, I developed an interesting story that felt good and rang true. The story fit. I was comfortable with it. My mind and head were aligned on the frequency of the narrative, and I started seeing beyond what was immediately filling my head from the readings. There was no stopping where my mind raced.

The open pages of my internal book told a story of a young lieutenant, a platoon leader in the Fifth Panzer Regiment attached to the Twenty-First Panzer Division fighting in North Africa. The lieutenant was the leader of the first platoon of the second company of the first battalion commanding a group of German Mark 3 tanks. He was engaged in the Crusader battles and met his end, suddenly, on the outskirts of Tobruk in mid-December 1941. I went on to research further, this time using the nascent internet, but was not able to identify the name of that young man.

I carried the tale of the Crusader battles, German tanks, and armored warfare for the following months, always hidden away in the further reaches of my conscious mind. As I placed my meditative mind into the being of a German Heers Panzer Platoon leader, information came to me that portrayed sudden outbursts and spiraling events of battle that finally simmered down to country living and family events.

The story I then developed goes something like this: He was born in 1920 in a small town on the outskirts of Munich. He and his family were small farmers. Aside from tending the farm, his father repaired mechanical equipment and renovated homes. His son, me, our panzer leader, attended his father at work from an early age. Life was spent in study, working the farm animals and machinery, and family activities. Devotional activities occupied his Sundays as they would for all Roman Catholics in the region. Munich in the 1920s and 1930s was a political epicenter. The politics of the time were not something his family tended as there was enough work to be done, and life was full.

"There was plenty to do, eat, and ponder without having to resort to an interest in politics." His father was fond of that saying.

The drumbeat for war could not be ignored and our young man found that joining up and entering military service was a requirement. His education, some university, and his knowledge of mechanical vehicles placed him in a highly desirable position joining the newly formed panzer forces. He really had no choice in the matter. He was placed, ordered into the panzer forces upon receiving his commission.

The platoon leader missed the early actions of the Second World War and started his short career in North Africa as a member of the Fifth Light Division. Combat for him started in late March/early April 1941. The Fifth Light was assimilated into the Twenty-First Panzer Division and saw combat in the seesaw desert actions of the day. The British attempted to put a stop to the advances of the Afrika Korps leader, Erwin Rommel, with Operation Crusader, an armored attack against the advancing German formations.

Spirit Guides and Angels

From the personal perspective of a panzer platoon leader, it was all noise, heat, dust, and the constant jolting of the body as it sat within a moving iron coffin. It ended with the sound of an ear-splitting, crashing clang as an armor-piercing round entered the turret from the right. The round penetrated the armor of the Mark 3 tank, splashing molten metal and shrapnel throughout the turret before ricocheting off the walls and coming to rest close to the driver's seat on the raised deck of the turret. It was over in an instant with no precognitive awareness of the event. Adrenalin flowing, the sound of the penetrating round as it burst through the side of the turret was noted and acknowledged—registered. The initial burning sensation as the molten metal scorched the skin was quickly followed by the peripheral, blurry vision of the penetrating round and the flying bits of steel that pierced the skin. It was all too much for the human body to absorb, and the life was over in an instant.

Silence and a sensation of peace immediately followed the din. A vision of his farm with his grandparents greeting him at the gate for an instant advancing him to a relaxing, floating sensation while he bathed in a cool, soothing, white cloud filled with white, shimmering light. And from there, he advanced onward.

Death and Taxes

Wayward Atlantean Priest

My compound sat atop a sheer cliff above the ocean. The cliff, a straight-up rock face, was four hundred feet in height. Ocean waves crashed against the foot of the cliff. The house was made from the same rock and in some places was carved within the rock. My vantage point was immediately between the house and the ledge. Only a waist-high rock wall separated my sitting area from the cliff's sheer drop and ocean. The weather was typically stormy. This last year I preferred stormy weather and required it to be so to match my mood and disposition. This day there were clouds but no rain in my vicinity, thunder but no lightning as the bright flashes disturbed my eyes. The wind was everywhere but absent from my immediate vicinity near me. I preferred to see its effect as opposed to feel it on my person. All was as I required it to be. I stood looking down into the ocean, wearing the robes of my office. I was tall and muscular with hands made of steel and a look that could shake the observer to the core.

My maidservant entered and offered me the bounty of the serving tray with food and beverage. She stood before me with her head bowed as was custom. She was to my liking: fair of complexion, narrow in the hips, and lithe of limb. Although she would frequently provide me with pleasure, this day she too felt the severity of my disposition and knew of the times that were upon us. Her breath was shallow and measured lest to draw my attention. I took the offering from her, and she withdrew, head bowed, never to show me her back. It was an angry day, and the meal did nothing to change the form or format of my mood or of the times at hand.

The seasonal change was concluding and soon all would be dark with agitated weather and colder temperatures. The season for conquest was typically then diverted to maintaining homely comfort and repair for the following year's exploits. This break would be different. From this time onward, conquest of other regions was secondary to the conquest of wind, weather, and sea, for our time as a nation was coming to an end. The earth quaked in more frequency and volcanoes were actively engaged in exhausting gasses and ash that blotted from us our sun for long periods of time. While we had the resources and power for conquest, we were at a loss to overcome the seizures overtaking the planet, seizures that we set in motion. The growing upheavals developed beyond our power of control. The balance of earth, air, sea, and fire we upset. The frequencies of the earth lost their harmony. What we did as a method to control other lands and our citizens would become our nemesis to our fatal detriment.

I could scape a mountainside with the power of my thoughts. Slowly, over the decades, I changed the face of my cliff, planting the impression of our order's sign. I added vegetation then stripped it away. Moved rock and earth as it suited me. All this I have done with my attentions, creating a physical and material world to my liking. Yet I was powerless over the events that would come next as the earth gained momentum of its own and the changes we set in motion were now out of our control.

We fashioned the earth, commanded the weather, moved mountains, grew and destroyed forests per our need, and set pestilence against our enemies per our want. And it was now all out of control. We created the beasts, the half man and half animal, to do our bidding as our slaves. They were now on the loose and taking their revenge. I took my pleasure from the populace as I wanted. Still, they served me from fear. My power was my salvation. I still had the power to destroy or manipulate the body, health, and mind of person or persons per my desire. My servants and slaves had nowhere to go to save their own lives, and they still feared my wrath, so they stayed and carried on with their duties as I required.

And so it was, at the ending of this era. The storm I created this day to match my mood never abated. It would no longer heed my command but had a mind of its own. It raged on till the end. I was not to see the sun or feel its warmth again.

Alchemist

One cannot turn lead into gold. It can't be done. It's a physical impossibility. One is more likely to manifest gold from thin air. That I have seen. It was during my travels to the Far East during my earlier years. Many things were possible there in that land of ancient wisdom and practice. There they raise boulders to astounding heights propelled by the blowing of trumpets. But even they cannot turn lead into gold. And so, they told me it could not be done.

I do not have the power, skill, or ability to manifest gold from thin air. And I certainly cannot turn lead into gold. But I will never tell the duke. Never. He thinks it can be done. And to disappoint him in his quest for riches would be a death penalty.

I am not afraid of death. I have seen the lack of value placed upon the lives of many around me. Never fear death for life is tenuous in this day and age. The life after death is so much more life than this life we have in our earthly bodies. The life after death is the real life while this one I experience is but an illusion. I don't fear death, but I must continue my work for it is my work that adds to the uplifting pool of knowledge that advances all humankind.

And so it is that I teach the youth of our nobility in the arts, philosophies, and the sciences. It is of value to those who will follow us. Through the lessons of art, I teach compassion and vision. Through the lessons of philosophy, I teach logic in thought. Through the lessons in the sciences, I remove superstition from their minds and show them the innovation of critical thinking. However, I tread a thin line. Wake up, my young charges, and see the world not as your forefathers would have you but of how it is and of how you would make it. But silently, subtly, and quietly do I teach my lessons for the duke's men are all about and he has an ear for the stories his men tell of ones such as me.

The province where I taught was Algarve in Portugal. We were in constant battle as the Moors, beaten off and removed from the area, were keen on returning and claiming the province as their own. Suspicion was all about for there were spies among us. And the need for gold was constant when outfitting armies to save the kingdom. I was not a spy, but I knew of and visited with the Moorish wise men for the purposes of sharing our scientific understandings and discussing critical, logical aspects of the race of men and of heaven.

My students would travel outward from our kingdom once they were of age. Some would stay and take up arms with their families and with the king, Alfonso. But the good ones would leave and continue with their studies in foreign lands. Many traveled with a letter of introduction from me to the teacher or nobleman they would query for sponsorship to continue with their studies. These were the jewels that would eventually be the teachers that replaced me. Influenced by me and enlightened in new orders of thought guided by wisdom and governed by compassion.

This was the gold that I created from lead. An awakened mind that would uplift our world ever so slightly and bring us to a new age. Worth much more than gold coins that outfit our armies.

An Italian Mother

Scrubbing, cleaning, feeding, lifting, sweating, always dirty, never filled with satisfaction or leisure. I was given all that I would have and must make do. I had no ability or license to get for myself. If there was food to eat, I was to prepare and serve it. If I was given food only for him, then there was no food for them. There were few that I knew outside of my home and family. Friends. What were they? Banter and celebration were words representing what others did, but they held no meaning for me. I was the first one up in the morning and the last one to bed at night. And at night is when I had to serve him. Him. I wished he would just spend his time in the brothels and leave me be. I could not go on another day, but I did. I could not withstand another setback or complication, but I did. Only death would give me rest. But my everlasting life was never guaranteed. Sunday, the day of rest and worship, was just another day of toil and servitude.

Then a Babylonian

I was in the flower of my youth. My parents were successful in commerce, politics, and war. My surroundings were the most pleasant and my education the most effective and fulfilling. I frequently walked up the hill stairs to my house. The gleaming white buildings with their hanging gardens were everywhere. The people about were the most pleasing to the eye and I fit right in with my clothes of the finest cloth. I bounded the stairs in strength, with the vitality of my years, in the flower of youth.

So Many Warriors

Swordplay is not play. It is a strenuous activity with only the integrity of my armor and the swiftness of my arm and eye that keeps me safe, alive. The basic requirement in conflict is to hack at another till they no longer represent a threat. If they threaten me, I attack them and move to pierce their skin with my blade. If they neither cease their threat nor retreat before me, then I press the attack till they turn and run or perish beneath my sword. There is no discussion of morality or question of values. I am simply placed into the environment. Events ensue and I act as needed to ensure my longevity and health. My life is not mine. I live each day as if death can visit upon me at any time. Life is short. Boredom is laced with excitement. One takes pleasure when possible.

The thunder of hooves is around me, my mount gasping and snorting under the load and intensity of the moment. He is swift but labors. It's been a long day of maneuver and battle. I am calm and focused. My attention pinpointed and my awareness all about me as I take quick accounting of my line, the horde. With crushing power, we burst into the enemy. They fall and are rebuffed by the momentum of our charge. Bursting through the first line, we encounter the heavier infantry. There are combat and maneuver as our momentum, still forward, slows. Enemy is all about me as I ride forward. My seconds guard my flanks. I pause and take note of the horde. Still, we move forward. Our opponent's numbers lessen. There are more of them coming from the right. I have four of mine who are idle immediately about me. They look to me, and I signal to finish up our work here then assemble, pivot, and move. A line of our infantry advances down the hill we occupied. The line encounters the flank of the newly advancing numbers. There is contact and commotion. I advance with my horde to brush the opposite flank of the advancing infantry, causing some confusion among them. My objective is the side of the main body that lies ahead, an arrow's flight distant.

I have ideals. I have honor. The encounter is no place for honor or ideals. The encounter is a place of killing or being killed. Quests and chivalry are concepts that are in literature only. One does and lives as strength allows. I am here to do the bidding of my lord and liege and to produce victory, thus reaping the spoils and riches of the day.

When I am not in armor and the active arm of my lord, I can be generous and tender. It is not, however, in my interest to be so carried away with the finer qualities of my life lest I become inefficient or preoccupied. Preoccupation during encounters means death. My worth is measured by the strength of my arm and the value I provide to my lord's need and requirement. I, otherwise, live my life to the fullest comfort and take my pleasure when I can. There will always be those who challenge me. And eventually I will meet my match and perish under the chopping and hacking of one who is stronger, fresher, and younger than me. Till then I have but one purpose: to vanquish the enemies of my lord and sponsor. I fulfill my purpose well. There are few better than me.

Spirit Guides and Angels

Chapter 7: Connections

Me and My Infinite

An infinite intelligence is all about me. It is within all living things. All things created are its expression. I am an instrument of the infinite's expression on earth.

I had the pleasure of having a conversation with a tree. The tree gave me its name. The name was Grandfather. I went to Goldmyer Hot Springs one fine autumn afternoon. After I checked in at the caretaker's cabin, I proceeded to the hot springs by walking up a trail. The trail takes a turn and then goes up a hill. On top of the hill is a clearing with a clump of trees in the middle. There are six or seven of them, all old growth. The tallest of the trees is the grandfather tree.

He talked to me. He said that he was old and wise. He had seen many years and had much knowledge and wisdom. This was obvious. This was not the message he wanted to give me, but the one that I expected.

The message that he then gave me was that he was a part of nature. He was always a part of nature. He knew his part in nature, and there was never any doubt about what his position or relationship to the whole was all about. Never at any time a doubt. Not for this grandfather tree.

His understanding was solidified not only by his perception of the truth, but that he knew no other way. That there was never any doubt, as that was the way it was. The world around him supported his identity and purpose. His understanding was reinforced by his conscious existence for hundreds of years.

He provided a home to insects, animals, and birds. He communicated with the wind as it swept through his branches. He provided service to us humans as he replenished and cleansed the air. He knew the universal truth and lived it always. He had the spark of nature within his consciousness, and he lived as one with the world and all creation and evolution.

I have this very same spark of nature within me, but I do not know it as strongly as Grandfather. I stopped living in the consciousness. I had hundreds and thousands of years of social culture covering my spark. Concealing it from me. Making it difficult for me to clearly see my perfection and my place in the world, and my role within the consciousness of the whole. I strayed far from my purpose.

But as my cultural challenges were significant and impactful to my being, my spark continued to reside within, and my role in nature became different from his. My spark within is expressed differently from the grandfather. My spark is the image and likeness of the infinite. And what I own, what

I can do, that Grandfather cannot; I have the power to create and to build, and as such, I am placed as a steward of this world we both inhabit.

The mind determines for my body which suggestions shall be followed. My consciousness is the mouthpiece of my soul to the mind. If I watch and listen, I see that my bodily actions and the words from my mouth are the signals of the powers or influences that are controlling my mind. My material interests or affinities may control my mind for a time, but before I can end my connection to this world, my soul must reign supreme over my mind and body. The time must come when all my actions and thoughts are governed solely by the dictates of my soul. This was the task given to my soul to perform when it was placed within man's body upon my entry into the cycle of incarnation.

I once taught high school. This program I taught was no ordinary high school program. I had a program that was located on my own campus. I served the ten Seattle high schools. I was the program lead. I coordinated all staff and volunteers. Wrote the text and curriculum. Developed educational programs or systems that supported our main technical undertaking for the school district. Facilitated internships and cooperative education experiences.

Represented the program throughout the community, the industry we served, and the school systems.

I regularly communicated with school board members, chambers of commerce, corporate executives, industry supervisory personnel, as well as workers, employers, and other nonprofit groups that worked in conjunction or cooperation with my program and campus. I also worked with the Department of the Navy, Transportation, the Coast Guard, and NOAA. I met with a member of Congress and a US senator. Wrote contributing columns to magazines and had the program written about in newspapers and trade magazines, as well as advertised on the radio.

During the run of the program, I would regularly meet with my peers. The people I worked with daily in the school district were educators, administrators, principals, and deans. All these people had teaching degrees, master's degrees, and doctorates. These were my peers in purpose.

The program took the kids from the school system who were cast away or those who were not on the college track. These kids lacked options. When they made choices in the past, the choices were poor ones and got them into trouble. Or they never made any conscientious and focused choice at all and just wandered about aimlessly. They were lost, or they had no one in their lives to show them the way.

I served them. I provided options and an avenue for opportunities. Or I required that they choose paths and actions and then saw that they were accountable for their choices and actions. Some worked out. Some did not.

The program was a small success on a national scale. Those in the maritime industry knew of it and respected it. The federal agencies that licensed marine personnel recognized it. The program spawned a nonprofit educational organization partnered with the school district. The nonprofit is in its twentieth year.

The kids experienced positive exposure. They did not experience negative. They received skills or knowledge about themselves or about working in the world that provided them with foundations for positive growth and change, and for many, for the first time in their lives. Their new perspective, one where they are the owners of their lives, was not limited just to the time they were in the program. The lessons they learned they carried onward for a good part of their lives.

The time I ran the program and taught high school was a very rewarding segment of my life. It all began one day in 1990. I wish that I could be of service. I wish that I could be in a place to give back to the community. In 1981, I worked for six months in a maritime school as a lead instructor, a mostly administrative position. I wished in 1990 that I could somehow find a situation like that again.

I went to the local community college where they had a maritime program; it was on its lips. I asked if they needed any instructors. They said they needed someone to teach a seamanship class for yachtsmen. I taught the class.

At this same time, there was a high school maritime program at the community college campus. Three months later, the teacher's wife, a navy officer, was transferred to New York State. The program instructor went with her. I did not know about the open position, but I was recruited for it and offered it without an interview or application process. It was mine if I wanted it.

I had no experience in regular teaching. I had no teaching or university degrees, just a high school education, a small associate's degree, and the experience of a maritime career. Up to this time, I had only taught this one seamanship class at the community college. In the past, I also taught as a fill-in instructor at the maritime school in 1981. But as the lead's job was primarily administrative or working directly with the industry, my classroom teaching time was limited. I had a little experience teaching in a classroom. I had never taught high school students. I had never dealt with at-risk kids. I had never developed, written, and published a full educational program.

And I had never received a regular university degree. Not a teacher's degree or a master's degree like all my peers I interacted with on a daily basis.

Yet I succeeded beyond anyone's wildest expectations. I succeeded where others with greater qualifications had failed. How did I do it?

I was consciously connected with the divine intelligence. During that time, I was the instrument for the expression, and I knew it. I brought the creative force in through my being and sent it out through my hands and fingers and my voice to touch the hearts and minds of those I served. I engaged in the act of cocreating. Owning my being and skills, I consciously engaged in a collaborative process that included me as a living part of the inspiration of angels and celestial beings. I was connecting with the universal self that resides within, the spark of God, and the infinite. Through that spark, all of heaven was available. During that collaboration, I was living as one with nature, as the grandfather tree would tell it. I was an active part of the whole.

My success was not all my doing. It was the divine will. Without my connection and without acting as an instrument to channel that divine will, I would not have been able to succeed.

That was the truth as I knew it. But I would not go around and tell others that I was an instrument of divine will. They did not know that I was acting as heaven's instrument. "They" were the ones I worked with in passing and every day: the students, teachers, school administrators, and industry collaborators, benefactors, and advisors.

During that experience, I knew in my mind that I was an active instrument and channel of grace, but I did not yet have that perspective rooted firmly in my heart. The intellectual understanding took a while to make an impression on my heart.

I know things intellectually in my mind. I see and observe and then interpret. I make an intellectual conclusion then act upon it. When I imprint my conclusion onto my heart, the principle becomes truly one with me, and I live the reality of my perspective.

So for me, for a while in this position, I did not completely own my success and the act of being an instrument of the divine. I did not take full and complete advantage of the power of the blessings. I did not accept it as a known and current fact. And I could have accomplished more had I relied on the living relationship between me and nature and my part in the existence and consciousness of the whole. I did not immediately recognize the magnificence and the honor and the miracles that were happening before me or how I was raised above my station in life in service to the light. And because of that, so very much more could have been done, but was missed. I was not as firm in my identity as the grandfather tree.

When the grace is flowing through me, when I am the instrument of divine power, when I work as an active and involved member of the nature relationship and consciousness, I can do anything. All things are mine for the asking. All accomplishments can be mine as an instrument of divine will. All blessings are upon me as I act as a wire to transmit the flow of the divine presence and expression to the beings of the world. All that is needed from me is to know this, acknowledge it, accept it, and go with it.

During this time, everything that I needed to do at work, at home, and in all places was accomplished no matter what the odds and no matter what my limitations. I did the impossible and I did it effortlessly. This is the power and the intention of the infinite intelligence as an expression of my relationship.

When I am an instrument of delivering divine grace, everything is possible; nothing is impossible.

It is my birthright to live a fulfilling life filled with love and accomplishment. It is my birthright to succeed and to be happy. And so it is for all of us here in life. The closer I am to being the instrument and to living and working as an integral part of the divine expression, the more the impossible will be mine to accomplish. The infinite is expressed through love. I see it everywhere. I know that I am loved.

I test the hypothesis. I dream. I dream of something for myself. It doesn't matter what it is. It may be impossible. It may be for wealth, or it may be for health and happiness, or for love and companionship. I dream of something that I have always wanted or that I want now more than anything.

I ask for it. I ask the divine, and I ask every day. I expect the request to be fulfilled. I own that it will be a part of me as I am an expression of that consciousness I reach out toward. I think about my dream every day.

Miracles do happen. I have seen instant healing. I have seen others healed by holy people, shamans, and healers, and I have been responsible for some small acts of healing in my own right. I have seen people healed by the prayers of a loving aunt, mother, or grandmother.

Thoughts create things and circumstances. Asking and desiring initiate the act of creation. When the thought or request is something that will provide service to others, or increase the love in the world, or position oneself into a co-creative relationship with the divine and nature, then *something* will be created. Have I not already in my short lifetime experienced the aspect of this natural law numerous times over?

I ask and I expect. If I needed wealth, I may see an opportunity that I would not otherwise have seen. I may hear of something that I would not otherwise hear about. If I need health, I may learn about a food type that is better for my immune system. I may start to nurture healthier habits. I may do something that I would not otherwise do, but I would certainly open pathways for blessing to come to me in the areas of my requests that would not otherwise be there were it not for my desire, my request, and my attention. Nature and the divine seek to place me into the consciousness of the whole and for me to take my rightful place as a full participant in the flow of blessings from heaven. My thoughts attract like physical situations.

I then propel my dream by serving others.

I know my part. As I am of service, I remember that I am emitting healing and assistance, love and understanding, and I consciously bring the flow of the infinite into my being and send it out to my charges through my hands and my voice and my love. I know and own that I am an instrument of a divine expression. I accept the grace that flows through my body and my being. I acknowledge the source of my inspiration and grace. I bring the love of the divine into the world through my being as a product and aspect of my service. I dedicate my service to the divine. And in so doing, I feel the divine presence flowing through me and out to those I am serving in the physical, emotionally, and spiritually, touching their hearts.

As it is written by James Churchworth in one of his magnificent manuscripts:

The great mysteries of the Hindus, Polynesians, Egyptians, and of the Biblical miracles are and were the results of working the soul force. Christ was the perfect example of the soul force being in perfect control over the mind and body. Christ was placed on earth as an example—to teach and to show what we eventually must become. The development is now going on. We must become perfect; otherwise, the great divine law will have miscarried. As the law is divine, it cannot miscarry.

A Grown Child Marries

At the start of our relationship, her mother brought her over to my apartment. I was hosting a dinner party. There were other children there, so I thought it might be fun for her.

I had an old apartment with large rooms and hardwood floors. I had this hallway that connected the bathroom, kitchen, and living room. All during the party, she would run up and down the hallway stamping her shoes on the floor. She made a perfect sound, and she had the perfect shoes for the job at hand. Slap, slap, slap, each step crystal clear, sharp, and precise. The sound reverberated throughout the apartment and echoed into the living room.

The sound was neat, and I didn't mind one bit. Especially since the neighbors in the apartment below me were two girls who danced in the clubs and would be out working. Beyond that convenience they would always let me know they were home from work. They would routinely come home at 3:00 a.m. and make enough party noises to wake me from a sound sleep. Taking that into consideration, I figured her bustle this night would be OK. I did not hinder her activity and her joy of making a perfect stomping sound.

I wondered what could make this sound so rich and clear. After all, here she was, just a little pint-size sprout. The sound was disproportionate to her size, but then I looked at the shoes and investigated. They were patent leather with hard leather soles. The width was as long as the length, a perfect square. I surveyed the feet. They too were square-looking and took on the properties of a square palm of a hand. It was no wonder the sound was so clear and precise. The stomping of the square shoe provided perfect dissipation of the sound as it radiated equally from all sides of the sole.

Who would have believed that twenty-four or so years later, I would be walking this square-footed sprout down the aisle and giving her hand away in marriage? In the time since the days of the square feet, she has grown into a beautiful woman and a remarkable adult. She is competent, strong-willed, assertive, compassionate, sensitive, loving, helpful, and beautiful in mind, body, spirit, and heart. Her mother and I are proudest of the woman she has become. We could not have asked for anything more for her than for what she has become.

She moved into her own home when she was eighteen. One day, several years later, she is running errands and comes over for fifteen minutes to pick up something her mother had for her. She brings a male friend. While she repairs to the upstairs to fetch the items, he sits with my wife and me in the kitchen. During that time, he tells us his thoughts and visions, his feelings and beliefs. He engages us and speaks to us as individuals, not as parents. In the fifteen minutes he sat talking with us, he spoke more than all the others she ever brought home to meet us.

Since that day, we have come to know him. He is kind, passionate, honorable, principled, caring, and dynamic. He wears his heart on his sleeve, and his love for our charge is clear for all to see. Throughout her time coming into her adulthood, he was always there, sometimes on the periphery and at other times close at hand and directly involved. At all times, he had her back and was patient and tender with her.

Spirit Guides and Angels

It is the joy of every parent to know that their little square-footed sprout has found someone who is as loving and caring as he is. And more joyous still to know that she has someone she loves to share in her adventures in life. It is to the joyous adventure that I write this passage. To the joyous adventure of the one I raised up from childhood, and to the one with whom she shares her life. They have found each other, and they know it.

Those Passing and We That Guard

I didn't know why I was sitting here alone in this empty room, but I knew I had to be here. Before me lay the occupied casket of an old friend whose journey here was ended. The traditional viewing of the casket was scheduled for another couple of hours. The room was newly prepared. They wheeled him into the room in his Sunday finest in a box made of fine American walnut. It looked good and was nicely finished. He would have liked it.

The funeral director set the schedule for the funeral program. The viewing room was prepared for him, and he would soon present himself to friends and acquaintances for this, the final chance to see his face. I knew I had to be there as soon as he was wheeled into the room. I had to stand watch and see that he was not left unattended. Some deep-seated, internal trumpet sounded and called me to that place to sit and stand guard. Some long-ago cast-off military ingrained discipline brought me here with this sight before me as I sat in one of the folding chairs in the back of the room, before me lay the material reminder of my dear friend of twenty years. We had seen much together and shared in life's common milestones as friends, keep and kindred fellows.

He was older than I. His role was patriarchal, while mine was a passing mariner sharing life with his offspring. We collaborated, cajoled, and cavorted together in a friendship founded upon respect. We respected each other's character. We knew our roots. He knew of my capacity, potential, and ignorant honesty, while I knew of his unshared thoughts and the company of his silent presence, dreaming of the jobs of his war.

We knew of each other. We each shared that same experience in life, needing, wanting someone to believe in us, requiring ourselves to be reliable and honorable. We knew of the arduous days at sea. The utter monotony as we put all else aside, just wanting to get the job done and finish this thing that we didn't start. We never exchanged words in conversation to this effect, but the recognition was there in a solid glance and passing as I peered into his eyes. We would sit in the drawing room after dinner and gaze silently into our own private thoughts and worlds. We knew from our familiar comfort that we sat this way together before many times, in other instances, places, and in other lives together. I would trust his presence as I extended my mind to the hinterland between sleep and waking. This sojourn here and now was not our only meeting. This was not the first time we sat about in the comfort of our deep thoughts while others stood by, lost in their own kindly world.

Perhaps I had a personal need for that last "after-dinner sit" where I could escape one last time with the old friend sitting, but now lying, in some comfortable spot in an otherwise empty room. The urge was strong within me, but I could not identify its source. Something very old within me was taking hold in the softest manner. I took my leave of those in my company at his home and traveled to the viewing room to sit, be in attendance, and stand watch.

I must have been there for an hour or a bit more. Silently sitting in the last row as I surveyed the room. All was quiet. Everything in the room was perfectly in place, and the colors were subdued, all very peaceful and calming. The family would like this. As I sat there alone, I couldn't help letting my mind wander. Lost in my thoughts, I contemplated our times in the drawing room for our after-dinner sit and wondered, *Why is this so familiar?* Countless times, unknown times, sitting like this in silence, escaping into thought with him, my friend, there. Close by. I let my mind wander and explore, but I always stumbled upon the same question. *Where have I done this before?*

As I rested my eyes and sat back and tried to relax on the uncomfortable chair, I felt the soft sound of clanking and clapping armor. Unhurried and at rest, the sound lingered in my ear. The whinny of a pony behind the trees added to the sound of frogs and critters alike. The fire was banked low and cracked a puff of smoke to add to the smell of unrushed, restful activity about me. Low, muffled mutterings reverberated inside my head. There were words whispered or spoken softly, devoutly. There are men-at-arms about me, all my brothers' cause. They are resting the respite of the deserving. Their day, long and eventful, taxed their bodies and the wits that they were to retain. This was the respite in the night. This was the time of tranquility that breaks when every battle or exploit ends, and we marshal our resources and take what rest we can. This night, we assess the toll and rewards and count our honored dead.

A tent was erected, and its perimeter was lit with torches. Within lay the body of a fallen kinsman. There were men-at-arms placed in attendance of his person as we watched the whole night long to sit one last time with whom we shared much life. I can't tell the uniform or accoutrement period, as there were many. None to stationary remain and say to me that this was the one memory of our meeting. We sat many times in quiet and ease, well enough to unleash the tethers of our minds and float freely, undefended, while in trusted company. We, those standing here, shared that trusting security. And he was our brother. He was one of us.

How many different scenes could I remember? I couldn't count. The uniforms, forever shifting. The flag never remained the same. The languages mattered little. The faces ever-changing. As before me his being would stand in armor while at rest, and the next he would be fallen and laid out with honor sleeping within the tent of the slain. The scene replayed itself over and over for the hour I sat alone in the back of the viewing room. Never repeating any one spot, not creek nor camp, nor farm nor forest, the litany of visions all based on this theme repeated over and over in my mind, interweaving the personalities of the slain and the living as I sat there on an uncomfortable chair, resting my eyes.

I would try to pull myself away and think of other, more temporal times and events we shared together, but always I would be drawn again back to the campfire and the calmness of repose in the late of night.

Guests started to arrive, and the place was filling up quickly. At first, they would trickle in and give their greetings to the one he was. They would sign the guest book and retreat into their solitude and their own shared memories. The family arrived, and the program proceeded. It was now time to go to the church. He was getting his own Mass, and his body would be laid to rest. I departed with the family.

The ride over to the church was a sad one. We, my spouse and I, did not have much to say. We were just proceeding through the tasks to complete this ritual while not wanting to think too heavily on what we were doing. It was a sunny day in the autumn, and I opened the sunroof. The wind took my hair, and as I felt it rustle came a familiar *whack, whack* on the crown of my head. *What was that?* I thought. And again came that familiar *whack, whack*. Throughout my twenty-year association with this passed-on friend, any lapse of coordination in body or mind would receive from him a three-finger whack on the crown of my head. This rap that I now experienced was very proverbial, being numerously received, and was detailed down to the three-finger width that was typical of the living experience. I found it odd to be receiving it now. I hadn't done anything uncoordinated, but it was so like him to be disrupting the status quo of my state of mind and, as typical, at the most inopportune time. But here it was. While it did help to add some spice to a somber car ride, I was not about to be shaken from my solitude. I remember saying, "Cut it out. Can't you see I'm grieving? I'm grieving here. And you're messing my hair." The whacks ceased for the time being.

I was then allowed to proceed unmolested. Arriving at our destination, I remarked to my spouse about the incident and was to learn that she too was whacked on the back of her head. She did not want to break her thoughts, so she did not mention it as I had. That's so like him. I was to later learn that I was being grossly uncoordinated at the time by grieving his loss too much.

I entered the church. He was a Roman Catholic who was devout and true to the teachings of his founder. It was fitting that he would have his private Mass here at his parish. I was to speak for a minute and relate my experiences with him to the litany of spectators and speakers, mourners all, on this one last tribute to a fallen friend.

He never told what it was really like when he went to war. But when his eyes took on that faraway look while sitting in the drawing room or at the dinner table, he was really standing on the deck of an aircraft carrier, wearing his flight suit, carrying his chart, and looking over the horizon, getting his last reading of the weather before he took off. He did not want to be there. But he did not want to leave. He didn't care to take leave or have some time off because he had a job to do. He wanted to stay in it till the job was done and the war was over.

That was the mission: to finish the job, end the war, and live in peace.

Those who went to war in the forties were defined by the experience. His experience revealed itself to me as I sat in the drawing room all those evenings and alone with him before the memorial. I understood the honor of our meetings these last twenty years. I understood that between were many other meetings throughout the intermission of the battle. He lived his life as he soldiered, caught between the actions on the field and the clash of swords in the charge. For his time from then till now was but a lull in the encounter and a time to rest up and eat heartily in the peace that he won.

The time came for the casket to be brought to the altar for the priest's blessing and the celebration of the Mass. I was one of the pallbearers. The day had thus proceeded in a very contrary manner. At first, it was the night's bugle call and my watch at the camp, and then his familiar tap on the top of my head interrupted my grief. My grief unbroken but for these, his appropriate goodbye, I proceeded down the aisle to the altar. This was the final opportunity for him to show his true feelings regarding the event of his passing. We proceeded to wheel the casket up to the altar, and he expressed himself to me the one final time.

How does one feel after crossing over the gate from this life to the next? What are the emotions of the soul and the elation to the spirit? Do the thoughts and memories of those so gathered invoke a celestial answer to the questioning I pose to him? As I wheeled the casket down the aisle, my mind slipped back to the viewing room, and I could not help but enter a slight meditative state. There, besides me, I see a reflection of what he once was dancing on the coffin that carries his physical remains. *Odd,* I thought. This was quite contrary to what I thought was an otherwise solemn moment. But there he was, as I saw him, dancing, doing a jig on the finely crafted American walnut casket purchased from the funeral home. The look of his purported pleasure and excitement took on that of Snoopy dancing atop his doghouse, feet quickly stomping and arms stretched out, cavorting.

This was not enough of a display for him. No. He would not leave me with this last look of joyous humor and carefree dancing. Onward he lifted from this immediate position next to me and continued to race around the walls, hollering for joy with a long-lasting cry of "Whoopie!" Around and around the inside of the church, he ran till my attention was required to position my fallen charge for his final honors.

The remainder of the service proceeded through the traditional program one would find at a Catholic Mass.

Throughout the service, I found myself slipping in and out of my current physical awareness as I delved into my memories of our shared experiences on this world and others. You might say that I was in an extremely receptive state of mind for those energies and influences that are being projected by those nearby. We were all thinking of him, and his spirit responded. My focus was drawn to the living memories of which he was to such intensity that I began to feel him around me and before me. I sensed his presence and caught the whiff of his cologne. I could feel him coming close to me in spirit as I slipped from any sustainable consciousness in this here and now. The boundaries of who I am and this spirit essence before me blurred, and I lost the awareness of my physical body for short spells. He was within then without me. His being pulsed as the concrete thoughts of him intermingled with the perimeter of my being and with who I was.

Those gathered who were celebrating the Mass stood in unison and offered to their neighbor and those standing around them peace and blessings. The expression "Peace be with you" was passed around and whispered like a mantra, often repeated. I turned to the person on my left, his sister. I spoke and said the words "Peace be with you," but the voice I sounded was not mine, and the vision of him standing in greeting was what outlined me. I thought it was I, but I looked so different. "Peace be with you," she said in return as she took my hand in a soft and gentle embrace.

I turned to my other side, and to his wife I extended my hand and again spoke the words "Peace be with you" and was met by the widow's longing gaze as I added, "My love." It was a term he used often when speaking with her. As it was said, recognition flashed from within her eyes. I shuddered as I became aware again of where I was and what the circumstances were.

The program finished, and we left the church to continue with our day and the final moments of our memorial for the fallen.

Several days later, I was in his old office cleaning up the place. Someone had to make sense of the books, computer equipment, and drawings that were piled onto every horizontal space available and otherwise. I decided to store some of the outdated papers that were technical in nature, some long-ago contract designs implemented and placed into service. I pulled from the supply closet an unopened box of plastic garbage bags. After reaching down to pull the first bag out, I snapped the bag open and fully extended the mouth as I readied the load of papers. There, at the bottom of the bag, was a shiny medal object. Curious about what this object could be in this newly opened plastic bag, I reached in to retrieve a silver medal depicting a bright and shiny being. Upon closer inspection, I identified the being as the Blessed Virgin Mary, Mother of God, and read an inscription. "O Mary, conceived without sin, pray for us who have recourse to thee—All who wear them will receive great graces."

The finding was very out of the ordinary. I could not for the life of me figure out how this medal came to find its way into this bag. It must have been from a line worker at the factory. I placed the medal into my pocket and continued to clear out the papers that had gathered over his last four decades. Finished, I tied up the bags and carried them downstairs to the basement for sorting. On my way down, I came across his granddaughter, who was also cleaning up the house after last week's mayhem.

"Take a look at what I found in a new plastic bag as I was getting ready to fill it with papers." I handed her the medal, and she took it in her hands. Immediately, her face became twisted and crunched up with a look of surprise and a hint of familiarity. As her hand went up to her mouth, her eyes welled up and she began to cry. "What's wrong? Why are you crying?" I said softly, extending my free hand and touching her shoulder. "Don't be sad. It's just a little medal I found, and you can keep it."

For the first time since receiving the medal, she slowly took her eyes from it and looked up at me. "This is his medal. It's his Miraculous Medal. They couldn't find it. He always wears it and never takes it off. But when everyone went down to the hospital, no one could find the medal. Not the medics or nurses. Not anybody."

We took the moment to look at each other and the medal. We said nothing of any substance to each other. Our only words were some malformed syllables sounding close to the words *what* and *how*. She took the medal up closer to her eyes, looked, and started pointing and exclaiming, "Look! See the ring that passes the chain? See? I broke it when I was little. I pulled it off his neck when I was one year old. I pulled it off and broke the ring. He soldered it back on. See? He fixed it with solder and look! It's the same medal!"

She keeps the medal in a special place in her house and within her heart. She wore it pinned to her wedding dress the day she got married. This friend who passed into the next life left his mark and remains one whom I will remember as I kept watch at the campfire after a day's duty.

Watching a Dog Go to Heaven

We were on our final walk, this old dog and me. He really wasn't a very old dog as dog years go. But this breed of his was prone to such surprises. In just two more hours, the vet would come down to the beach house where we'd be waiting. I'd even let him up on the couch where he could dine on thinly sliced cheese that I'd serve him in comfort and splendor to his heart's content.

I could never figure out why, for a dog that never, *ever* went swimming, the beach was his favorite place. He'd run right down there next to the salt water but never go in past his hips. I imagined that he preferred running on the soft and temperate sand to the hard surface of a city street or the stony outcroppings in the wooded backyard. But the beach was his favorite spot, so here we came to take this one last walk. He was a good dog. I was happy to be there with him.

Perhaps my eyes were bigger than my stomach for taking such a long walk with him this afternoon. Or perhaps I never wanted to turn around and return to the beach house to make our appointment. We'd go around another point and then turn around and head home.

To landward stood the bluff. The bluff was a steep, windblown cliff that was eroded and weathered over the years on end. Each year, a little bit more of the bluff would come crashing down in a mass of rock and sand, falling victim to the pounding rain and ever-present wind. The bluff stood two to three hundred feet high and ran the length of the entire beach, terminating at the spot known as Double Bluff. The bluff had ample vegetation to keep all the animals that would frequent it. Occasionally, you'd come across a fallen tree or a slide of sand and rocks as they fell to the retreating landscape. From time to time, I would see an eagle riding the wind, searching for food, or perched in the treetops that stood upon the tall bluff.

This day was quiet with few visitors to the beach, human or avian. My friend and I walked in solitude. Coming to a point in our walk where I had to decide if we had had enough walking, I scanned the area to survey the ridgeline of the bluff above. There in a tree, sitting quietly and intently scouting the waters for food, was perched an osprey. The osprey took flight. The dog, now firmly on the beach before me, found his friend the heron in the water. The heron that inhabited this section of the beach was very familiar with this dog. Many times in our history, we'd come across the heron standing on an outcropping of rock several yards off the beach or wading knee high in the lowered tide. The dog, not letting a bird go by without saying hello, ran his way over to give the usual greeting. The heron would, of course, take off flying. The heron would always fly down the beach in the direction we were walking. Landing a short distance away, the dog and the heron would repeat the interaction all over again. There were times, I knew, when the heron was messing with the dog. The dog wouldn't harm a feather on the heron's wing. He was just so happy that he couldn't contain himself but had to run out there and join in the heron fun.

Moving my attention from the dog and heron interplay, I notice the osprey alight on one of the trees outlining the ridgeline on the cliff above me. There he sat with his watchful eyes following our every move. We kept walking. The bluff was lower here. There was a manicured pasture on the land above us, beyond the bluff that provided but few trees in this section. The trees here were clumped in groups along the ledge of the bluff. I noticed the osprey above and off to my right, behind me, sitting in a tree. As if following us, the osprey launches off his perch, descends in slow, plunging flight paralleling our movement down the beach, then, swooping up, he alights on the next clump of trees to again sit and watch, following our every step.

As we advanced, the sand cliff came closer to the water, narrowing the beach to just a sliver. The weather in this area was very active, and winter was not quite over yet. Frequent days of high wind, wave, and rain eroded the sand bluff, dropping trees and boulders onto the beach. Close and to my right were the signs of a newly uncovered boulder of compact sand. The boulder was very inviting and being newly uncovered from the depths of the cliff, I could not help but touch its surface to feel the texture and know its age. As I touched the sand boulder, my palm print was left remaining. The boulder seemed the perfect place for me to leave a written epitaph and display to all the merits of this good ole dog by my side. I wrote his name and the years he resided in this world. At that, I dropped my stylus to the ground. *I wrote enough,* I thought. *Let's keep moving. We've got a little time yet to walk farther.* As we rounded the nearest point, I noticed the osprey farther down the beach above us. The osprey was still tracking our every move.

Immediately after we rounded the point, I saw, farther ahead, that a rockslide containing a large boulder blocked our advance. We still had some beach to walk yet, but we'd have to turn around when we got to this large slide area and boulder just thirty yards ahead. The dog bounded off into the water to visit with the heron. As I watched both dog and heron flying about in the wind, the osprey again leapt into my view, gliding about in a semicircle over the water and dipping down in its flight once over the dog and heron, only to again alight upon a tree atop the bluff. I tilted my head upward to mark the osprey's perch one last time. The boulder that stood before us caught the rays of the sun peering out from behind a cloud. I looked, and there I saw carved into the boulder the totem of a solitary osprey.

Death and Taxes

As the boulder stood before me, I could see the faint lines of a totem standing about six feet high and presenting an osprey with its wings spread wide as if preparing for flight. I stopped and held my position. The dog, having chased off his friend the heron once again, returned to my side and stood there panting while unmoving. I looked closer at the boulder. Were those shadows I was seeing? As in response, the sun came farther out from behind the clouds and cast its full light upon us. What was once the shadows of this charcoal sand-encrusted boulder were now filling in with colors of red, yellow, blue, and white. The totem slowly changed from its charcoal gray shadow to white, gaining dimension, protruding out from the rock. Blue marked the outline of the bird as red filled in to form boundaries that stood between rockslide debris and totem, framing the bird within a crimson enclosure. The background of this vision was yellow, like the sun above reflecting off the water. I looked down at the dog. *What do you think this is all about?*

Looking again at the totem carved into the boulder, I saw an additional form take shape. Above the osprey, I beheld a sitting dog with droopy soft ears and ever-noticeable jowls. *A good old hound he is,* I thought. As the sun disappeared and reappeared from behind the clouds, the dog carved into the side of this eroded boulder took on the color of a dark tiger with a white breast and four white socks. As the sun again came out from behind the clouds in full strength, the image of the dog took on the same crimson boundary as the osprey, and the form of a totem pole came into being as if carved out of the solid rock and shifting sand. While looking down at the dog, I asked, "Is this you?" The sun then disappeared behind a threatening cloud, and the totem was no more. All that stood before me now were this rockslide and boulder on the beach as I first saw it, charcoal gray with encrusted sand all about. There was rain coming. It was time to head back.

As we walked back down the beach toward the cabin, the osprey above tracked our movement and shifted its perch to keep up with us as needed.

The osprey totem was mine. Decades ago, on a mountaintop in Oregon, my spirit guide, the osprey, found me. I have carried the aspect of its spirit within my personality ever since. The osprey was the foundation of my totem. It would make sense to me that if I am going to see a totem carved out of a boulder, it may as well be the osprey. Then, as I was watching the light play tricks with the shadows, there appeared the dog sitting above. Totems present the foundation spirit at the bottom. As new and additional spirit guides align, or as spirits of the animal kingdom become integrated into a soul, they're placed higher up on the totem, above the foundation. The osprey found me long ago in my youth. This was the only known totem that I claimed, having not knowingly bonded with any other spirit of the animal kingdom since.

How now comes the dog as the second inhabitant of my totem? And then I understood. As I was preparing to end my witness of this animal's journey on this earth, I stood here for him, on his last day, engaging in this lasting activity, together, as we had so many other times before.

The dog came to me as a rough-and-tumble rescue from the humane society. He was rambunctious. But behind all that exuberance for life and the company of people, he was gentleness and empathy. He knew who his people were, and he knew he was one of us. The leash slipped out of my hands on our first walk, and he took off running. Thanks to the kindness of the stranger down the trail, I was able to regain control of his discovery run and bring him home. From this first walk with his uncontrolled joy at running and meeting new people, to walking with me anywhere in the city, at heel with no leash. That was the extent of our journey together. It wasn't obedience school that taught him to heal with such dedication. It was the love he possessed and the desire to excel and be the perfect dog to his people. I provided him the environment and the opportunity; he did all the work and became one with those about him who loved him. I escorted him through a journey of heavenly advancement as a member of the loving family he cared for and protected. Now, this day, I would escort him to the next world that waits.

I never asked the spirits that inhabit this land for the honor of the dog totem. I never traveled in the woods seeking the guidance of the spirit. I never contemplated the honor during my life with this companion. I simply lived each day as I had, remaining in touch with the living spirits of nature and paying my respects to caretakers of the truth that is stranger than fiction. The spirit of the shamans' underworld, the guides of the four directions, the keepers of the four elements, and those celestial wonders that knew me so well bestowed upon me this honor. For now, my spirit was imprinted with a dog and all that his character entailed. Throughout the life of the companionship we shared, we grew together, becoming one in thought and heart, and developed as more loving, compassionate, and empathetic beings. It was in appreciation for the life I provided, the manner with which I lived it, and the growth in being that we shared together. It was now for me to be so rewarded by that spirit of the dog.

The walk back to the cabin was difficult for the guy. With all this bounding about and seeing his old friends, the dog was walking back in labor; the lump growing in his throat was hurting him every time he panted. There wasn't far to go.

Death and Taxes

We both arrived at the beach house in good repair. The dog was quite subdued. I was acting brave. We settled on the couch, where one by one I fed him shavings of his favorite cheese. What a treat. The vet was a little late, and I didn't mind one bit. Knowing the dog and the dog knowing me, we did not fret about the journey he was to undertake beyond this world. For him, it was all very natural. His body was a good one, strong and healthy. It was this one thing, this one large and growing lump that got in the way. But for him, it posed a clear message that his time here had come. And now he was to take his leave. He, like me, would never tarry or hesitate before a new adventure. And while he was not now as bouncy as he could be, he was ready and happy to leave his pain-riddled bag of bones for the bliss of oneness.

He knew the vet, and he liked her. She was one of his buddies. Yet there was no excitement upon her visit. The living room took on a somber tone, and we all went about the business at hand. They say that the healthier the animal, the quicker the medicine takes hold. And so, it was over even before it seemed it started.

He bounded out of his body. No, floating gently above and giving your last farewell, not with this doggie. He bounded out with a force and presence that had me dodging quickly over lest I get in his way, and he knocked me over. As he had done so many times before, he took a running leap to jump over this final gap between where we were and where he was to be. As he left, his front legs were leading. With his tongue fully extended and hanging out from the side of his mouth as if being driven by the wind of the car's advance, he bounded up and outward, and I quickly lost sight of him.

Although I could no longer see his image or shadowy body, I was still attached to him. He was heading to some destination, and he was not letting me go. There was still something between us. Something that he wanted me to experience with him, outward he went, never slowing. "Follow me. Follow me. I want you to look at something."

Ahead of him was what looked like a stream. I watched as he approached it. This stream reminded me of the graphic representation of the jet stream that I see often on the evening news and weather reports. The jet streams circle the Earth, dipping and rising in latitude as if driven by some unseen levee system. He was heading for such a stream, and I was right there with him as he entered.

Entering the stream, I heard the laughing, the barks, and the playful sounds of puppies. Looking closely, I saw no single dog that I could identify by image. There were no shadowy bodies or souls, spirits, or ghosts of dogs that were visible. There was just something in the air in that stream that had the mirth and energy of playful puppies. The stream was a whole community that had one being. I was struck by a whirlwind blend of affable personalities among this single community. Each was like a whiff or a jingle that, when combined, created an aroma or a sound. I could feel the presence of my friend close by at my side. Yet while I felt him beside me in his familiar place, I also felt him behind, around, and away from me. His being was all about me, lost in the stream of personalities that had one being, one purpose, and one life.

To one side of the stream were those aspects of the whole that were leaving and entering another dog's life. The scene reminded me of an open car door with furry companions ready and eager to jump in and start the next journey to wherever it was they were riding to. Within the car, I saw for the first time within the stream a shadow form of an animal. Taking residence within this shadowy body was not one spark of personality but many. Where there was one body to be occupied, there were many personalities of the stream that would reside within, all in harmony with one another as they lived the life of one dog.

This body that was forming and getting ready to arrive at its appointed time and place was destined for a grown woman. The woman had several dogs during her lifetime. She had fond memories of each one and made lasting friendships bridging the species line. Now in her waning years, she decided to take on a new friend to comfort and be comforted. Into this shadowy body of a dog strode the personality sparks of several who were at one time her pets. The aged adult woman would soon and often remark to her friends that this new dog reminded her of not one but three of her old hounds. This new dog had the temperament of her old English setter, the energy of her boxer, and the closeness of her old lapdog mutt that her father picked up for her when she was just a child.

And so it is that when we get a new dog, we sometimes see traits of personality or character in this one new dog that remind us of our old, passed away dogs that we loved so much. Before the new dog arrived at her side, he resided as a scent within the stream. And just before the new dog comes to life, the car door opens, and all those wanting to take a ride jump in together as one. To live in harmonious joy as one. Her old dogs could not resist the opportunity to visit and make a home again with one they loved so much. And so, they jumped into the car, and when she met them, she recognized them for who they were from days gone by.

With this last vision and shared experience, I left the stream and returned to the here and now. There was work to attend to. I had to help the vet this one last time. I did not have the time or opportunity to tarry with the dog in his new home within the stream. It was his place now, anyway, and not for one such as me. I appreciated the visit and the last urging from a friend I could always trust to lead me to something interesting and exciting for us both. I am sure that we will meet again, this dog and I. And the next pet I meet will have some small spark that belongs to this one, my friend and companion for a decade and more.

Spirit Guides and Angels

Chapter 8: Bumps and Balance

Energy

Throughout the years, I ran energies that brought me to the brink of stepping through the curtain and residing in both worlds, not just at a spiritual level but on a physical level as well, or so I thought. I felt that I was on the verge of taking my foot and stepping through that circle of light. I fully expected to be whole in body on both sides of the veil and to have the ability to create physical articles and happenstance per my thoughts by materializing my desire into the physical, concrete reality. And then it all just ended. The opportunity ended. The door swung shut. Silly of me to think that a mere mortal could physically walk in two worlds, two dimensions, that my thoughts would immediately manifest concrete creations, or that I could materialize objects from thin air per my intention.

Fortunate, it was that the door slammed shut regardless of how close I was getting to the secret because I was but human and flying too close to the sun, again. God help the world, my family, and those close to me, were I able to manifest all my thoughts into concrete creations. Some of my thoughts are humanly uncontrolled and not meant for the light of day, much less some concrete creation foisting itself upon others' required attention. And now this current two-year foray into the spiritual metaphysical immersion was to end, and the rebound effect would be upon me. All this, I knew, through my experiences decades ago when I first flew too high and reached too far.

As this wave of immersion into the metaphysical crested, what then followed was the trough, of course. And for the second time in thirty-plus years, I experienced the opposite side of spiritual growth and development. This wave had all of me. My involvement here was at the personal, familial, vocational, and social levels as well as metaphysical. There was no aspect of my life buffered from the work, practice, and community I was involved in. When the door slammed shut, it would reverberate within every aspect of my personal life and throw me to the floor. To say the least, this shift from crest to trough was traumatic.

What followed was the loss of many friendships as well as social and developmental associations. The tension that accompanied friction between my dear spouse and me was at an all-time high. The reverberation on all fronts would last for half a decade. That was the temporal measure associated with my fall from this height, for each tendril of my personality was associated with one isolated, nontraditional church and attending community. I married my metaphysical practices to this church and community. Upon the sudden withdrawal of my tendrils from the subtle energies produced by the living dance, my core shuddered with a repeating shock wave as the walls all about me caved in with resolve and increasing pressure.

I stayed away from any organizations after that one. I refrained from sitting in circles that did not consist of only my silence and me. I sought silence. No longer did I seek the discourse with the heavenly host. I did not want to see them nor know of their presence in my personal, solitary sphere. My conversations now were of an earthlier tone. As tension in my home grew, the earthly tone that distracted us became all there was about our communication and partnership. My personal world and family life took on a catastrophic existence. Anger, isolation, and fear gripped the household, my wife and Me. We were our own antagonizors. Our bodies responded to our emotional decline in kind by bringing one sickness and calamity after another. What a ride it was.

The organization of my sole attention was not without controversy in its forty-year history. This was the place where all the great local and regional mediums studied and participated in the operations of a spiritual church and center of learning. This was no spiritual center that hosts the occasional motivational talk or guided group meditation. This was a church that existed and focused upon communication and physical experiences coming from beyond the veil, with active representatives of the heavenly host. Such communication was part and parcel of the Sunday services. Classes taught the technique and enhanced the gifts of the participants. The organization maintained a consistent program taught by respected leaders of the spiritual community.

Then in the 1980s, the congregation scattered, the mediums left, some disavowed the church, and the organization foundered. The abandonment of the organization was likely political in nature. Power plays and personal ambitions are present in all gatherings of people. The more intensely individuals exercise ambition and covet power over others or the groupthink, the easier it is to fracture the bond between the actors. In the case of this place, the union between the participants dissolved within a relatively short period of time, and the place became an afterthought in the local spiritual community.

I came across the place when taking a sabbatical from my occupation. It was a sabbatical. I wasn't fired. My employer and I mutually agreed to separate after ten years of service to one another. I was good with that agreement and eventually took the next fifteen months to idly follow my pleasure and passions. Here would be an opportunity to participate in the mixing of the spiritual, physical, and metaphysical, and to practice the work with the pillars of the local movement. I jumped into the organization with both feet.

I entered the program with my dear spouse as my constant classmate. Together, we became a part of a large spiritual community that stretched across several regional metro areas. We took classes, participated in focused discussions, sat in a circle with fellows, and actively interacted with representatives of the heavenly host.

This was a community of mediums and practitioners of metaphysical spirituality. This community regularly communicated with spirit while maintaining the concepts aligned with the continuity of life. The afterlife is real. The spirit and soul of man survive after the thing called death and transition into that afterlife. Speaking with those transitioned spirits confirms the continuity of life. Physically interacting with the heavenly host confirms that the secular life experience is a shared partnership between dreamland and earth. The heavenly host is with us now, at the hour of our birth, and at the hour of our death. It is upon the death of the body that we leave the illusion of this thing called life and transition to our spiritual and heavenly home. Who we are here, living, we are there, living in the duality of spirit. Our soul and spirit are eternal.

For those community members who lived by this creed, the interaction between spirit and physical took on a concrete existence. The heavenly influence, for many mediums, would solidly interact with their physical day-to-day lives. This interaction would occur to some degree at any time during the day. The most involved exchange would come when many joined to form a circle, enter a deep meditative state, and slide open the curtain and greet the heavenly host. Who were the representatives of the heavenly host? For this group, there were many. For this group claimed and practiced audible and physically apparent communication and interaction with the archangels, the ascended masters, the Christ, the teachers, and physicians in spirit that are in service to the One Source and Center, God, and to us living the human, incarnate, experience.

The general population may know something of mediums and interpret their purpose as speaking to dearly departed Uncle Harry because his widow needs to know where he hid the key to the secret room. And there are mediums that will interact with Uncle Harry and other souls that have passed from this life. Many of these notable mediums will appear on television shows, radio shows, and print media. I can't help hearing about them; their marketing is very effective.

The mediums associated with the community to which the organization was tied, while never hiding in the shadows, were a close-knit association of seers, seekers, priests, and facilitators. They were dedicated. They were serious about it. They were not into speaking to Uncle Joe but to Archangel Michael instead. They would gladly teach and discuss aspects of their gifts and their community's interaction with the heavenly host. But perhaps the degree to which they participated in the heavenly relationship was beyond the average Joe's or Jane's interest and commitment level. It took some looking and investigating to find this bunch and to commit to their practices. I was ripe for this. I readily cast off the lines to any earthly grounding and immersed myself to my full ability and potential.

The church was a shadow of its once bright beacon when I found it. Attendance at the Sunday service was in the single digits, if anyone showed up at all. Donations were practically nonexistent, and the church survived on the estate of a past benefactor. Evidently, a successful life of spiritual pursuits does not exclude the ability to accumulate earthly, material commodities. The benefactor's endowment was still going strong in its fortieth year. The endowment paid the bills, keeping the lights on and the doors open. The staff of the dedicated few was down to one custodian pastor. He had his close-knit group of friends. His friends were the congregation. They were to practice their skills among themselves. They were an isolated lot. Keeping to themselves, they lacked that merging of diverse gifts that generates higher levels of understanding within any given group. That was all fine for them. They liked it that way. They were in command of their own small ship, and they navigated where they chose and picked the waters to sail upon that were to their liking, fulfillment, and personal comforts.

All would have continued for them unmolested were it not for a small crack in their door that allowed others to enter. The others were gifted practitioners and priests who were filled with energy, innovation, and enthusiasm. I was numbered among the others. The isolated church group satisfied their interest in learning from the new priests' gifts. Several of the isolated members wanted to become well-known mediums and of notable repute, so they stayed engaged. Events and classes were scheduled and implemented. People came to see the priests and to take their classes. With momentum being achieved, it was unavoidable that the church would again become a beacon to the spiritual community. The facility was being frequently used for classes, demonstrations, and services. The isolated church group had no other choice but to go with the flow and allow a level of integration that mixed diverse visions for growth. The small church group soon lost control of their ship. Others were at the helm and requiring purpose, direction, and follow-through as the facility and the group serviced the growing regional spiritual community. The whole situation was a challenge for the small church group, especially so for the custodian pastor. There were now others.

When I came to this place, I was emerging from the general, unaffiliated spiritual community of physical mediums and clairvoyants. I was looking for involvement and service to the community, and the church provided that opportunity. I was keeping an active schedule with my own studies and practices. Involvement with the church would add to the opportunities for growth in my skills and exercise but would require a physical effort and involvement in the running and administering of the mission of the church. Jumping in both feet first, I took up the role of associate pastor and board member. My self-defined duties included conducting Sunday services, producing events and classes, teaching, and community outreach. I was on sabbatical from my occupation. I had the time. I wanted to do it. Church work became my full-time voluntary occupation.

During that chapter in life, I worked the metaphysical spiritual angle beyond anything I had experienced in the past. I was sitting in circles a minimum of twice a week, teaching two classes a week, and organizing and conducting Sunday services weekly. My work with the church involved collaboration with others. We collaborators grew close. The lines between social, home, and vocational blurred to where my dear spouse and I were regularly socializing with a growing community of church-associated families. I no longer knew where my church role and my personal identity began or ended when it came to that church and community. I no longer observed clear lines of debarkation between my pastor duties and my family responsibilities. We were all one community of seekers and practitioners. We were mediums and clairvoyants who shared the purpose of this movement and this church. There were no clear boundaries. That type of association also meant that there were no buffers between the spiritual community and my personal home and family life. Cast a stone into the community, and I felt the ripples in my living room, kitchen, and bedroom. As I said, this association was all-encompassing, and I jumped in with two feet into the deep end of the pool. I would maintain this level of involvement for eighteen months.

Politics, to my understanding, encompasses the attributes of ambition and the need for power expressed through control. Politics is everywhere, especially present in groups responsible for the administration of churches and organizations. My association with this church did not lack the political aspect. Our measures over the last eighteen months of involvement brought the church a significant increase in membership. Participation in Sunday services left almost every row being utilized. Donations, gifts, and income increased along with the activities. The increase was exponential. The books exploded, and we lost count of the incoming revenue. It was that much. By all measures, the church was growing and succeeding in becoming a regional spiritual center that focused upon demonstrations proving the continuity of life and the living connection with the heavenly host.

The original custodians, the small group of isolated church members, were losing uncontested control of their ship. They grew insecure. Through insecurity, they acted to wrest control back to their isolated circle, spawning conflict, consternation, and contention. The environment and movement suffered. The growth sputtered and ceased. Many who were active in the church's success left as the environment was no longer conducive to peaceful, healthy living. Nor was it a safe environment to propel the spirit and open the clairvoyant centers to all mysteries, unprotected. With the collapse of the administrative infrastructure, the isolated group filled the vacuum, thus regaining control of their once comfortable but solitary ship. In short order, they had regained the helm and set the sails appropriately to their liking. Sunday attendance returned to the single digits. Classes that were taught by many gifted seers transitioned to one or two close friends who increased their income by teaching as they supported each other through the purging of this last cycle of interlopers.

Death and Taxes

When the movement ended, it slammed shut the door I regularly walked through on my spiritual, metaphysical journey. The event reverberated into my home life. The sudden change impacted existing social friendships and the interactions between the various families and groups of people who were associated through the community. The toll and consequence on the physical and social aspects of life were considerable and deeply felt by all involved. The impact on the spiritual and metaphysical aspects of life, particularly my personal practices of heavenly intimacy, was felt at my core level.

This was the second blizzard of spiritual growth and development that I experienced in life. For like being caught in a mountaintop blizzard, I emerged frostbitten, numb, shivering, blind, and suffering from altitude sickness as well as sudden compression into a changed pressure gradient. At one minute, there is the spectacular view before me—mountains, valleys, and sky from a high place—and the next minute, the blizzard is upon me. I was to learn that this rebound would provide me with the greatest and most valuable opportunities I ever had in my studies of the metaphysical, the spiritual, and the personal me.

As opportunities go, this one wasn't immediately recognized. It took hindsight to distinguish between help and hindrance associated with various events. If the heavenly host were close by and holding my hand through this period, I would never have noticed. I was preoccupied with managing my life and reacting to physical stimuli. All would settle out, eventually. That eventuality required me to make a choice to live or die, be miserable or happy, and to recognize the beauty and mystery of this illusion or to remain blind and bump through the ticking of my years in forced ignorance.

Prior to recognizing the opportunity, I unconsciously delayed making choices of any sort, especially those that required me to do things differently or think beyond my current milieu. Life was stressful. I do not outwardly react to stress; a doctor told me. I asked this doctor to evaluate my mind and my neurological system from toe to crown and beyond. I needed to know where I stood within the scale of my age bracket. Spiritual life or not, I was a boomer and wanted to know how my counterparts were doing in their mental and neurological bodies and how I was doing per expectations and the evidence of my years. How did I compare?

I carry my stress inside. I can carry significant loads of stress, and the world may not know of my load, nor will they see it. Verily, my load, one way or the other, may not even impact the people and institutions around me. Yet my stress impacts me. High stress loads bring about one of two conditions, as the good doctor told me: depression or poor health. I react to my stress by having poor health. And I did have poor health for three years, which I can directly attribute to the swing of this pendulum. Poor health in the body as exhibited in infections and lumps to be removed. Big lumps. The impact on the mind was emotional loss of power; people could get into my head, as well as my own penchant for cultivating self-destructive and abusive attitudes that I took out upon myself and others close to me. I'm telling you it was a heck of a ride for those who loved me. And in this facet of life, I also had to choose mayhem or choose peace.

The choosing is the opportunity, and without the swing of this pendulum, it would never have appeared. The choosing requires I either accept life, its wonder, and to bask in the presence of it all, or not. Many choose not. I would not be alone had I gone this route. I'd have company within the masses of those who have spurned the gifted touch, in sharing feelings and emotions, and conversations with angels or even with their earthly mates. There are many who spurn the touch of looking within and sitting in the silence of their own spirit. I would not be alone if I decided that this was it for me, no more potential for rebounds and flying too close to the sun.

The opportunity brought choice. Choice requires action. Is it not what life is, but action that operationalizes changes in heart and mind? My choice was to live peaceably with my body, mind, spirit, spouse, and community. My choice and actions would bring balance to my earthly universe and presence, a balance that is most important for me to achieve. I flew too close to the mystifying light of heaven while standing here in this earthly bag of bones. My spirit does not lack the means or the desire to look into the eyes of God. It is myself, my ego-driven self, that was not prepared for the journey. We cannot look into the eyes of God till we have faces, till we are whole and loving in this physical illusion of life.

Personal strength, strength and clarity of mind, purpose, and soul combine to produce an environment filled with harmonious energy patterns. Positive energy patterns reinforce the pursuit of peaceful, loving, and grounded living. The energy's initiator: me. Through my changing attitude and by taking up healthy life practices, I eventually created an atmosphere of positive growth and loving intention. My actions, motivated by my choice, created the positive energy that eventually permeated my world. As the properties of energy go about their business, they soon become the cause as opposed to the effect of the initiated action. When positive energy becomes the initiator, positive physical creations follow. Then comes the momentum. Momentum propels the traveler into an ever-increasing solid state of bliss and contentment with the physical and spiritual world in full cooperation and balance. This is the metaphysical balance I sought to own from the very beginning of my existence on this world, but till now lacked the means required for the possibility.

The metaphysical results, once the positive energy momentum is established, are astounding. This mere mortal earthly spirit can fly to ever-higher climbs. With the security of positive energy heaped about me, leveraged by a loving household and peaceful living, grounded in this earthly living, I can live in confidence that accelerated soul development follows the norm for my life as opposed to the infrequent, unique experience.

During the two blizzards mentioned over the decades, my material world was in flux, and I was self-centered. I was the architect and the doer who drove my life's direction to my choosing. Harmony with the heavenly host and with creation was not something I thought much about at the technical level, in detail. I did not associate my gift with who I was. I thought I was beyond that requirement. It was just a gift and had nothing to do with my character, individuality, or the person I was in life. I treated my gift as something external. Silly of me to think that my gift was proof that I was a well-developed, peaceful acting soul when the relationship between my gift and me was quite the opposite at times. My success in psychic development didn't readily mean that I was mature in the attitudes, thoughts, and actions that represented the emotional, material, and diplomatic states of being. Absence of balance manifested the blizzards.

The first blizzard occurred during my twenty-third year; the second blizzard arose close to my sixtieth year. This second blizzard, this current opportunity, brought me the vision to clearly see that I am the owner and wielder of my gifts. And I am the owner of the spirit in me.

Expressing a desire to grow spiritually brings about a chain of events. The events are created by my desire and intention to grow. As I express my desire for growth in my words, prayers, and meditations, I reach out to the heavenly host and make the entreaty, "Help me grow." And they do help. They take on an active part. Together with the creative ability of my thoughts, the situations for growth appear, and I get to choose at every step of the way to participate or pass. I would never pass on an opportunity for spiritual, metaphysical growth and experience. The growth combusts and creates energy, pervading my being in all aspects, not just in regard to my gifts but to the very core of my being, me. My gifts are not an expression of my talent or uniqueness. My gifts are a part of who I am. I cannot develop my gifts to a high degree without also developing my character and personality. Balance must be maintained when working with high levels of energy lest all hell break loose as had during and after the two blizzards I lived through. The weight of my character balances the reach of my spirit by keeping it firmly ballasted in peaceful, loving contentment.

My latest opportunity then was to develop the peaceful, grounded, and calm persona that I reinforced by expressing and accepting love while in service to self, family, and others. Integrity and honesty play into the mix when weighing down that centerboard. By requiring myself to be as honest with myself as possible, I have the ability to maintain and nourish the peaceful, loving world about me. Should changes in surroundings or energy intensities occur, I am now better placed to ride out the tempest and maintain the navigation of peaceful life as it was intended. My grounding enables flight to heights never attained.

I, the student, am worthy of the lesson. The lesson, if not mastered, is repeated. With this principle in mind, I review these two great development events that were separated by three-plus decades. I see that the lessons given were products of my intentions and desires. Each attempt to physically cross the curtain left me dazed, but chiseled away the imperfections in this granite soul, imperfections that blocked the fitting of this square peg mortal into the round hole of eternity and the universe. I looked into the eyes of God, and I did not have a face. I stumbled and could not sustain myself. I was then confronted with a choice, an opportunity. I took the opportunity and made the choice. I then retreated to create loving, peaceful, calm, and to live in harmony with all, spirit, and earth.

Keeping my metaphysical energies in balance maintains my health. The higher I climb in my spiritual pursuits, the more grounded in peace I must be. I know this now. A strong grounding regulates my interaction with the energy I receive from spiritual pursuits. Having health and happiness while residing in a house that is peaceful and in balance with nature, heaven, and earth enables me to generate, manipulate, and live with significant levels of energy. There are to be no further rebounds in my life development. My foundation is finally strong and well-cast. Opportunity knocked, and I rallied to the call for action. God, keep me, and God, bless the Holy Host about me.

Doing the Gut Check

Veracity is truthfulness and accuracy. Veracity in the heavenly messages I receive from others is at the highest level when I first receive the message from my center, myself within, for I, the individual, am the best interpreter of the subtle messages that come to me at moments of quiet and stillness.

I may go to a clairvoyant or a spiritual counselor to get a reading or a message from Spirit conveyed to me by said individual. As I place myself into a receptive state for the practitioner's message from gods, angels, or ascended masters, I receive instinctive and intuitive communications from the same source on my own. During a reading, I process and interpret the message given to me by this other oracle as well as monitor the experience I am then having on my own as I sit and listen to the speaker's voice.

I'll evaluate the speaker and the message content. When sitting across from a clairvoyant, it is easy to excuse or deny my instinctive feelings. After all, I am experiencing the love of heaven and the inspiration of a mystical communion by a respected seer whom I chose to sit across from and take advisement. Still, I must give heed to my immediate instincts. Instincts come from the "gut," and the "gut's" anatomy is centered about the heart and solar plexus, both spiritual cores to our being. I think of an instinctive thought as a sentence coming from my higher self, and I am required to give it my full attention.

When I get a reading or speak with a spiritual counselor, I must remember that the words are delivered after being interpreted by someone else. I am receiving the messages from the lips of others, in this case, the provider. The messages from on high travel through the personality and character of the provider, and I call that a filter. The very nature of delivering the message and of the relationship between the provider and me is influenced by the life experiences and ethics, the filter, of the counselor. In all, there are many dynamics in play when visiting a clairvoyant and being counseled on the metaphysical aspects of life. It is the duty of a counselor to present or transfer the message to me as accurately as possible and to remove from the presentation all manifestations of their personality and character while acting with the highest ethical standards.

Messages from mediums and clairvoyants have their place and their limits. I find that messages given to me from others confirm much of what I already know about myself. In many cases, I will find that I have already established a relationship with the celestial beings that originated the message brought in by the message giver. The information delivered by providers does, however, give me another perspective on my manner of interacting with the world. The very nature of hearing someone else's views adds perspective.

As I seek clairvoyants for messages, I remember that clairvoyance is a gift. This gift can be cultivated and expanded upon like any other gift. There are concrete and natural laws that, once acknowledged and observed, enhance one's gifts and abilities and eventually build a skill set that assists in presenting the messages with consistency and dependability. To freely use the gift of clairvoyance that all persons possess, all one must do is develop the skill.

Everyone has the gift of clairvoyance. Some simply never heard the voice from within. Or should they sit in silence and eventually hear the inner, silent voice, they seldom recognize it from the noise of an otherwise active and physical life.

Clairvoyance does not bestow a level of godliness on the holder. Clairvoyance does not make one pure, nor does it necessarily signify purity. High levels of clairvoyant development do not mean that the owner is that much closer to God. No. It means that the owner is skilled using the gift and understands its dynamics well enough to receive and interpret the intuitive impulses. Through practice, all skills can be honed and brought to a higher level, no matter what the personality, character, and ethics of the owner.

Thus, when I consult with another and receive a message through their filter, I must first do a gut check and validate the veracity of the personal message received.

As opposed to receiving messages from spiritual counselors, I value receiving the message from the self within myself, from my own heart. I cultivate the relationship I have with the self and my connection to the celestial. The mechanics of establishing a relationship with the celestial are the very same ones that assist in discovering the inherited gift of clairvoyance. Living a spiritual life and establishing a relationship with gods, angels, ascended masters, and nature will lay the foundation for ethics and purity. Messages sought and received from my own personal center of purity ensure the messages delivered are of the highest standard, the standard of honesty that I establish as my very own. And in so doing, they ensure the veracity of the message.

When Others Speak for God

Having arrived at an understanding of my own clairvoyant dynamic and establishing a relationship with nature, the life force, and the heavenly hierarchy, I proceed to live a spiritual life. I strive for a high level of integrity and personal, internal honesty. Once the habit and lifestyle are achieved, I find that I don't need a man of god to tell me what god is saying. I can listen on my own. I don't need a teacher to interpret lessons for me from angels. They are my messages, and I can receive them myself. I don't need someone who leads a mystical life to tell me what is before me. I am my own master, and I can converse and consort with heaven and nature whenever I want and on my own dime.

All persons have within their circuitry the ability and wherewithal to receive the inspirational messages from angels;

the informative and teaching messages from ascended masters; and the offerings of spirit, creation, and nature.

Some would say that they couldn't hear or see these subtle lessons or feel intuitive impulses. They say that they lack the sensitivity to feel inspiration and receive neither the communication nor the vision to see the work of angels and gods.

So, they listen to others, accepting that others are the only ones to know the words coming from god's lips to their ears. They will accept the interpretation from ministers of all faiths and persuasions. They will bestow upon the holy man or woman the sole power to divulge the messages that are from the celestial to the human.

Prior to owning my spiritual life, my initial reaction when I received a message from god delivered by a holy man was that I was honored. I could feel that the godly energy was there. I was high on the celestial light and love of the master, angel, and spirit of god that the holy man was delivering to the audience. I would question myself, "How could what I am hearing from this learned person's mouth not be accurate, of value, and worth, and not what I am supposed to be hearing right at this moment?" And before acknowledging and accepting my own gifts, I also figured that the speaker had a gift and sensitivity that I lacked, attaching even more credibility to the speaker.

At times, I could not hear the words coming from within. I felt that I was not sensitive enough. I listened to others who exclaimed that they have the authority, learning, talent, sensitivity, and skill to be the interpreter. The authority of the speaker drew me in. When I allowed the consciousness of another to be my filter, I gave away the power to interpret the words of heaven, and I placed myself into a vulnerable position. I was at the mercy of the personalities, characters, and ethics of the self-proclaimed holy men.

When I listened to others speaking for spiritual beings, Jesus included, I would have done well to understand that allowing others to interpret personal messages from god or spirit interfered with my own innate ability to listen for myself. Words of the others, as they interpreted the voice of heaven, distracted and deflected my own innate ability to hear for myself from within. Their voices caused noise. Their pontification stood as my excuse to remain ignorant of my own personal power and God-given gift.

The words of gods, angels, and masters are for me as well as for anyone who wishes to listen and participate in the dialogue. Anyone can receive heavenly inspiration whenever they want. As the saying goes, "From God's lips to my ears." The saying applies to everyone.

I gauge inspirational and heavenly messages that come from any speaker for veracity. The practice keeps me out of trouble.

When I Need a Quick Pick-Me-Up

When meditating, I like to listen to bells or Tibetan singing bowls. They help to set the mood. I produce the keys of G or F, and then usually sit for thirty minutes at a session.

Frequently, when insecure and in confusion, I relax, sit, and listen and attune myself to the sound of bells. I match my vibration to the frequency of a bell's vibratory rate. I then find myself in a field. The Romans called this place the Elysian Field. I look about and all is calm. In the clear distance appears a purple fog. I intuitively know that this is the expression of the violet flame I've heard so much about. I have no fear. The fog emanates from the energy of forgiveness and renewal. It brings me rejuvenation and a feeling of being alive. I feel protected and living in a world without judgment. The fog approaches closer. It wraps around my feet; it rises about me. It is now all that I can see as I stand within the cloud of the purple mist and violet flame. I breathe in the violet flame, taking it into my body. The flame merges with my body at a cellular level. My body starts to vibrate, and all I hear are the tones from the bells and bowls singing in the key of G. Then suddenly, the fog lifts.

In the close distance is the faint outline of a temple. My immediate impression tells me that this is my temple and my place of refuge and peace. The temple has four columns. The four columns represent the four primary forces. The four primary forces were commanded by the Creator to bring order to the universe at the time of the creation. There is a door to the temple. On either side of the door is a guardian standing tall and unmoving. I approach the base of the temple and look ahead to the two large, stone-faced doors. The door to the right slowly opens. As the door cracks opens, it springs forth a sliver of light. The light touches me and delivers an immediate impression of innocence and purity, love and kindness, youth and vitality, and exuberance. Out from the light and through the door emerge three beings. The being in the center is flanked by what appear to be two angels. They bid me to approach, and I do. I take note of this individual in the center. He is wearing a white robe. I look to his face and take a moment in study and see that it is me. The face is blemish-free. There are no lines of worry or tension. The face is free from wrinkles. The skin is tight. It has the look of youth but the expression of ageless wisdom in its eyes. This face has known no worry or tension, no fear or dismay, only tranquility. The eyes are clear and sparkling. The scars I gained from chickenpox are absent. This must be my eternal self.

Come. My eternal self beckons me into the temple. He turns and then enters ahead of me. The angels escort me in, one on either side. In the center of the temple, I stop and stand again face-to-face with my eternal self.

My eternal self speaks. "I love you. You are loved by all in this realm. I forgive you. You are forgiven. But there is nothing that needs to be forgiven. I carry for you the light of forever and the candle of hope for all things. For all things are of hope. And hope is your destiny. I am always with you. I am always here to light your way and to chase away the shadows. To help you lift the loads. I petition the divine facilitators and sing your praises to the angels for you while you live as you do now."

I then speak to my eternal self. I tell of my hopes and wishes, dreams and aspirations. I recount my fears and worries and give before my eternal self all the burdens that I carry. And I feel lightened and relieved.

"Your loads will become lighter. And your heart will become brighter. Your wishes will come to pass and become truth. Speak your words, for they are true and honorable. Our time together for this visit is ending. I will always be here in this temple upon the field. We will be reunited often, and in the end, you will be the eternal one."

And with this last statement, the audience concluded.

I turn, and my escorts turn with me, and together we walk out of the temple. Through the doors and beyond onto the field, I turn and look once again at the temple. The doors close. The sliver of light abruptly disappears with a snap.

As I stand before the temple, the familiar violet fog gathers again. It is again about my feet. It is rising around me. I again instinctively attune myself to the vibration of the bells that I can now again hear, and I breathe the violet fog and flame about me. The fog lifts, and I am standing again in the familiar field of Elysia. The temple is gone. I open my eyes.

All day, I kept the feeling of having a good talk with myself. I maintained that connection between my eternal self and me. I walked with my soul and was one with my spirit throughout the day and into the following week. All week, I was connected to the heavens and knew that my very nature is one of the divine.

Death and Taxes

Chapter 9: Maturing Me

Chance and Fortune

I love this place. It's been a while since I just stood and hung around in this part of the property. Standing here and taking it all in, I realize how much I love this place. This part of the property was once all trees and a muddy bog. The trees fell away to my chainsaw several years ago for firewood. And right glad they did. For those that were not harvested fell to one windy winter or another. Had I not harvested the alders, one would surely have fallen in the wind and crashed into either the yard fence or the deck. One remaining tree came down three feet from the fence line, the winter before last.

This place was a small valley between the hill the house stood upon and the one that separated me from my neighbor's property. The valley sits between two rising vortexes of energy, as physically signified by the hills on either side. The rising land created an upwelling of energy at the summits. The deck of our house upon the hill was the perfect place for pondering the future and planning the activities that brought that wonderful future to fruition. This valley represented the intersection of two upwelling vortexes producing this valley of low, calming energy. The perfect place to enhance introspection. Now with all the trees gone, the place took on a parklike appearance. The felled trees left in their wake giant ferns and green bushes that climbed the hill between me and my neighbor's property. All about me was nature's green, refreshing green. As I stood in the quiet, motionless, I again confirmed my love for this land in every aspect.

These were to be my years of golden pleasure. I would spend this last decade and more tending the property and its inhabitants. And there was much for me to tend in this place where my dear spouse and I chose to live our waning years in peace among community and nature's gifts. Taking my count of this review and assessing the current outcome, I am more than pleased, contented, and comfortable with my landing spot. Yet it was not always so. My road traveled was rocky. Emotional toil and extremes, as well as rebellion, marked the passing of my years by impacting my macro as well as micro worlds. But for now, for this phase of my life, for all the wear and tear, for all the trials and tribulations, I was now pleased and at peace.

It was all worth it.

Life for me prior to taking up this residence and place of mind was a blur of rebellion and agitation. On a macro scale, I was appalled at what had become of this world. The greed, violence, hate, discontent, and ever-present visuals I saw of the poverty about me struck to the core of my soul. How could this be? How could this happen? Why was the opportunity squandered? The world was not to my liking, and I simply wanted to refashion it to my preference. Of course, that was never to be. The world will be as the world will be, and for me, this realization signaled much discontent.

I had many opportunities to complain. Hippies were to be loving and inclusive. They were not necessarily so. In my experience, they were competitive and cliquish. Organized religion and the leaders were to be forgiving and nurturing. Yet as I saw the dynamic, organized religion was a form of social control, and the leaders were self-serving, condemning, and in some cases illegally abusive. Politicians were to serve their constituents, but all too often, once in office, turned a deaf ear to the pleads of the populace and proceeded to become corrupted with power and riches. The truths and realities conflicted with my idealistic beliefs, and this conflict drove me crazy. I then became a rebel to authority in any form. My rebellion fueled my anger. My anger at the world, at my world, was evident in my everyday interactions with those about me.

Living as a rebel has its costs, and the expenses were felt mostly in the workplace, in the occupational aspect of my life. Throughout many of my vocational pursuits, I had the knowledge, drive, and technical skills to be of profitable importance to my employers. I am sure many would have loved to be done with me, but the value I delivered justified the inconvenience of having me around. Or so it would work out till patience ended, and I would eventually be shown the door. Where I lacked the skill to be of true value in the workplace, I settled for low pay and a degree of freedom and flexibility that comes with lowered expectations and responsibilities. But even in these situations, I would be problematic to supervisory staff, and if I didn't get the boot, I would simply grow tired of the job and leave as the feeling suited me. Rebels to authority are difficult people to employ. Or at least I was.

In the micro-perspective, that is, my family and personal life, those close to me were put through the ringer. Pity the poor soul who sought intimacy with me, for they were subjected to a constant wave of discontent and the constant comparison of who they were, as opposed to who they should be, per my impossible standards that defined how they should approach life. That approach encompassed the daily technical aspects of life's mechanics, as well as the degree to which they can act with strength by following my requirements of self-discipline. That was all nearly impossible for any human to fulfill. Yes. Pity the poor soul.

Ans so it was for me throughout much of my journey to turn interpersonal and occupational gold into lead because of my deep-seated and subtle anger. And the odd thing about my choice of living persona was that it was the most contradictory choice, one that was counter to my spiritual being, and I went about it with a vengeance. It was the persona I wanted to be known for. This screwy concept of what I required myself to project would cause me much discontent. The dynamic took on a life of its own after some years, and while in the beginning of my adulthood I may have cultivated the rebel persona and practiced it with precision, as I grew into my senior years, I had no power to abate the momentum of this façade with any effect, no matter the level of pain and discontent it brought to me and my kin.

Had I had the power to fully exercise my anger, I would proceed to level the world around me and to strike out at the transgressors who would corrupt the world and pervert the blessing of life. Isn't that a contradictory tone? Yes, the avenging angel complex in me would strike like Roland's sword Durendal at the battle of Roncevaux Pass, where it is said the angels smote the enemy horde by extending lightning bolts from the tip of his sword. Is there any wonder why this mortal would be restricted to mortal means, limiting the expression of my hidden humanly impulses?

All this would change once I found help in arresting my complicated behaviors and acknowledging my willful choices.

Change led to calmness of mind and steadiness of emotions that would eventually empower me to accept peace and contentment.

This place I had come to love was tucked away on an island called Whidbey. Whidbey was away from the hectic city, Seattle. It would take a Seattle friend the entire day to visit by taking a quick ferry ride and driving to the residence. Not many of my Seattle friends would invest the entire day in the visit. Alternately, travel for me and my dear spouse into the city was frequent as we went about our business and affairs or saw to our medical needs. The residence we now enjoyed was not our first on Whidbey. There was another time when we resided here for several years. I was working in technology management on the mainland to satisfy the income and healthcare equation, and my dear spouse was managing the inn we owned. We took up residence on the lower floors. This first residence on Whidbey was anything but peaceful, as my anger was in full form. It amazes me, and amazes my loved ones, how a few years and a change of attitude altered my viewpoint and endeared me to this place where I now find peace, companionship, and rekindled love, and initiate those pursuits of my heart that waited decades for action.

I came to this place through the graces and wages of information technology, the newest craze. Manufacturing was on the way out for some time. Computers and those who could build, command, and control the flow of information were to prosper for the foreseeable future. I was drafted into this new field after the collapse of my maritime career some years ago by the demands of the market. Jobs in information technology were abundant, and retraining dollars were plentiful for technology students. The GI Bill provided via my Navy service helped immensely as it provided me a steady income and paid the rent while in study. I studied electronic engineering and entered the geek world of information technology as a self-admitted mercenary. I was in it for the money, pure and simple.

It was never my intention to look into my future and plot my occupational strategy. I was never that forward-thinking when it came to working and earning a living. The very idea of working to earn a living gave me the shivers. Where is the adventure in that? I envied those solid-minded kids and companions who had their plans all worked out. They would become firefighters, police officers, doctors, and lawyers by design. Many of the kids had parents coaxing them into choosing a future field and occupation. A few stood out as the strong-willed, old souls who knew their life's calling from birth and readily maneuvered the requirements of initiation into the field of their calling. Not so for me. I would stumble from one low-paying, menial job to another having no idea what a career, occupation, or chosen field was. I knew that whatever I was to do to sustain my material needs in the future would have to come to me.

And so, I initially worked in the navy and the maritime industry as an avenue of escape from the humdrum status quo that surrounded me at the time. The sea called me, found me, and then aroused deep-seated memories of the ships I sailed and the students I mentored while living incarnate, progressing the wheel of my soul's life. I was a natural for shipboard work and for teaching the masses.

Once I finished sailing the seas and getting some formal classroom retraining, I found technology. It was new to me. When it came to figuring out the social, behavioral, and productivity benefits of technology in the workplace, I was head and shoulders above my neophyte peers thanks to my diverse work background. Yet at the hands-on level of operating systems, hardware, and applications, I was slow to find my niche. Once I did, I proceeded on to a life of productivity and sustainability. Living in Seattle, and by now married with a ready-made family, was an expensive proposition. Work in high tech would have to fill the need for revenue. The hands-on technicalities were of little interest to me. The enterprise application of the technologies, as they integrated with business, generating profits, did interest me. With newer technologies, organizations had to adapt to change. The opportunities for organizational change provided me with a pretext to look at the bigger picture of the information age. To me, the changing dynamics took on the form of a living and breathing network diagram where people, technology, and processes evolved to become unified in mission and vision.

Information technology management was to be my forte as I mingled my way through the organizational layers of companies and corporations. I had ample opportunity to exercise leadership; there was always a team to lead. Solutions to problems came quickly to me. Pathways to efficiencies were apparent with my quick review of the existing business model and technical, organizational needs. I had a few limitations to my technical and business accomplishments. My nemesis: authority.

Deciphering an organization's business requirements and providing a technical solution is easy to do. Being the paid consultant, I had a certain expert's power over any given situation, and since I was typically a hired gun, the clients were more than happy to get what they were paying for. I did very well when working with clients while running my own business. When that business became so successful and I was in such demand that I was absent from family dinners, vacations, and reunions, the powers that be said enough. Yes, we all enjoyed the plentiful access to money brought about by my newfound cash cow, information technology. But my absence and preoccupation with work were becoming problematic on the home front.

I ceased working for myself, joined corporate America, and took a technology job in an insurance company as an intermediate-level systems engineer. Here I was, limiting my involvement as only a paid corporate employee could. My weekends, or at least most weekends, were my own, and I gladly shared them with my family. My workweek settled to the nominal forty hours, although I frequently exceeded that. I was no longer responsible for everything, with neither customers nor clients to satisfy nor employees and contractors to juggle. The technology possibilities in corporate America were limitless, and life became easier.

I could have continued from this point in my corporate career, being the solitary engineer, responsible for my piece of the puzzle and keeping the show in good working order. Many of my former peers did just that. Yet I could not. The opportunity to bring fruition to the network-like diagram visions that I maintained in my mind required that I take on more responsibilities and climb the corporate ladder like any other engaged in the rat race. Climbing the ladder to management, I was finally able to define strategy and choose the pathway to implementing plans and processes. It was good work. And I liked it and did it rather well. Sitting quietly at my desk, I would close my eyes and see the organization as a living, breathing entity. I would inject into that organism technical stimuli and watch the reaction as the impacts traveled through the beast and came out as profit or savings. It was all very simple to do. All I had to do was close my eyes and place myself in a light meditative state. The rules and natural order of things always carried through, as if rules and natural order were laws. And laws are infallible and predictable, like the law of gravity. When subjecting an object to the law of gravity, a known outcome is produced: the object falls. Gravity was to act upon me in some fashion, for from the height of occupational success, I was to fall prey to my predilections. Authority, and I just didn't see eye to eye. And for managers in corporate America, everyone is their authority. The authority demands and requires that the work be engaged in the fashion and behavior expected by a rotational expectation of professionalism. Authority's expectation of professionalism, no matter what it looks like, required me to be what and who they wanted me to be. And I just couldn't. I never could.

My natural ability to visualize organizations as living organisms and determine solutions to challenges was to fall prey to my contempt for authority. My long-dormant anger finally rose to prominence. Where did the anger come from?

My anger was from the world. The world was not to my liking with its prejudice, greed, inhospitality, and the requirement to maintain the status quo. The obstinacy of a pigheaded corporate population stood before my desire to bring solutions to requirements that would benefit humankind as well as the single mom, customer service lady who worked in the general call center pool. Triggers for my anger were all about me in corporate America. The technology would no longer matter as personalities became my bane, and I grew dissatisfied with the current situation.

If I were but a young lad, I could easily have packed up and joined the navy. I'd be swapping one of my soul's reflective muscle memories, organizational technology, for another, seamanship. However, at my stage in life, I was responsible for others and the head of a household. Leaving the cash cow would become problematic. However, it would also become unavoidable.

I could not count how many times on this earth, in how many incarnations, I manipulated technology and organizations, morphing what I found into sleek, efficient, breathing business machines. Being at this *working for a living* going on my fourth decade, I was gaining some understanding of my personal dynamic and how I come to work in one occupation or another. I did not choose technology and organizational design as much as I fell into it. I entered the information technology era and craze by taking the most basic of college programs and rose to a position that would typically require specialized university degrees and a proven history in the field. I would offer a proposition, many times acting above my station and position in the pecking order, the potential in my proposal acknowledged by those about me, we'd arrive at an agreement, and I'd get a promotion. Easy. Just close my eyes, and I can see all the moving pieces and personalities, and then the solution to their defined needs would appear. And they'd buy it. That was the easy part. The hard part for me was the authority my chain of command had over me. I could never resolve my issues, and eventually, my productivity and profitability became secondary to my sacrilege.

Every season naturally progresses without required effort. Natural rhythm leverages the work at hand into the next phase of being. This natural rhythm and synchronization bring productivity: plants, flowers, and vegetables. Things grow when in synchronicity with natural rhythm. People guided by their soul's rhythm, whether aware of it or not, fall in and out of harmony with any given fixed system. And so it was with me and information technology and the corporate world. My natural abilities in this arena quickly matured as I have lived countless lives so engaged. Yet no dam will hold back an overflowing lake. Applicably, the wings of change were upon me once again. The political aspects of my occupation became too prominent. I was not in a state of mind to smooth the waters while pressing for my given solution and maintaining my productivity. Recognizing and acknowledging the change of tide, it was all I had to do but to finally move on and find happiness, harmony, and productivity once again in some other line of work.

When younger and leaving one workplace for a newer one, I would go home and take a long, hot shower. This would wash the stink of the last workplace from me. It would wash out all inharmoniousness and discordant memories. I was done with that place. I'd start my new situation with a cleanly body. This washing ritual trickled into my mind and countenance. I was done with the old and welcoming the new. After forty-plus years in the workforce, my ritual for changing work evolved to something more than a long, hot shower. In this case, I would not be returning to the same line of work. After more than two decades, I would no longer associate myself with information technology or corporate America. I needed time to think and draw upon my inner well. I needed to seek and expect occupational opportunities, to recognize them, and to engage myself. What to do? There was so much to do.

For many years, I heard people telling me to take my bliss and find a way to convert it into income and revenue. My bliss at this point was this beautiful place, my slice of five acres. That and my habit of meditation were all I could muster for interest now. I was relieved that I had three months of work to do about the place, as three months would be the amount of time I allowed myself to sit and be idle. As I sat in meditation, I would scan the world of work and income and look for that harmonizing melody that played fancy with my persona and my soul. There would be something needing to be done out there, and I would do it. Perhaps service to others. Or perhaps I could find a situation where I can again be a business owner and be the point of contact with my customers with no corporate authority over me. Thought soon turned to action as I followed the money trail from my blissful anchorage.

The land. The land was my first lifeline. Maintaining the property and animals required my observance of routines and gathering of skills that were in demand by the local community. The island was home to several nonprofit organizations that provided animal husbandry and land conservation strategies to the novice small farmer or rancher. Land conservation provides lasting benefits to this generation and to those to come. There were several nonprofit organizations that facilitated the human-to-land relationship.

I found my organization through the urgings of my dear spouse. She was involved with one of our local conservatories at a board level. Being an avid gardener, she also took in the weekly farmers' markets and built a network of active citizens. I fell in line with the lessons of land conservation from sheer economic sense. I fell in line with the organization's mission through material necessity. The organization involved the lives of many kindhearted souls who generously gave of their time and efforts to sustain the conservation and husbandry programs. What the organization members pined for was a direction as expressed through a strategy and a steady stream of funding to carry them through the years. Quite by accident and spur of the moment, I asked if they would entertain a proposal from me to bring them opportunities to satisfy their needs. Surprisingly, without asking for details, they happily agreed to hear my proposal and, regardless of the details, they would accept my offering—whatever it was. My work was to be done on a commission basis. For every dollar I brought in from grant writing or an authored fundraising program and plan, I would get a good percentage in commission. If I didn't produce and they got nothing, I'd get nothing. If I succeeded, they would get something they wouldn't have otherwise and more than they would have gotten without my efforts. It was a win-win situation. I presented my proposal at their next board meeting. Unanimously, they accepted. I threw myself into the work the very next day.

Here I found no corporate authority limiting my thoughts and requiring me to tow an imaginary behavior line or appearance. Here I found only cooperation and helpful, happy cocreators who responded to my off-the-wall methods and out-of-the-box ideas with enthusiasm. For those ideas that were unclear or lacked the vision that leads to clear implementation, the members and board pulled together to brainstorm how the idea would work before throwing themselves into the effort, fully committed to its success. The camaraderie and innocent cooperation I experienced with this group were a breath of fresh air. Our association absented competition and hostile positions from all actors. We all pulled together in harmony for the service that we would provide to those in need. And after some time, after things got rolling on the fundraising program line, we had the assets to grow in membership and class offerings.

We extended our reach into the city, Seattle and partnered with schools. We worked with the Native American tribes. We took the senior citizens and helped them plant seeds for fresh vegetables. We represented our mission to the community at large and interacted with town and county governments, seeking their support and referral. We succeeded in expanding our service offerings to those who would benefit, and we grew close, with one another, as friends sharing in a dream and the work that propels it. These were good times.

The Pacific Northwest was still an expensive place to live, and revenue generation was my requirement. Bills had to be paid. Chickens had to eat. Horses had to be shod. And the car occasionally needed repair. More revenue was needed. I could not stop and rest upon my laurels with just the commissions from one organization.

Service is noble work. The benefactors are typically those who would miss an experience if not provided the opportunity by those in service. Yet being in service is a two-way undertaking. Being in service is as good for my soul as it is helpful for the needy. My method of assessing a nonprofit's current maturity and solvency and assisting them in building a strategy and implementation plan succeeded for this one conservation group. What if I could do the same for other nonprofits regardless of their area of expertise and the community they service?

I formulated a marketing plan and approached community-based nonprofit organizations. I had my list and network of associates to draw from. I had the credibility I established with the farm network. It all seemed like a good fit. As time passed, generating revenue was initially hit or miss. I found that for every three grants I wrote, one might hit. The organizations were doing well as the generated funding kept them in the black and supported their plans for growth. The strategies I helped develop were also hit or miss. Small nonprofits that rely on volunteers for much or all of their work had difficulties following strategies and working disciplined implementation plans. Not wanting to fuss over the lack of military precision, I blended with the wind and adjusted the individual strategy implementation plans to suit the individual and varied clients. The clients were happy with my methods, their accomplishments, and our group results, and I was happy with my newfound occupation.

The very aspect of adjusting to the volunteers' availability and unrushed ethic was something I found new and refreshing. If a plan was not on schedule but progress was apparent, the client was happy, overjoyed because they were seeing real progress toward their vision. Taking my cue from my clients' satisfaction, I fell into an attitude of flexibility and mellowness. If they were happy, I was happy. And one of the main reasons they were happy was my ability to work with them and make progress toward our goals, regardless of any bumps in the road. Life and my line of work looked very promising. And the income was enough to sustain the lifestyle on the ranch.

The intensity of my work never reached a hectic pace. With all I had to do for my clients, I still had time for myself. I ensured that my residence didn't suffer from my absence or preoccupation at any time. I did the work I needed to do, as it needed to be done. My horse suffered no neglect. I made sure that I always had time to pull out a carrot and hang around in his energy field. Riding him on the trails and arenas happened often enough that he was steadily losing weight and gaining muscle mass; he was such a foodie that he always had to watch his weight. And for the family life, I was the most generous of my time. The amount and quality of time spent with my dear spouse increased proportionately through the months, as did our shared involvement in one nonprofit or another.

Here, I found the harmony with colleagues, coworkers, and management that eluded me throughout my corporate technical career. We were all drawn together in service and usefulness to our community. Volunteers serve nonprofits because they want to; they don't have to. Working with people who are present because they are fulfilling their hearts' desires brought me satisfaction, peace, contentment, and many fine new friendships.

Idle Pursuits and Lofty Goals

Peace comes to me when I want it enough to work for it. I must be willing to do whatever it takes to build myself a peaceful life filled with occupational pursuits that support my spiritual connection, encasing me in a healthy environment. I am a lazy soul. Luck. I've been lucky. Luck can be a fickle mistress. I ofttimes, much too ofttimes, rely on luck being my salvation and bringing me the items and articles needed to build happiness and peaceful contentment. Anger contests my peace. Only through freedom from anger in all forms and its inner clinging can my soul be free. In anger's absence, I find true contentment, gratitude, and peace.

My daily life in this place that I love was easy enough. Wake up and feed the horses. Exercise my body and meditate my mind. Picking any number of the work items off my list, I would spend time piddling about the property and slowly but surely make the desired improvements or needed repairs that kept the place running. On many days, there was horseplay to be done when my dear spouse and I would load up the giants into the trailer and take off for a ride or lesson. My occupational work brought in some level of sustaining income. I was a self-employed program manager. I could manage any program that any nonprofit had on its to-do list, and if they didn't have a list or a need for a program to implement the list, I could help them develop one. It was good work. Not too taxing, and there were plenty of interesting people to interact with. It paid the bills. And it kept me in service to others. Life was good at this stage. It wasn't always so good.

I entered this phase of island life one year before I found my peaceful mindset. At the time I bought this place, I was anything but peaceful. My life, mind, and all that was about me were in constant turmoil. The last thing I ever expected as an outcome of those tumultuous years was a peaceful existence with nature or people. For it was during this period in my life that the anger within me, the anger that had found its roots in my spirit as a young child, the anger that had simmered throughout my adolescent and adult life, that surfaced from time to time and cause mayhem, was in full flight and on the face of every motion, thought, and deed that I undertook. It was a heck of a time.

For all I knew, I was born angry. It wasn't a reaction to an individual event that rubbed me the wrong way at some point in my development. No. Anger slowly intertwined into my evolving personality as a matter of course throughout my young life. I could not tell when or why it took root, but I found that I had an aptitude for owning and expressing it. I was never openly hostile, nor did I have any impulses toward violence. My anger rarely expressed itself through outbursts. I kept it inside. Simmering, yet it would become my own personal saboteur. I was the primary target. The world was unfair, unjust, and unkindly. I'll show the world. I'll sabotage myself, and the world will be deprived of the blessings and positive energy I would otherwise bring. And in so doing, I would thumb my nose at God for placing me into this situation in the first place. I went about life with a small invisible chip on my shoulder and a self-disabling dynamic.

My life growing up was not too unlike the lives of other children in the fifties and sixties, outwardly. In all other respects, my childhood was to be the product of a broken home. Yes. Like 50 percent of all married couples, my parents divorced when I was four years of age. Where does a housewife go when divorcing in the fifties? She goes to live with her mother. Mom and I packed up and moved from our home in a suburban development back into the city to live with the grandparents. The living arrangements in this era of history were unique compared to what exists in the twenty-first century, but for an ethnic family of the 1950s, it was all standard and unexceptional. Here, we, the family, several generations of us, lived in a large duplex where all residents were related through the same great-grandparents.

On the first floor lived my grandfather and grandmother as the primary residents. This first floor was a two-bedroom unit that sported a standard layout with a kitchen exiting to a path leading to the dining room and terminating at the living room that hosted the big black-and-white TV. Two bedrooms and a walk-in closet stood off to the side of the dining room. Room enough for Mom and me, right? Well, not exactly for in one bedroom slept my grandfather and grandmother. In the other bedroom lived my aunt, my mother's unmarried sister. Mom and I occupied the dining room. We moved the bedroom set from the suburban house into the dining room at Grandma's house and called it home.

The upstairs unit matched the downstairs and housed my great-grandfather, who came to the States from Italy, and my two great-aunts. My great-aunts shared a bedroom, and my great-grandfather had his own room. My two uncles, my mother's siblings, lived in the fixed-up attic, having the place to themselves with a level of privacy that was to always be afforded to boys turning to men. All in all, I then moved into a house that hosted ten family members who had roots in the Tuscan state of Italy. The house was well laid out and never felt crowded. It did lack a certain level of privacy for Mom and me, as our bedroom was on the flight path from the kitchen to the TV room.

We all picked up and moved from that house a few years later. Aunts and uncles married, leaving the hive to make their own homes. The family's patriarch aged and passed from this life. The core theme of living as one large multigenerational family remained. The new house would be big enough for the remaining family members. We continued to reside together and offer a room or a cot to any family member needing one, especially when they got divorced from their spouse. And there was always someone in the family getting a divorce.

Children of the 1950s grew up with TV as the primary babysitter. I was no different. With TV and a battle set of army men close at hand, I never lacked for entertainment or for something to keep me occupied. Interpersonal interaction with family members was kept to a minimum, as I appeared to be self-maintaining. This aspect of me doing fine on my own set the stage for the level of contact I was to experience throughout life at home with the family. Contact was minimal. I knew how to change channels on the TV and adjust the volume. I also knew how to position squads of army men and their tanks when assaulting a fortified position. What more would I need to know? I was then assigned to the care of my grandmother while those otherwise entrusted with my upbringing pursued life outside of the home. I would do fine on my own.

In later years, when reminiscing with old friends about our upbringing, we all had similar observations as to how we were prepared for life once we left our family homes. Most of us had a common gap in many aspects of life preparation. We were expected to go through our school years and, hopefully but not mandatorily, graduate from high school. Once graduated, we will know what to do with ourselves. We were resourceful. We were smart. We were self-maintaining. The truth of the matter is, we didn't know squat. And so it was that throughout my early years, I bumbled along and experienced the world bereft of any assistance or guidance, helping me navigate coming to grips with life in all its wonders and the emotions that would come from living. On my own, I didn't do very well. There was much lacking in my education. And I knew it.

Popularity was always a puzzle to me. Army men were easy. Set them up and blow them apart, then start over again when ready. The quiet solitude of being in my own world was reassuring. The rules of interaction and behavior were simple: enjoy myself and let my imagination take flight. Meeting people and trying to integrate into one clique or another was an issue. Merging my personality with the individuals and the group-sync had me changing one face to another like a chameleon with no idea of the type of foliage I was sitting upon. I really had no idea at all. I especially had no idea where these interactions and popularity things were going, or what the purpose was. My innocence and confusion were interpreted as vulnerability by others, and I was naturally torn apart like carrion by the vultures of those who were cool and socially prosperous. I played the part of a vulnerable idiot from that time forward, especially throughout my high school years. I was different. I was innocent of the most basic emotional concepts about how I was to react to the offhanded treatment I received from the cliques. I struggled and thought that this was the way it was supposed to be.

I struggled to find a role and a foothold in the society around me, as exhibited by the company I kept. I struggled with the attitudes I was exposed to and with the words that were thrown at me from one cultural group or another and the cruelty of the crowd. I wanted friends and assumed that a price must be paid for admission into the brood; I must first pay the piper and suffer appropriately before being accepted. Expectations of the masses, being what they were, required conformity. Dress, walk, talk, and think alike, or suffer the consequences of being different from the mold. To do otherwise would become catastrophic.

During my sophomore year, I found the great social equalizer behind the neighbor's garage. It tasted foul. It inebriated the mind. It made me one with the crowd. It gave me something in common with the horde. It quelled my seething anger. I avoided the emotional toll required for social initiation by joining in with the group. Drinking alcohol to excess replaced playing alone with my army men. I would spend my remaining high school weekend nights getting drunk with my friends. And as I learned much later in life, freezing any future emotional growth and sabotaging any real potential I had to fully develop my gifts.

I found the pleasure of self-medication to be a staple of my life from that period onward. I treated all that ailed me with one form of intoxicant or another. Here, within the throes of self-induced delirium, I never had to worry about coming up with the appropriate emotional response. Take another toke and party on or keep on trucking, but whatever I do, don't think. Interpreting this methodology as living in the present, I jumped in with both feet and was rewarded with popularity and company around me. It would turn out I built the foundation of my persona upon a ground of shifting sand and mud. And as we all know, there would be cracks a plenty in the house so produced, but for the time being, everything was groovy.

It is a testament to the stoutness of my soul and to the strength of my mind that I was able to rise to the heights I had achieved in career, soul expression, and intelligence, regardless of the methods I chose to quell the anger I held within. Being no ordinary soul, I was able to burn through the self-imposed fog of intense partying and resulting self-sabotage to carve an irregular path to achievement. Was I not special and different and made of sterner stuff than the average Joe? Yes. I was unique, all right. I had myself convinced, and my successes validated my lifestyle and method of anger avoidance; I simply ignored anger. I medicated, partied, and played it away, stumbling through my evenings with my fellow get-highs. My methods worked. All hail to my uniqueness and to my stout soul and strength of spirit. For I have prevailed over anger and the limitations of my past. I have become the man I am, regardless of the curse flung at me by the masses and kin alike and the obstacles placed before me by the god that created me. I was special. My distinctiveness and success became my anger's protectors. But beware, the structure built upon a shaky foundation, for the laws of nature and gravity will prevail.

My work brought opportunities for travel. Reporting to a ship in San Diego, I visited my friend I knew while living in Hawaii, Mel. For entertainment that evening, Mel and I took in a psychic fair. I sat with a clairvoyant for a reading. Her theme for me could be summarized in one word: abdicate. Whatever did she mean? Abdicate? Like a king born to reign, abdicate the throne, and become one of the people. This clairvoyant was giving me an early warning. The message received from the heavenly consciousness had accuracy, but the listener, I, wasn't ready to interpret the meaning. The message was a prophecy that my uniqueness, intelligence, and practiced spiritual attunement would lead me into a false and misinterpreted understanding of what it is to be distinctive and grand. My gifts of clairvoyance and success were my Achilles' heel. I utilized my gifts because they were there, and I had the technical skills and know-how to apply them. The gift of clairvoyance is no imprimatur crowning the owner as particularly deserving and wise above all others. The gift does bring the responsibility to know oneself. With the gift came the responsibility to know myself and to be a clear, pure, and innocent channel of the universal graces that come from heaven, through me, and into this physical world of illusion. The clairvoyant I sat with that evening initiated the angelic choir's call. "Free yourself. Abdicate."

Abdicate. Surrender my ego-driven response to my insecurities. Surrender my need to prop myself up as protection from that entire world that constantly validates my inferiority. Reminding me that I am different, that I am not one of the crowds. I am not accepted. I can't relate. I know nothing of life. I have no clue what emotions I should be feeling for any given occasion. I was never taught. I was never mentored. I don't fit in. I will never make it in this world and will amount to nothing. With every turn I made, with every situation I tried to fit in, I found constant reinforcement of my failings, my shortcomings. My emptiness. Yet my uniqueness, intelligence, and ability to get things done would be my shield. I would wield my shield like a banner over all others and elevate myself beyond any true value. I was unique, special, intelligent, and able, and they were not, even if they were the credentialed popular leaders who had authority over all under their domain. Abdicate. Why would I even give it a second's thought?

When I first joined the in-crowd behind my neighbor's garage, I found that I became one with them. I was accepted. So long as my speech was slurring and I could make good, drunk, cynical jokes, I was to be regarded as one of them. I made it to the big time.

As I aged and moved among social groups, I took on varying degrees of intoxicating methodologies. The sixties and early seventies were the years of the hippie. I was to be considered one. Peace, love, sex, and rock and roll were my passions. In reality, it was all about partying and getting numb enough not to think. I had plenty of company. As far as that peace and love thing went, it was only a mantra, an empty one for me. I didn't really care about peace so long as I was having a good time. Why would anyone want to start trouble anyway? And love was something that came to me in the form of a warm bedmate. God, help me if it required a responsible relationship of any sort. A relationship would require behavior contrary to the dictates of numbness. I was the dirt farmer of my life. Live on a farm and have some property absent a crop to harvest. The farm's productive output: dirt. Once I establish the image of who I am, nothing more is needed. Substance is irrelevant. "Abdicate."

I could be wrong, and I could make mistakes. When anyone crossed me, when anyone brought up my inconsistencies or called me on the carpet for my outlandish self-truths, my anger would righteously come to my assistance. I would vanquish the usurper of my pride through verbal conquest or by turning those about me into my allies. Together, we would turn the tide and attack the accuser. When I did not prevail, the most likely cause being the truth of the indictments against me, I would scurry away into a corner, medicate myself, and further sabotage my efforts. This tactic, of course, caused failure, excusing the indictments against me. Such a dynamic I created! And why or how would I do otherwise? Failure was a product of my origins, the origins that produced the broken actor that I was. I played the part. Somewhere deep within me was the call to be the person my environment and upbringing destined me to become, the failure. What better way to silence the call than to capitulate and sabotage myself by remaining in a constant state of intoxication and numbness, a numbness that allowed my anger to simmer unmolested?

And so, life would progress through my twenties and into my thirties. The partying abated somewhat. The need to self-medicate never left me, as the old insecurities never left me, and my need to reinforce some inner value and worth remained as strong as ever. Occupationally, I moved from the Navy into the merchant marines. I plied the waves starting out as an able seaman, rising through the hierarchy at a steady pace, and in short order secured my "Licensed Master Upon Oceans." I passed the exams with my usual flair, having never spent time studying. I just sat in the exam room and wrote out the answers to one question after another. I knew my stuff. That I would pass the exam was never in question. Wasn't I special and a cut above the rest? "Abdicate."

It was during this time that the merchant marines and all governing agencies that were established to ensure the safety of the traveling public instituted a zero-tolerance policy toward any form of intoxicants. My intoxicant of choice at that time was cannabis. Ah, sweet Mary and Jane. It was mellow. Not hard on your body like that foul-tasting swill Carol brought to the party behind the neighbor's garage, the swill that contained just a little bit of everything that her father had in his liquor cabinet. Weed was different. And to my richer enjoyment, ingesting it prior to meditation brought me to new heights. Or so it seemed. I traveled around the world stoned, reposed in my personal numbness while reinforcing my uniqueness. I had such a damaged past that I needed to be medicated, and others did not. And I survived my past, and if anyone else were in my shoes, they couldn't. What did they know? It didn't matter. Needless to say, it was time for me to find a new occupation as this zero-tolerance policy might cause me some trouble. The scrutiny from the Department of Transportation was getting a little too invasive for my lifestyle.

When it came to money, I was lucky. Luck is the only way I can describe it. Opportunities appeared, providing me a means to sustain my family and myself. My needs were always provided for. That I was able to adjust my income potential to match my needs helped quite a bit. But as the responsibilities of family, to which I was the head and chief income earner, mounted, the need for more income arose. Still, I was lucky. We never were without the necessities needed to maintain a comfortable living. Life as a merchant seaman or deck officer migrated to information technology management with a side gig in teaching. Always below the surface simmered the anger rooted in the insecurities of my youth. Thirties, forties, even the fifties, the decade mattered little for the tiny, alone child was ever-present within my psyche, reminding me of my inefficiencies and shortcomings. Shortcomings that would never have existed had I someone, anyone taking me under their wing and showing me, tell me, what the world was about and how one lives within it. If I just had a little bit of help when it was needed most. Damn my fate. It wasn't fair, and I would take my anger out on the world around me in subtle revenge.

I cannot live in a conflicted world. I cannot maintain conflicts within. Anger and self-flagellation are contrary to self-love and peace. To profess a strong countenance and peaceful persona while harboring a self-destructive personality with supporting habits labels me, the speaker, as a fraud. And it was in this regard that I was a fraud. I practiced my gifts with all the insight of the heavens and the highest intentions of holiness. Yet when it got right down to it, I had no control over my baser instincts and the outward actions that manifested, created by those very base instincts. I maintained a comfortable numbness that fed my blindness while professing myself to be a holy man reaching the highest levels of the heavenly hierarchy. For God help me if I were ever to look at who I really was. I would have to do something about it, and I knew from the start that I would not; I could not. Continuing with my program of self-medication garnered some questions from those close to me. For a spell, I drove the developments of a spiritualist church. I led the congregation. How could I lead when not adhering to the integrity of self-honesty? How could I lead when, after Sunday service, I'd go home and once again alter my mind's state? How? Was I not special? What did it matter, as the message is just as true regardless of the weaknesses of the vessel. "Abdicate."

These were the inconsistencies and conflicts that I owned that plagued my life and left me incomplete. Avoidance of anger and resolution blocked any real peace I would ever find. Without resolution, I would never have true peace. Without surrendering to my past in all its gory detail and forgiving others and myself, I would never be the intact vessel of heaven's message. Without quiet acceptance of the world and my history, I would never dispel the anger that seethed within me. Exclusive of absenting my spirit of anger, I would never free myself from the self-destruction I sought.

I offer praise and astonishment for the elaborate, imaginative mind within me that I brought into this world. For without it, I would never have lasted as long as I did in my numb bliss. But the energy generated by the life of my soul's development has a mind and life of its own once created, cultivated, and loosed upon the life of the creator, me. The universe has a funny way of providing scenery once the life's navigator sets the course. I set my course on development and a true merging of my mind, heart, and soul with the light of the central sun and created energy that would propel me through the years onto my intended path. My denial and forced ignorance through my intentional numbness would last only so long before the moment of truth came upon me. The choice I had before me was to continue numbing myself and allowing my mind free rein over my inner, sleeping thoughts, or do what had to be done to address and resolve the anger I harbored since childhood. Usually, I'm not one to balk at a challenge, especially one that brings opportunity for growth and a real shot at peace. However, the subconscious and its partner, the ego, are tricky little devils. They will do anything to keep on with their methods and modes of living. And when their existences are threatened, they would rather bring death to the body than change to the heart. The fight was on. It was to be a bloody war I waged within me. The fallout was everywhere within and around me.

If I had the strength of mind and convictions, there may have been an easy path to resolution and contentment. If only. The path typically winds its way through spiritual living of the highest order, joining with the heavenly hosts and closeness to the angels about me. And for the temporal me, there is professional help from any of the doctors who specialize in the resolution of patients' deep-seated issues. Help was available, and all it would take were acknowledgment of the issues and willful steps in the right direction.

However, during the crucial time in question, my connection with the heavenly host and the angels about me was closed. I forced the connection shut through my dissatisfaction over the direction my life had taken after my last mountaintop blizzard of spiritual, metaphysical development. I could no longer trust the guidance I was receiving from the heavenly host. I questioned the value of maintaining a dialogue and decided to step away from all things metaphysical and spiritual. I knew that there was a connection still. After all, was

I not created a member of the heavenly hierarchy? I'd step away from my spirituality and not concern myself about the ramifications. What are another two or three incarnations, anyway, when turning the wheel? I have 5 million years to get this human experience thing down, and if not this lifetime hanging around these human souls, then maybe the next or the one after will settle this issue. I closed the door and darkened the light. I preferred numbness. Being connected and aware was causing too much pain and disappointment.

The material world required more and more effort on my part to maintain. I sought alternate solutions. Prototypes required purchases and cash outlays. The experiments did not solve the problems, and I was left much depleted in treasure. These alternate arrangements didn't work out. I blamed God.

Close ones around me failed me. It was not just that they did not live up to my expectations; they also caused trouble, they brought trouble in from sources external to the immediate family core, and they generated need and stress that taxed every fiber of my being, stretching me till I finally snapped and broke beyond repair. My body physically reacted by generating low-grade spasms that would always transit my body at random locations and throughout the day and night. No one could see the spasms, but I could feel them.

Death and Taxes

On a sunny afternoon, I sat and attempted to still my body while sitting on my patio. As I sat in my chair out on the porch, I felt the spasms. There were hundreds of pulsating nerve and muscle bundles firing off in any given part of my body. First, there was the upper right arm. Then the lower left leg and simultaneously the right cheek under my eye. A little shake and a sputter from my left index finger, and I would lose control of my grip and drop the item I was holding. I sat attempting to quiet and still my body while spasms hit me everywhere without interruption. I felt I was being bombed by a Boeing B-17 Flying Fortress dropping its full payload upon me and then a second B-17, and a third, and then another, nonstop. I gave up the attempt at stillness and chose instead to seek numbness through Mary Jane and Jack Daniel.

The noise from those close to me never abated and would increase in intensity with each passing week. My dear spouse was having health troubles. She needed help. She was alone, abandoned, and estranged by her family. There were issues of estates and inheritances, theft and negligence; she was the innocent target of swindles brought about by those who were her kin. She was betrayed. She accumulated stress and released it all around her, but mostly to me. I reacted to the stress by protecting myself. The method of my protection, the only one I knew at the time, was to step back and become numb. I closed myself off to all her protestations and conditions of malaise. Having previously forced shut my connection to the holy host, I now had to break any connection with my dear, longtime spouse. I could not handle what was before me. My body was failing with the load, and my mind was growing darker and darker, seeing neither path nor potential for a positive outcome.

Running away was not an easy undertaking. It would not be all that cut and dry. There were threads and vines that held me down to my current life and mode of living. The status of marriage that spanned several decades took on more of a corporate entity than a simple marriage. There were offspring. Yes, they were grown and lived their own lives, but they would be impacted and their lives changed by any new arrangements. There were possessions that had been accumulated over the thirty years of our association. The disposition would have to be settled. Then there was her health. She was frail. Yet she was also stubborn and proud. She would profess that she could handle anything that came her way and would prosper throughout. "I'll take care of it," she'd always say. But she couldn't take care of it. She couldn't take care of her affairs in the long run without help. And to this, my response was apathy. I didn't care. I had had enough, and I couldn't take any more of the intricacies of living in the life that I had created. I needed respite and the freedom to cast this shell from me. And throughout, the anger grew within me.

Death and Taxes

I was angry that the gods abandoned me: their messages and guidance conflicted and were contradictory. I could not then trust what I heard, saw, and experienced when interacting within this realm. I was angry that my dear spouse brought me only worry and trouble. Rarely speaking a kind word and routinely picking fights with me to ratchet up the misery quotient in the house, I had no pleasant moments in the spectacular house that we resided in. I received neither thanks nor gratitude for all that I delivered, managed, facilitated, and lived through. The problems she brought me were not mine and not of my doing, yet they became a never-ending conveyor belt of burden delivered with regularity to fall upon my tired and weak shoulders. I was incensed that I could not just leave and remove myself without the most trying complications that would tax me beyond belief. I was furious that I felt burdened by my responsibility to her while I still loved her. "Curse my sense of responsibility. Poor me. Pity me."

Materially and environmentally, I thought the solution and first step was a simple one: get her a place in the country while I live on the yacht. That would be the ticket. She never appreciated the spectacular place we lived in high on a hill with a view of Puget Sound and the Olympic Mountains, but she always wanted to be in the country. I devised a simple solution. Buy a house on Whidbey Island that could accommodate a horse or two. She'd integrate into the community. I'd live on the yacht upon the water and stay in the city while I continued to work my occupation, bringing in the cash that would generate the lifestyle. Eventually, over time and the natural course of order, we would both get into our respective communities and lives and draw apart, making the subsequent separation and disillusion an eventuality via natural progression. A brilliant idea if I don't say so myself. We would both get what we wanted. I would get freedom to pursue whatever came next for me, and she would get her country living and her horses. Eventually, she'd get some inheritance, and I would no longer be financially responsible. And when that day came, I would pack up and move abroad, alone. A genius win-win proposition.

Life in the country took work to maintain and make the mini-ranch that we purchased livable. I remained residing on the boat in the city, a short drive to work, during the week. On the weekends, I'd pack up my overnight bag and travel up to Whidbey. Splitting firewood, mowing the lawns, and grooming the property were all I needed to do to keep the place going. She pretty much had everything in her hands and capabilities during the week. Yet it didn't take me long to discover that nothing was getting done during my absence other than her making a small meal for herself and caring for the dogs. Anything requiring manual labor was not within her catalog, and I would find a list of chores to be done over the weekend.

I didn't mind taking care of business. It was the least I could do. Throughout this experiment of maintaining two residences, I was never able to step away from the responsibility I felt I had to care for a spouse of more than twenty-five years. She enjoyed my visits. She always felt the place would be our family home, and she longed for the day that I would join her on a daily and permanent basis. I must also admit that I was taken in by the place in its natural beauty. There were plenty of woods on the parcel of five acres. Woods, ferns, hills spotted about, and the field and barn needed for any type and number of horses a couple would want. Falling for the place and finding a level of comfort were not in my plan. Weaning off the responsibility to care for her was in the plan. And the plan was not going as I had intended.

In the still of the night, as I sat upon my flying bridge, the final conflicts started. Life was not going according to my plan. I could not shake the responsibility I had for her, and I could not dispel the love I felt for her. A love I knew I would always have, but one that kept me attached to a life and being that was driving me crazier with each passing year. How could I love someone who brought such trouble into my life? And someone who seems to thrive on conflict and over-the-top emotional displays, as I felt she certainly did, would cause the end of my physical and emotional life. My only method of living in some type of personal calmness was to numb myself from the constant stimuli that came my way. Numbness. Any numbness would do, and any manner of getting there would work. I ratcheted up self-medication as the conflicts within me grew, those conflicts of love, responsibility, and that which I had from dangling that sweet, lovely lifestyle in front of me, the turmoil I felt would find no outlet. I sought only to numb my mind and emotions. To turn to stone and feel nothing while I went about my implemented plan and waited for time to pass, time that would hopefully bring me freedom to run away.

Conflicts were not just confined to my family life. Right at the time I purchased the ranch on Whidbey, I changed jobs. This was to be my retirement job. There was a promise of an acceptable and healthy work/life balance as well as an opportunity to make a significant contribution to the institute of higher learning that I joined. I left private industry and took on a manager's job at a university, a government job. Little did I know at the time, but I was soon to learn that university workers had all the characteristics of the stereotypical government worker. They were not lazy but worked at their own pace regardless of the organizational need to do otherwise. They were not unskilled, yet the skills they did command were antiquated and long ago dropped by private industry. They were not diligent in their care of the institute and lagged private industry in technology, practices, and process by ten years. And they didn't mind it one bit at all. They cared for the institute's needs. But their priority was maintaining the status quo. Nothing could impede the status quo. I was soon to find that life at this university was all about the status quo, as if it were some sacred cows that we all fell in line to worship. Status quo maintained the main actors' roles, jobs, power, and authority. The status quo was never to be threatened, for those doing so would be isolated, alienated, and then retaliated against in the most unimaginable ways.

I was hired as an agent of change. Picked from private industry to apply my skills and experiences, and to eventually drive improvements for managing staff as well as reducing the inventory of infrastructure work backlog. And to this effect, I excelled. My successes violating the first rule: never threaten the status quo. I suffered the consequences of my actions. I became a target, and they got inside my head. Any shred of peace I could find by immersing myself in my work was torn from me. They were in my head when I sat on my boat at night, and when working my property, pulling down trees for next year's firewood. I could not get them out of my head. And it drove me even crazier. Home, family, personal, and work lives were all going not at all as I had planned, and I was in conflict like never before in my life. I was becoming angrier by the day.

I was incensed that I could not shine at work without drawing the ire of my superiors or the complacent, cynical staff. That I could not free myself from my yoke of responsibility to my family. And I was angry with myself for still loving my dear spouse. My mood would find no outlet. I chose instead to obliterate myself nightly with any intoxicant I could find. Cannabis was legal and plentiful. Scotch and beer were on prominent display at any grocery store I entered. The availability of intoxicants was very convenient and helped feed my desire to escape all forms of consciousness. In any given day at the office, I would have one hour of honest work to accomplish. The flow of work coming to me from my superior was nonexistent. Perhaps he felt it an unwise strategy to place me into a flow of accomplishment. That would certainly disrupt the status quo to a higher degree. I received no assignments. I left the office at 4:00 p.m. and retired to the boat, alone. Wishing to sleep by nine for lack of anything to do, I would proceed to bring myself into the appropriate state needed to pass out. And by 9:00 p.m. I lay crashed upon my bed, looking forward to repeating the cycle again the next day till Friday. Friday, I will drive up to the ranch on Whidbey and work all weekend during the day and intoxicate myself all evening and through the night. Upon my sixty-second birthday, I noted that my mind's instability and level of intoxication rivaled that of my twenties. Being forty years on and not having the strength of a twenty-two-year-old, I wondered how long it would take before I could no longer sustain my current lifestyle, body, and mind.

It was during this time that I concluded that I could not continue. I could not live the way things were any longer. I started to devise my newest plan that would take me out of this ridiculous world and abort this ill-advised mission of whatever it was I needed to learn or accomplish. It was obvious to me at this time that I had failed. I failed in everything. I didn't have too many chances when getting started in this life. Indeed, things could not have been any more disadvantageous for the young lad I was. I carried no tools from my childhood that would provide me with any utility for times such as these. I was done. That was that. It would be a bane for all those whom I left behind. There would be insurance money. They could sustain themselves off that. There would no longer be my voice calling for sanity from the back room. No more pleads for my dear spouse to get up and take care of herself, to fight or to move on from that which cannot be won. I would no longer be mired in the illogical, self-sustaining status quo of a workplace that was built and maintained not for the institute but for the personal careers of those with job longevity. I was done with all of it. And so it was that I made my plans to end it.

I had multiple options at my command to carry out the deadly, life-ending deed. There were always the handguns. I had several of them. I was an accomplished marksman and could be quite efficient in a gunfight. But that would be messy. Yes. A forty-caliber does quite some damage as it passes through enough membrane to do the job. But the clean-up is such a mess. I didn't want to cause a mess or to put the survivors through the viewing of my distorted and damaged head. And then I realized that there were drugs to do the job. Not just any drug that one would find on the street, but certified pharmaceuticals with a guaranteed outcome if taken in large quantities. There were always drugs available. This was one of the benefits of being married to a woman who had an incurable neurological disease that brought high levels of constant pain. There were always drugs about the house if I looked in the proper places, which I did. Then it would be drugs. I wrote my letter and mixed the tunes that I would have liked to hear at my funeral and made a reservation at a local fleabag motel north of town. There was no need for me to wait once I had the materials on hand. I'd visit the hotel on Monday after another full and invigorating day of work. That would be the ticket.

The weekend came and went. More work accomplished than usual for me, as I wanted to get ahead of the chores as much as possible. My dear spouse would be busy and not have time to fill the firewood bin the following week. I also wanted to accomplish some tasks that had been on my list for several weeks, putting an end to them. I put in a long Saturday and Sunday, but when finished I celebrated my accomplishment in silence by sitting on the deck with a $250 bottle of fine scotch while my dear spouse took up her usual position on the couch, napping in front of the television. The alarm woke me on Monday morning. I got in the car and made the 120-minute drive through the usual heavy traffic and arrived at work to find that there was absolutely nothing for me to do. What a job! At least this will be the last time I have to waste the entire day surfing the web or reading the two local newspapers three times over: enough of this already.

I left work and arrived at the fleabag in good time, considering the high volume of traffic during the evening commute. Checking in, I found a standard room having one bed, one chair, one TV without premium cable, and a bathroom. I'd shower first. On second thought, I'd likely lose all my internal fluids, so why waste the water and time? I'm going to be a mess anyway. I opened a fresh bottle of water and got ready for the task at hand.

Why did this all seem so easy? How could I proceed with my business without feeling nor hesitation? I had years of practice numbing myself and closing off all thoughts, feelings, and expressions of emotion. There were no angels coming to my aid, striking down the glass as I put it to my lips. There were no mystical visions to deter me. No one would mourn my loss; they were all so self-absorbed that this would be just one more bump in their road to get through. No big deal.

And then, as I brought the vial of the finest our pharmaceutical industry could provide to my lips, I hesitated. I could not bring the vial to my lips. I fought the impulse to stop. I won over and brought the vial up to my lips. "One step at a time, old buddy," I encouraged myself onward. I tilted my head back and poured the contents, and not waiting for the water, I swallowed. *How would they ever go down?* I wondered. They didn't, and I started to choke. The choking became uncontrollable, and it was all I could do to breathe as I coughed and spit and cleared my airway of the blockage. *Well. If at first you don't succeed, try it again. I got plenty more.* And then my mobile phone rang. Who would be calling me at a time like this? Who had the nerve to throw a curve into my plan this time? Can't I do anything without having someone pee on my leg?

The caller ID showed me that Jayne was calling. Jayne. Jayne was a casual friend who chatted with me from time to time. Every three to six months, Jane would give me a call to see how I was doing or ask me what I was clairvoyantly seeing with her love life. She must have had time on her hands this day. I first met Jayne when seeking counseling twenty years ago. Jayne was a nurse practitioner and my counselor. The counseling relationship lasted about one year. Jayne knew of my gifts of clairvoyance and always had questions about the gift, as she always thought the topic interesting. Jayne also wanted to know about herself. She wanted to know what I saw in her future. Many times, throughout the year, I would answer Jayne's call, and the first words I would hear after her greeting were "What do you see?" Over the long years, our relationship reversed 180 degrees as I became the counselor providing clairvoyant insight and Jayne became the querent. Jayne was calling. I had to answer the phone.

I don't know what came over me at that instant. Perhaps it was that I didn't want my kids to be placed into the position I would be placing them. Or perhaps it was the love of my dear spouse and the worry, work, and toil I would be causing her. If only I could find peace within me, the place up on Whidbey would be so sweet to call home for the rest of my life. Or maybe it was the realization, no matter how dim, that all was not hopeless. Whatever the reason, it was enough for me to answer the phone.

"Jayne. It's Wayne."

"Hello, Wayne-o. What do—"

I didn't let her finish. "Jayne, I need a name. I need someone from your professional network who specializes in substance abuse and self-destructive personalities. Give me a name."

Jayne got right on it with all the professionalism that could only be found in thirty years of being a therapist. Her only remark to me was "So you're finally going to do something about that, huh?"

Jayne gave me a name and number. He was a psychiatrist practicing one a town away from Seattle. It wasn't optimal as the traffic getting there was enough to drive me crazier, but I figured it would have to do. I didn't convey to Jayne what was immediately on my mind or what personal task she interrupted, but I did remain in pleasant conversation with her for a little while longer. I told her that I wasn't able at that time to advise her on her love life, so we settled down to the mundane family matters of her daughter's partner and her son's aggression toward him. The down-to-earth talk calmed me down and took my mind off what ailed me at the moment. I looked around me and thought it over. It all seemed rather ridiculous and personally embarrassing. I gathered my personal effects and made it out the door, but not before flushing the illicit contents of any incriminating and self-destructive vials in my possession. My early room checkout brought an inquisitive look from the night desk clerk. I simply smiled, signed the checkout sheet, and left.

I placed a call to the good doctor the very next morning to be told by his assistant that he was no longer accepting new patients. I asked for a referral to another doc and got one for a psychiatrist in a local Seattle practice. That would make my life easier. I wouldn't have to fight traffic, and I could easily take the time off from work, for lack of a better term, to have an afternoon appointment.

Contacting that doc, I learned that he was booked solid for the next four weeks. I accepted his next open appointment and requested that they let me know of any cancellations. Four weeks was a long time from today, and I was worried that without some help, I'd easily slip into the final plan again, and it would be fatal. As luck would have it, the doc's office contacted me the next day with an opening later that afternoon. "Would you take the appointment?"

Damn right I would.

My initial meeting with the good doctor was brief and to the point. He asked the questions, and I gave the answers. His questions were pointed about a central theme that did not touch upon my mental state at the time. Indeed, he didn't ask a single question about what brought me to his office or about the articles of my pain. No. His questions led to the written history of my drug and alcohol abuse. For that's what it was I was doing, plain and simple. I could call it what I will: seeking numbness, escape, self-medication, or maintenance. Whatever I called it, the fact remained that I was abusing intoxicants of all forms, and this abuse started when just a young lad learning the ropes behind the neighbor's garage. We didn't talk much about the why or what of it, the doc and me. He simply gave me an objective reading of my history mapped out from early youth to the present. That was it. The excesses of my coping mechanism may not be the problem or the central focus of my malaise, but without arresting and ceasing the intoxicating behavior, I would never have a chance to understand and address the root of my anger or anything going on within the deep recesses of my mind, for that matter. Further discussion would be a waste of his time and mine until I addressed the elephant in the room: my drug and alcohol abuse.

With my complete agreement of his assessment, he then provided me with a list of spiritual-minded communities that addressed long-term aspects of life without intoxicating coping practices. "Here's the list. Try them out and see what you can do on your own. Come back next week." And that was all there was for my first meeting with my first psychiatrist.

I recall the relief I felt when I came to the agreement and realization that I was a drug and alcohol abuser. That title is impactful and a difficult one to wear, but the fact of the matter was an accurate one. The doc didn't seem interested in my mental anguish at the time because he knew, as he told me, that without ceasing the confusion brought about by smoking dope and drinking fine scotch, we would never be able to see what is really going on.

This was not the first time in my life that I was given this admonishment. The last time I was told this very same truth from a doctor was when I sat in St. Barnabas Hospital in New Jersey. I just bombed out on my first attempt to leave the family home and strike out on my own, ending up with pneumonia and who knows what else instead of independence. The three-week stay in the hospital was a long and boring one. A friend regularly supplied me with joints to smoke in my boredom. The ingestion of cannabis masked any symptoms and clouded the doctors' diagnoses. I had to stop smoking that stuff. My uncles eventually informed my friend that if he didn't stop the supply, they would break his legs or get him arrested or both. The supply stopped, as did my smoking. I left the hospital twenty pounds lighter with no one ever knowing what was wrong with my health in the first place. This doctor in the present wasn't saying anything I hadn't heard in the past. This time, I would follow the doctor's instructions of my own accord, without my uncles' intercession.

Spirit Guides and Angels

Maybe it was the close brush with my own mortality. Or maybe I was ready to drop the façade and become true to my being. I'll never really know. I wanted peace. I needed peace. I was so tired of the conflicts and the internal arguments that haunted and plagued me every day. Even in my best days, my highest mood riding days, I always had this shadowing cloud that stood in the way of the sun's light. Some may call it clinical depression, but I wasn't stamping my identity with that label, regardless of the reality. I wasn't ready for it. There was just this one little item that was standing in the way of my complete happiness and peace, I thought, and at times I could pierce the membrane and drink from the joy of the sun's light, but only to recall like muscular memory the anger that seethed within. I wanted peace. I surrendered to the need. I surrendered to the circumstance. And I surrendered to the heavenly host and angelic choir that stood by me for all my days on this earth. Peace was to be my salvation, and my celestial brethren were the steady allies, never relaxing their vigilance.

My practice of self-medication ended. I could never end it on my own; I needed help from others. I needed to be bathed in a positive energy emitted by people who also strived for peace. In this endeavor, I had the help of a fellowship that brought me encouragement and positive reinforcement. Many in this fellowship were like me, angry and foreboding. Many found the peace they were looking for once they ceased their intoxicating ways and took up the path of spiritual living. The journey to peace did not stop at removing the cloud of intoxication. The journey continued onward, cultivating a rewarding relationship with the spiritual self and the beings of heaven and nature that whisper to me within. Many call it what they will: the higher power, the spiritual, nature, God, the higher self. Call it what we will, but for me, it was a reintroduction to the life around me and the aspect of creation that expressed itself to me. The celestial beings I communicated with and felt about me were always there, close by, regardless of the depths of my despair and the force I employed to shut the door to their presence. They never abandoned me and were always looking out for me. They always presented me with positive, lifesaving opportunities set before me. I could take them or not; it was up to me. They laid the groundwork. They worked energy, enabled synchronicity, lined up circumstances, and cheered me on to the final moment that I would find contentment, peace, and happiness. They were always there, and so too was my peace. All I had to do was see it, acknowledge it, and then accept it. It was right there all along. I could never do it alone. I had help from this physical world around me and the celestial world above me.

Once I got that failing self-medication practice out of the way, I found it relatively easy to see the true nature of my life at that juncture. Sure, there were some challenges, but all in all, it was a pretty good life to be lived. And most importantly, I was loved. Loved by the right people in my life and cared for, worried over, and supported. All I wanted was a peaceful existence with my dear spouse, family, and the animals on my ranch, and harmony in my community. It was all there for me. All I had to do was accept it, be present, and live it.

It became abundantly clear that changes in my physical situation had to happen if I were to maintain a positive, reinforcing attitude. Work at this university within their culture had to end. The daily four-hour round-trip commute had to end. Money would be tight, and I'd have to keep on my toes lest I risk healthcare, food, and shelter. It wasn't just me I had to take care of. I had my dear spouse as well as dogs, horses, chickens, and the property. The weight of responsibility was heavy, or so it could be. Yet I found no fear or worry for our future. I really couldn't say what came over me. I wasn't afraid or concerned. I knew it would all work out, and I would be provided for by Providence. How could that be? I was in no way set to retire and live the life of a leisurely country gentleman rancher, yet here I was placed in that position as a necessity to establish my foundation for a peaceful existence. What were the conditions of mind and spirit that brought the absence of fear and worry?

Death and Taxes

I was supported in my endeavor. My dear spouse was thrilled that I would be home with her daily. As time progressed and I became more relaxed, peaceful, and unstressed, she responded in kind with a nod of gratitude and additional support that came in increasingly higher levels.

Since I now had the time to hang around the Whidbey community, I was able to provide service to nonprofits and fellowships. My offers of service were accepted, but not because I was merely available. My service was accepted because I was present as a participant known for a steady mind and accepting, personable outlook. Providing service exposed me to new communities, extending my local, at-home network. My exposure provided the opportunity to be who I am among others. Those about me held me in sustainable regard. Through friendship came business opportunities that created income. The income enabled my sustainability and allowed me to invest more time in my local community, leading to a return of more income. The income/healthcare equation was solved. Solving the riddle locally enabled me to cut ties to the city and the commute that came with it. And so, it would continue spiraling upward after gaining a rising momentum of prosperity with each cycle fueling and enhancing the next. And this was just in the physical realm.

What brought peace? Many are the truths said in jest and in clichés; a faithful, confident, positive attitude is all it took. The momentum toward peace created by faith in a positive attitude cannot be calculated on any given scale within the physical realm. Positive attitudes present me vision to see the opportunities that lie before me. Positive attitudes decipher the map of blessings that all others and I possess within our spirit construction. Faith in positive attitudes gave me the confidence to act.

I first needed a few wins to get me going in a positive direction and away from the road I most recently traversed. Starting out, it was a bumpy road to say the least. My stamina, emotions, thoughts, perspective, and outlook were at all-time lows to the point of hysteria—quiet, simmering, deeply held, and silently expressed hysteria. But now I was in fellowship with others of like mind. They gave me an opportunity to voice the specter my frame of mind had become. They told me of their experiences. Together, we compared notes and shared our heartfelt feelings and our truths, as we knew them. Their fellowship gave me confidence to regain my power and bring to the surface of my living experience the core of my being, unhindered by any self-sabotaging and self-berating personality traits. They joined me in my celebration of success. I no longer self-medicate or abuse drugs and alcohol. And I was relaxed about it while enjoying every minute that I was present in life as opposed to numbingly covering my spirit from everyone's view. I felt alive and real for the first time in my lifetime. This was the win I needed.

But it wasn't enough. Once enticed, confidence wanted more. Confidence raised the bar. Discipline. It now wanted discipline from me in my mind. Discipline to silence my internal whispering and distraction. Meditation provided the classroom while log splitting proved the real-life application of discipline. It was all very simple and reasonable to me when I realized that silence was calling for me and she wanted to be obeyed. Splitting wood or sawing logs into rounds is a noisy proposition. I must wear hearing protectors, or my ears will go bust—again. The work is repetitive and could be tedious. I must remain attentive when working with a chainsaw or hydraulic log splitter, but there remains much time to listen to my thoughts. Yes. A day working, muffled up, slinging a chainsaw, produces the opportunity for many hours of internal dialogue. And I could think up a storm on any number of tangents. Having a predisposition to beat myself up or get wrapped up in an emotionally charged problem that is all mind, all-encompassing, was causing negative impacts on my positive attitude. I brought in the discipline to still my mind from Buddhist meditation techniques, thanks to a helpful suggestion and book given to me by a friend during one of our backyard conversations. Stilling the mind removed the nagging presence of people, things, and emotions that plagued me. Stillness. Stillness brought the rest that I needed. It helped me pause upon the subject at hand and rethink it or approach it in a different way. It placed the issues in perspective and brought sanity to my very contorted brain. Problems fell away. A session of meditation became relaxingly invigorating. A day at chain sawing became a pleasant experience, never tiring of the task. My mind was still. It was another win. Confidence was satisfied but not satiated.

It was about that time I came upon a Buddhist tome—a prayer and convocation that calls me to do its gentle bidding. I declared with this prayer my values and primacies. I vowed to be awake and present. I vowed to own a grateful heart, to smile at the hearts of others while sharing my love and easing their burden. I will abide within the dance of life, practicing kindness, generosity, acceptance, and tolerance. And I will thus uplift the cause and benefit of all worldly citizens and all living things.

My new practices created an extremely positive momentum. Others about me reacted. What I was doing was not obvious to others, and I was not one to profess my salvation technique or engage in any gospel preaching of any type. I just went about being present and counting my blessings. The world around me and those occupying it relaxed. Everything took a step down in intensity, drama, and stress. Everything connected to me via a thread of involvement tugged a little less. Yet it goes without saying that in the world of behavior and interpersonal activities, people still had their problems with other people, and I was close to those people. Where I once entered the beast of the fray and paid an emotional toll with my method of involvement, I now knew what my part was and was not. I took neither ownership nor sides and was able to be a sane, quiet voice of calmness.

My battle with and within myself was drawing to a smooth conclusion. I found the glimmer of peace and accepted life on my harmonizing terms. It was sweet, and it was to remain so for the remainder of this one life on this earth. Now it was time in my life to live being alive and present. To count my blessings and to harvest new ones ever replenished. I loved life and living and found pleasure and purpose in the simplest of tasks. It was a long battle, and for a while it could have gone either way. I'm glad it turned out well.

Consider the task at hand. I have no clue as to what I am doing on this world. I am no statesman. I yield no influence over the masses or individuals. My best friend is a Norwegian Fjord horse who loves me and awaits a never-ending stream of carrots and apples. I provide no material benefits to anyone but the few that are family, and to this effect there is no largesse. I have no following and am without congregation. I have no students. I teach no one and am no one's apprentice. My gifts I keep close and will display to others only when absolutely required. And it is required that I display my gifts infrequently at best. Throughout all my days, I simply tend my fields and animals, love my dear spouse, and live a quiet, peaceful, and obscure life among friends joined together in service to others. Yet here I am, possibly or apparently and likely beyond belief, an angel in human form, bound within a human life, and sharing the destiny of man.

I am an angel in human form, bound within a human life, sharing the destiny of man. I am not here to wield power; avenging angels are products of Madison Avenue advertising firms and their predecessors in the clergy. I am not here to dispute opinions to the contrary or of those that are contrary to my definition of the heavenly hierarchy, angelic choir, or existence of celestial beings. May we all understand our universe in our own way and in our own time. I am a weary traveler come recently from lives lived in strife and in battle. I come for my repose, for my peace. Yet nothing comes without the potential to accomplish or without a price of admission. I have paid the price and seized the golden ring. I am now here to live my life in my peace and to reside peaceably with my kin and hearth. It is through the natural, simple pleasures of life that I draw my strength and tranquility to recharge awaiting my next cycle at turning of the wheel. I spend the remainder of my life in service among my fellows. I have freed myself from anger's grip, and I am renewed.

Chance and My Dear Spouse

Thirty-three years is quite some time to be living with someone, married to someone. Me and my dear spouse have that longevity. It's more than half of her life and almost half of mine. Soon, she'll be sixty and I seventy. I've known her since she was twenty-four. Knowing, being with, walking with, living a life with anyone from their twenties through their sixties is not a trivial matter. It's a milestone that can deserve some introspection based on observation and experience. For after all this time, here she and I are. We are together, and in a pretty good place.

Now I'm just a city boy from Newark. The armpit of New Jersey. Where I landed and am living now far exceeds any possible outcome of where I thought or imagined I'd end up. Life when I was younger was a killer for me. Not only the family life but the overall environment. New Jersey and its culture back then was a very difficult place for me to live peacefully. I knew that being a member of that culture and society would not be healthy for me. I, of course, made matters worse by becoming a mess of a kid in every way possible, self-destructively so. You can't imagine what my late teens, early twenties were like. I am quite surprised that I survived. But I did. Once I broke free from that box that they all built around me, I survived, and I thrived, and I built quite a life for me and for those others close around me. It wasn't easy, but I had and have a strength that is unmatched by many in this world and a mind that sees beyond dimensions, or so my grandfather told me so.

And here now she is, living with me through all these years, family. Not only is she family but her child is as well. Did she ever wonder where she'd be now without me through the last thirty years? Or what kind of person her child would have become if I was not a significantly influential part of her childhood? We have been through our times; we have us two. And while I, since striking out on my own so long ago, have climbed to the top of my revenue-generating and occupational potentials, first as master then as worker to senior manager and college teacher, she lies stricken with an incurable disease that only gets worse and of late is also taking from her the peace of sleep. Now she can't sleep.

Yet I sleep like a baby and all through the night. It could be argued that sleep and peace of mind are related and tend to go hand in hand. Certainly, one supports and bolsters the other.

Death and Taxes

I am at peace with myself. My conscience is clear. I have happiness to an acceptable degree. I am contented. I have done all that I could to make a good, safe, and secure world for me and her while helping to raise her child as my own. And now I am in my olden age, my golden years, there is nothing left that I must do. And so it is that I play with my animals. Walk the village I have chosen to live by. Enjoy the park I have cultivated on our small section of land. And I sit in the living room with her as she, exhausted from continuous pain, lies on the couch and watches TV, and I am at peace. The universe has spoken to me, and for the most part, I have listened and lived harmoniously with this life we have. Within my abilities, as best I could. And that turned out to be a good thing.

And here we are together, still, after thirty-three years. I don't know if that's the way it was meant to be, our sharing our lives with each other to this degree that we have. Practically, I think I'm here and I've done it so might as well not complain about it or second-guess it. I know that love has something to do with me being here with her for all these years because I love her. That's a simple truth. And I know that I am the love of her life. There's a lotta good in what we have.

I also know that I have an unhealthy sense of responsibility. And with her I have placed her needs above mine. Her ambitions above mine, too many times. I have made things possible for her that required sacrifice on my part at a cost of reaching the full potential of my will and heart. There is so much of our lives together I made possible for her by skewing events through my strength and will and energy so that we could be comfortable or satisfied. Like the fool, I provided for her and succeeded in bringing about a life that was comfortable, plush, and envied by many, even though contrary to what I at times though was wise. Love? And some sense that we were meant to be together through the end no matter what transpired and no matter what it cost me, my soul, my spirit, or my purpose. Those things for my advancement I put behind me and elevated her needs above mine. Not the thing to do for anybody, anywhere, at any time perhaps. But she had, has, and will continue to have so many, *many* needs that living this life and keeping it all running takes everything that I've got. *Everything!*

There's an old saying that goes, "To thine own self be true." It means to do for others. But make sure you do for yourself first. Take care of yourself and do what you need in life for you, *first.* One must establish the healthy boundaries that protect and cushion self from the full array of whatever can and may happen during the living of a lifetime relationship. And once the boundaries are established, maintain those boundaries at your own peril. Avoiding the opportunity for regret. And bolstering the odds that when you depart this green earth and jump into the heavenly real world, you're pleased with where you're at. Not feeling that you were a sucker and shortchanged yourself because you fell for the old tricks and placed others' needs before your own a wee bit too much and out of proportion where and when it mattered most.

I tried to leave her. It seemed that it was the only way I could grab my life back for me where it was important, and for my own health and peace of mind. Each time I left her, or wanted to leave her, my spirit screamed out to me to be free of her, her troubled soul, and all her trials and all her problems. I longed to live my life for me, if only for a little while before it's too late. Because with her it would be impossible for me to live my life for me. I can't get enough oxygen for me. Her need is all-encompassing. She has a way of sucking out all the air and energy from the environment around her and most especially, from me, just so that she can maintain a steady presence or lack thereof. It's not intentional. It's not willful. It's a matter of survival, and it's really all she knows. It's real, not imagined. But here I am. Still calling the same address home. No matter what the conflict, no matter how urgent my need, I just could never seem to leave her.

The universe had a message for me that I willfully ignored. The message, like so many from the universe, was repeated all around me. Like from the MS caregiver support group, for example. The consensus of the group to many of the spouses' situations was always the same. "You didn't sign up for this. It's their life and their karma that is at work. Go live your life and let them live theirs." I didn't follow the consensus.

But like she says to me from time to time, the universe tells you something or gives you a lesson and you either listen and comply, or the lesson gets harder and harder, and the voice gets louder and louder. Pretty basic. I know from being with her all these years that she knows the meaning of the basic concept, and she knows it from experience. As many times I have witnessed the universe trying to tell her something that she acknowledged but refused to process the message, and the voice got louder, and the lesson got harder. I can think of a couple of experiences she's had to this effect, and one of them is happening right now.

The bed is shaking every other night, and it woke her up. The bed was physically shaking. I didn't feel it, but she did. She told me about it in the afternoon after it happened the second time. And in answer, I mentioned what I thought the cause and the why of it. It was the Old Man who lives in the cedar tree. He's a remnant of the days when the Northwest Natives harvested berries and eggs from my neighborhood. He likes us. He watches over us and our animals and tries to keep us safe. He knew the universe had a message for her and he tried to give her some advance warning to spare her the hard part. His message was to be nice to me. That she wasn't being particularly nice and that she needed to treat me better. And that time was running out for her to act. Message delivered by the Old Man and before she was slammed by the hand of God, just like he intended. And what did she do about it? What did she do with this advanced warning? Nothing. She still treated me in the same manner that she's been treating me for more years now than I can count. And now on top of it all she can't sleep. *"What's going on?"* Her words.

Christmas comes and she gets the traditional annual Christmas letter from me telling her that I was at peace and contented and that I loved her. She was nice for a couple of days, and she finally got some sleep. The bed ceased its shaking. Then it was back to the same ole behavior and treatment that I have experienced from her for almost a decade.

And what is that same ole treatment? (I'm going to use simple language here. I don't want to be offensive or for it to be taken as such, but I know no other way to put it. So, I'll just lay it out.) That she has been and still is a real jerk to me and treating me like poop more and more every year since I can remember when. To say that she has been a witch would be putting it mildly and insulting the poor female nature worker involved. She's been treating me poorly in just about every way she can. Yes. It's not intentional. She's miserable. She's always sick. And she has no energy or motivation because she's always in excruciating pain. But at this point it doesn't matter whether her treatment of me is intentional or not. For I believe and hold that we, as adults, have a responsibility to other people to treat them based on how we would want to be treated by them and not to take our frustrations, misery, and failures out on others. Especially when those others (me for example) are the ones who make their living with some semblance of comfort and grounding possible. All adults have a responsibility to manage their stress where they don't harm and hurt those around them because they are having a stressful time of life. Especially when that other around her (me for example) is the one who is the only person making her daily life possible by doing all the daily tasks and efforts it takes to live.

She told me a story last week that keeps coming up over and over through the years. A reoccurring theme. The story of Vegetable Man and the family's trip to Europe where they left her at home and let Vegetable Man stay at the house to supervise her. Vegetable Man was her sister's then boyfriend. I first heard of this story through what her Auntie told me. Auntie told me that she and her husband, Hubs, felt so bad about how her mother and sister conspired to exclude her from a family trip to Europe that Auntie bought my dear before-spouse a trip to Europe the next summer out of sympathy. This event was the capstone of my dear's relationship with her mom and older sister.

She told me that her sister put her in a box. As early as she could remember, right from the start, her sister put her in a box, and she didn't like it one bit. But from what I can picture after Auntie's conversation is that it wasn't just her sister that put her in that box. It was also her mother. What I got from the reoccurring theme of hearing this story from her auntie and herself through the three decades of our association is that it was not only her sister but also her mother who conspired against her to put her in that box and excluding her from the family trip to Europe. And what was in that box? Was it the family screwup? The family's litigating fanatical failure among all those accomplished people? And that's how it was from day one for her. Mother, sister, and then aunt and uncle placed her in that box. They all defined who she was. And she was defined as the screwup. Some people must have a whipbird they can point to in their life so that they can feel superior. And for whatever reason, they needed my dear spouse to be that whipbird from her childhood through adulthood.

But she knows all this. She knows of this box-building aspect among her tribe who raised her. She told me about what she knew and how. She told me of how Older Brother and

Auntie treated her father like an old shoe regarding the beach house once the Older Brother came back from working twenty years in Alaska. She told me that after twenty years of her father taking care of the place, they just waltzed right in and said, "We're here now and we'll be calling the shots without discussion from you, so off you go, little brother." Auntie and Older Brother did to her father what her mother and sister did to her. The phenomenon was generational.

And that box-building went on throughout her entire childhood. It was the event in her early adult years with the Vegetable Man and everyone's trip to Europe, everyone except her, that brought it all to a head. A big, pus-filled, festering head slamming her right in the face in a way that she could not avoid, knowing that this is how it is and is how it has been for as long as she could remember. She saw it then! It all clicked! She knew it! And then she had a choice to make. Live with it as they wanted her to live with it, in her box. Or live her life by calling this treatment what it was, recognizing these people for who they were, and getting her ass out of there to live on her own … Or not.

I had at nineteen a similar choice. Acknowledge what I was living within the family dynamic and the general environment of New Jersey. Live and play my part or get the hell out of there. Now in the process of making that decision and getting to a point of action, there was some internal conflict. And for this conflict, I turned to partying, drugs, minimum wage jobs, and animal living. I was a mess as stated earlier. But then I decided when and how and I acted. Fifty years later here I am. Where father and grandfather never made it to sixty, I'm going to hit seventy. Where every member of the family had multiple cancers, I've had none. The universe gave me a lesson, and I listened. The result is scribed by me to those who reared me. I have health as the physical manifestation where they did not. Cancer and death would have been my fate had I stayed. Staying was not my destiny.

At nineteen the universe shouted in her ear also, and she had a similar decision to make. Live in the box they placed her in or live her life for herself and on her terms. In such cases, one either chooses to leave the family home or stay. She stayed. And the mechanism she used to justify staying and living with herself: denial.

Denial creates a conflict between spirit, mind, and body. We cannot live with conflict such as this. Conflicts like this, if left to fester, create *dis*-ease. *Disease.* There are those who have said that they do not see MS in her. But that is what the medicos say she has. Whether MS or not, it may be a result of the universe trying to pass her a lesson (and a hell of a lesson at that) and her not listening. So, the universe made it harder and spoke louder. And she still didn't listen. Got preggers. Married Bobby. Conflict. Abuse. Sibling rivalry. Living in the box. Keeping up with the denial and rationalizing the truth of it. And at some point, here comes me. "Maybe with you she might get grounded," her auntie told me before we were married. Yeah? That depends on whether she continues living in the box everyone built her into or not. That same box that she filled with denial. Do you think that she'd stop living in the box after so long in denial about it? Or after joining a husband and building a family, would she drop that coping mechanism off by the wayside and gain freedom from the constraints others would place her under? We'll see.

So here we are some thirty-three years later. I listened to the universe when I was nineteen and have health and am alive. She didn't listen to the universe when she was nineteen and she has what she has. All that and now she can't even get a full night's sleep because she's being a mean and nasty, toxic jerk to me by continuing to treat me like poop after being warned by the old shaman down by the cedar tree to stop. Not listening at nineteen through sixty cost her health of mind and body as well as close to half a million dollars from what we spent in lawyers as she argued with her sibling over estates and inheritances (money most of which I brought to the table) or lost by her almost being disinherited for pulling some garbage with her auntie that her lawyer and husband told her not to pull. She didn't listen to us either.

That's the way it is with my dear spouse and me, and I'm OK with it. I don't really have a choice about it because at this stage in our lives it's just she and me. That's it. I got her and she got me, and that's all there is to it.

We have a slice of heaven here. We made this place. Yep. I did most of the work. I provided all the steady income so that we could live above our means and have those nice things we always wanted, if only for a little while. Yes. We'd drive down the road hauling our horses to the trailhead for an afternoon ride, and she would tell me she was living her dream. She did get to live her dream, which is much more than many in this world get to do. Did my efforts, work, and drive make her dream come true? Would she have been able to do it on her own? I don't think so. It took a long time and a lot of work to get where we're at, and I did the heavy lifting.

Throughout the last several years, my goal was to get us into a spot where we have some level of security, safety, stability, and comfort. It was no small task working with her where money was concerned. She approached money and finances a bit like a teenager. Perhaps late teens? Because just as when she was nineteen and her father had to bail her out of credit card debt, she now still demands the ability to use money and spend as she wants but refuses the accountability to make and manage money in any constructive manner. Knowing I had to work with someone with money-handling hang-ups, it was my sole objective to get the house paid off and then to get a certain amount of cash in the bank. That would establish our footing and give us a chance in this very harsh and expensive world. And that's where we are right now.

My dear spouse has some choices to make. I am happy (happy enough). I am contented. I'm satisfied. I'm OK with sitting on the other couch in the living room reading a book or playing with the dogs while she spends twenty hours a day lying on the couch watching YouTube because she's too tired to move or expend any energy while her body fights constant pain. I'm fine doing the work to make this place work for us. I could use some help from her in ways that she doesn't seem to comprehend, and if she does, she doesn't seem to want to provide. But that's fine. And if she wants to continue being a giant toxic jerk treating me as such, I guess I have no choice in the matter so she can just go ahead and spit venom wherever she likes. I'm not going to take any steps to punish her or to strike out even though I can't stand it! If she wants to tell the universe and the shaman down at the cedar tree to go screw off, then she can go right ahead. She has MS. Her energy is at the lowest level I have ever seen. I will not let her vamp energy from me anymore so she's on her own in that department. She can't sleep at night and she's as miserable as anyone can possibly be. Is she going to keep it up?

But! If she'd like to try something new for a change like showing that she appreciates the life we have by not acting like such a horrible monster or acknowledging that she was dealt a lousy hand and didn't play it very well and realize that it doesn't matter in the long run because I had her back and look what we have now, then she might just start to unwind, drop the violin tension her father talked about, and realize that we are in our golden years, we have each other, and we are in a good place. We don't need the aftereffect of trauma anymore. Life can end at any time. Especially now with all this stuff going on around us. There's no need to carry all that baggage anymore. It's too heavy. We don't need it. We have whatever we need. Just take what life we have left and enjoy, chill. Take what time we have left to get it right. And remember we might not have as much time as we think. Don't put it off another day.

Chapter 10: We Are Here at Long Last

A Day in Paradise

Idyllic. That's the word that describes sitting here on my back deck in the morning. The sun comes in through the trees in patches. Warmth here and a little shadow there, where I stand or sit depending on my preference now. Trees all about me except right before me and down the hill where sits the barn and the field. Dust clouds swirl about as the animals change their positions while talking over their morning call for breakfast. They await my visit. Ever attentive to my softest sigh or movement, they stand at the ready watching my every move. "Is he coming down yet?"

"No. I think he's still having his coffee. Stare at him harder."

Coffee finished, I start my typical daily routine. Today the routine suffered from a little sinus or bronchial congestion. I was a little slower than usual and having to rest frequently to catch my breath, too frequently for my comfort, but nothing I couldn't handle. But that was a by-product of the joys of grandparenthood. The stepdaughter had kids who are now three and a half and two. I babysat for the whole day five days ago. The kids are home now and the three-and-a-half-year-old currently has a high fever and is screaming and crying diligently as everyone at her house walks softly lest they come down with something also. I have been feeling under the weather since yesterday afternoon. Not too bad now but not too good either. I've no time to be sick.

Down to the barn I go to fill the wheelbarrow with this morning's ration of hay and supplements. Anticipation. They love their supplement. They stand at the ready hovering over their assigned mangers waiting for my tap on their nose and drop of the morning dose into their supplement bucket. Then in goes the hay. They will be chomping and chewing for the next sixty minutes. Chore number one: done.

I love the walk back up from the barn. Calling the dogs back to me before entering the gated yard, I get my treats ready for their reward and pleasure. They come to me so much the easier if they are compensated with a small doggie treat. Into the yard we go and back into the house, or the deck for that matter, whatever they prefer. They're good doggies. They'll just lie about in a patch of sun taking their morning nap. I'll get me some breakfast before starting the day's work. My work for the day: cutting logs into rounds to stack for next winter. It is good, honest work done just like the pioneers before me. Of course, I now have a little assist with a powerful chainsaw, tractor, and hydraulic log splitter but still, honest work in providing for my family.

Spirit Guides and Angels

These days the family numbers that I provide for have dwindled down to me, the dogs, horses, and a few eggless chickens. I'd do something about those chickens if I had a mind to, but my dear spouse promised the original owners of those chickens that she would not eat them when they became too old to lay eggs. I'll feed them and clean up after them because my dear spouse made the promise. I'll keep her promise for her. It's the least I could do for the chickens and her memory. I miss her.

I lost her six months ago. It was all very sudden. The illness that first came on decades ago advanced its purpose, and her body could no longer rule over its effects. I'll always miss her. This hole in my heart shows testament to this very day that I miss her presence. I'll always love her. I've always loved her. Everything was fine this one day. We were the best we ever were with each other in all the years we were together. Over the last many months, things got better between us and for each of us every day that we lived. Every day I could not imagine my luck having someone who loved me like she did. Her love for me was so kind and gentle. She was vulnerable now and weak. People would call her frail. She trusted me enough to show me that. She was that too, for me, trusting. She was a gift to me. And I miss her being with me on these mornings when we would go down to the barn together and greet the boys. We'd banter about for the morning before our breakfast, salute the boys, then fill the wheelbarrow and disburse the bounty.

We went riding horses the day before. It was an uneventful ride where the boys were at their best behavior. At the end of the day, we soaked our sore bodies in the hot tub and then lazed around the house, me on my recliner and her on her couch. She expended much energy this day and needed an evening nap. The next day she was so tired she couldn't get out of bed. That was new. We always played Ping-Pong with the fatiguing effects of her illnesses, but we both attributed it to her being tired from yesterday's activities. Rest is in order. Rest and I'll take care of things. She was finally up around 2:00 p.m.

The day was a lazy one for us both with me just hanging around the deck working on a writing project for one of my nonprofit clients and her just resting on the couch. We fed the boys their afternoon snack, adding in a session of carrot and apple eating. No need to swat at flies this afternoon; fall was coming, and the flies were finally gone. We impartially shared out the cookies we took down from the house, just for them. Cookies. She always called any treat for the dogs or horses cookies. The horses knew what it meant when we came down the hill and shouted to them, "Cookies!" as we cut power to the hot fence. This was just another blessed day where we hung around the house. She rested and I just did whatever. Always we observed the afternoon cookie and snack break. It was a tradition.

Getting back in the house, she felt extra fatigued and retired to the couch as usual when in this state of tiredness. But unusually so with this nap, she fell into a deep sleep and stayed as such though the evening. She never really woke up from that sleep. They called it organ failure. Her body just had had enough. It stopped working, and that was it. That was all anyone could do. I was there throughout, never leaving her presence for a moment. Friends took care of our animals for us so that I could focus on her and be at her side. We talked. Or at least I talked with her. She didn't move or open her eyes. I felt her kiss as she left. I felt her cheek upon my cheek followed by the kiss of her soft lips on mine as I looked into her closed eyes. I didn't see her leave. I averted my gaze from the celestial world because I didn't want to see. I just wanted to be with her for whatever time we had remaining. Be with her fully with every fiber of my spirit and presence and never to leave her side. But now she was gone from me. Gone from my life this point forward.

I didn't say goodbye. I said, "See you later." I know what awaits her spirit as she recommences her journey in the celestial realm. It is life, unlimited and unfettered life, and health of mind, spirit, and the body of light that she will become. I know what awaits her, and I know of her happiness. I know, but I did not want to think about it, any of it. I just wanted to be here at her side and hold time between the heartbeats. But I am only human and mortal, and I could not hold time and the movement of our physical lives. Sitting here with her was all that I could do. Sit here with her and feel. I bid her adieu and let her fly unreservedly and freely. And for this flight and all that we lived together through the decades, she touched my cheek and kissed my lips.

I could never fill the part of my heart that she occupied. I don't think about where she is and her joyous journey, because I will not. I don't want to reach out to her and attach a thread. I want to feel my emotions here within and not distract from the present. I was losing her from this life of ours and I was in pain. And I knew that I had to feel everything I was feeling to the fullest, in the flesh. She is in good hands now and I don't want to interfere in any way or tie her in any way to this world. I don't want to give her concern over me. She'll be a part of me again, of course, and we will again make a home when the turning of the wheel generates the reward and requirement. I have a life to be lived here in the flesh. When I take my deepest meditations and reach into the heavens, I will not look for her. I don't want to disrupt her rest but instead know she is recharged on the bed of light attended by angels of the highest order. "Rest. I'm always here. Rest. Time is nothing to us now. Rest. I'll be here, my dear."

The plan was that the other one, the one who survived the longest, would keep living at the ranch till it was impossible to maintain or sustain. Knowing my health, we figured that would be yet another several decades of tending horses. We figured that Spike would live to be thirty-five. Someone had to be around for him. He was too sweet to ever give up, so I would keep him. Well. I'm the one who is left so I figure that Spike is my job now and I will do as she bid me during our many talks should this situation arise. Keep Spike and take care of him. No condo on the beach with maintenance people and maid service like some of my contemporaries who live the golden years of leisure. Not me. I'll be slinging horse poop and hay till I can't walk, whenever that is.

I stayed at the ranch and did honest work providing for my family of dogs, horses, and chickens. And it wasn't as though one fewer person in the roost reduced the need for less firewood to make it through the winter. I will always need five cords and cutting rounds throughout the year was part of the ritual. The work for me really was no problem. I was in great shape for someone of my age. My fitness tracking device says upper five percent for my age group. I exercised regularly in my studio just to hedge my bet. I may cheat on the workouts by cutting them short or not hitting my full count but moving a bunch of wood from tree form to the firewood stacked in my shed was hard evidence that I was in shape. I'll be here, I figured, a long time.

The logs were at the path leading up to the round pen. The round pen is where we exercise the horses using voice and hand signals. No leads attached in the round pen because the animals can't go anywhere. The pen is round. And it's not that big so when they slack off their exercise and training and start sniffing around the ground for no reason at all, and in the middle of a lesson in the first place, I just walk a few feet over to them and tell them up close and in their faces to stop slacking off. Get a move on. Eat later. We got that pen a few years ago and used it enough to drop one hundred pounds off Spike as the doctor ordered. Spike and I both were in good shape. We'll be around for a while.

The path leading to the round pen hosted our Folly. We wondered why an English innkeeper had a single, solitary door standing alone in his garden. We asked him. He tells us it's a Folly. We nod to each other signaling that we needed to remember this and retired for the night. It would be an early morning the day after we learned of a Folly. The next morning, we had a private, self-led tour at Stonehenge when the sun came up. While we didn't have a door on the path from our barn to the round pen, we had a patio set of wicker chairs and table inviting anyone to stop and take a break. So long as the visitor refrained from sitting at either of the chairs, all would be well. The chairs were so placed more than a decade ago and were now barely wicker. Weeds and rot would render the Folly into one of nature's works of art. But there it was, our Folly out on the path. The sun was shining through the trees and branches. With the slight breeze coming out of the north, the sun's light danced upon the chairs and table. I had to remind myself that they weren't moving, that it was just the swaying light playing tricks on me. And there up the path, where the logs awaited my attention, the sun shone down through the break in the trees in the clearing that the round pen required. I approached my quarry and settled in for what I estimated to be the next four hours muffled by my high-end hearing protectors and buzzing up my chainsaw with the newly sharpened chain. I couldn't have a better day to do the work. I was glad I put it off from last week. This day was sunny and cool with a refreshing breeze coming over the fields to cool my sweated brow.

The work was easy enough under normal circumstances, me being not sick with a cold or flu, so long as I took a long break every time I had to fill the saw's tank. Sitting on a nearby stump, I looked to see two eagles riding the upstream provided from the reflected warmth of the field. Perhaps the eagles would find a rodent or two? I'd love it if they could get a meal off me. It took me a second to recognize them as eagles. As they swung their arc to the west, the sun brightly reflected off the white tail feathers and head. The white tail was unmistakable. They were eagles. As they left the visible sky, I stood up to get back to work.

The work wasn't hard for someone in shape such as me, but there's no stopping age and age is what I had plenty of. That and some lung or sinus malady building up in my upper torso. And then somewhere along the line a few years ago I started to get back pains when I never had back pains. The back pain I really found interesting was the one that traveled down my left leg. My leg especially complained when I bent over. Silly leg. Everyone knows that cutting rounds is nothing but bending over. The only time I stood fully erect was when I threw a round onto the pile of wood. Cutting rounds was all bending. And at times when I stood erect, my head would spin and I'd become short of breath. A little dizzy would touch me for a moment and I'd lose my breath. The doc I've been seeing for the past twenty years tells me that it's normal. He told me that it was my blood pressure adjusting to my change of stance and blood flow. Still, I don't remember having this issue when I was in my thirties. But I probably wouldn't have been able to cut, split, and stack five cords when I was in my thirties. Or I wouldn't want to.

My next break came when the chainsaw ran out of gas again and I had to refill it. I sat on the stack this time, it being solid enough to hold me. *What new body pain would I feel this break?* I wondered. Yes, my left elbow. That's whose number was next. I compressed my elbow when I took up archery after a thirty-year absence. Christmastime was neigh, and my dear spouse asked me what I wanted for a present. I wanted a bow, I said. When we were first married, I set up a small archery range using a couple of bales of hay that would have otherwise gone to her horse. I was pretty good with the bow and arrow. I was a natural. I must have had ingrained archery skills. "What else could be the reason?" was our running joke. My dear spouse got me exactly what I asked for as a present, a fifty-pound longbow. Silly to think I could jump right into pulling a fifty-pound bowstring after a thirty-year absence. After two months, my right shoulder revolted and would no longer draw the string. After being on strike for a year from any such work, my shoulder transferred the watch to my left elbow. My left arm was compressed and pained me for a year afterward. It pained me now. And my chest started feeling heavy with me having to concentrate on each breath I took. I could understand the pain in the elbow, but the one in my chest was worrying.

The feral cat came by while I was stretching my left arm. He just sat there looking at me. There were several feral cats in the area, and this one was the friendliest. Although if I moved a muscle in his direction, he'd run and disappear, but for as long as I sat here relaxing, he was fine with lying or sitting some ten yards from me while studying me over. After several minutes of our silent communion, I arose to get back at the job. The cat disappeared.

Harvesting rounds is never ending bending and straightening. With each of my prolonged bends, rising erect produced a dizzying effect and shortness of breath. *It must be that blood pressure thing to the brain the doc told me about,* I thought. *And this cold isn't helping any either.* Nothing usually deterred me from completing my day's tasks. After heaving over three abnormally large rounds, I sat to regroup before settling down to finish the job. I arose and leaned upon the stack. There goes that lightheadedness again, but holy cow! Now I can't breathe. I decided to call it a day and head back up to the house. For some unearthly reason, I felt it extremely important to get back to the house quickly. I'd excuse myself for leaving my tools out on the job site for the time being. I'll rest up and pick up later before dark. I've done enough wood working for now. I figured I'd take a moderate break and return to the task later once rested. All very odd for me to leave a job in the middle, unfinished.

The vertigo was minimal this time around, not like the others of the day that had an edge of intensity that took me by surprise. Vertigo be damned. I couldn't catch my breath. I instinctively staggered toward the house as I struggled for air. Up the hill taking one sure-footed step after another, getting into the backyard I entered through the nearest gate. Closing the gate behind me, I doubled over, having felt like I was hit by a Mack truck. My trouble with breathing intensified. I was struggling and could barely breathe. I tried to push the air out of my lungs. It didn't want to flow without effort. I'd pant and push the air out. Then I would recover and take in a short hiccup like inhaling breath. Pushing the air out of my lungs then gasping for as much air as I could pull from the atmosphere around me. No matter how I tried, I was not getting enough air to suit my needs. I felt like I was suffocating.

But I don't understand! I just have a small cold that's hardly getting in my way. Right? And I don't get sick! *Right?* And as I question my stamina, I collapse to my knees, no longer having the strength to stand upright. Kneeling was not working either. I shifted and lay prone on the grass in the backyard with a large, white dog sticking her nose in my ear, wondering what's up with Daddy.

I wasn't in this position very long before I started to feel what can only be described as fear. Finding myself lying there on the grass grasping for air and coming up short, I think I started to panic. Thankfully I listened to my son-in-law long ago and installed that Mesh network as he suggested. I'd have mobile phone service through the upgraded Wi-Fi. I dialed 911. They answered and I immediately blurted out my name and address to the answering responder. The responder got the message and was able to ascertain with minimal dialogue that I was unable to breath and needed help. Someone would come to my aid. I simply had to wait for them to get here. The responder would stay on the line and wait with me. I placed the phone into speaker mode and was able to carry on a short but frequently interrupted conversation. It seemed like the medics were taking forever to get here. Then I realized one of the drawbacks of living in a rural setting. First responders take forever to get to you even if your need is immediate. I felt I needed that hurry-up effort, although I couldn't understand why. I waited. The 911 responder waited with me.

As we waited, I was able to blurt out a message requesting the responder to please call my stepdaughter, Marie. I provided the phone number. I asked the responder to contact Marie, give her a quick summary of what's going on, and that she comes to the house to take care of the animals. Marie was my emergency contact and power of attorney. All official contacts of my life and death were transferred to Marie upon the death of my dear spouse. Knowing I'd be up at the Hospital in

Coupeville, I asked that Marie come to the house and secure the animals then come up to the hospital to pick me up. I was slowly but steadily sobering to the reality. I was having a medical emergency. Holy cow! Help!

The medics arrived. The 911 responder signed off, but not before telling me that they were in contact with my stepdaughter, Marie, and she would meet me at the hospital.

What immediately followed was a jumble of flashes, sounds and g-forces that I had difficulties following. I do have a couple of vivid memories of that immediate time when the first responders arrived. They were doing much shouting. Why were they shouting? I had my hearing aids in my ear, didn't I? No. I didn't. But I learned that medical providers always yelled when they want the patient to understand what's being said. And in this case, they were doing a good deal of yelling at me. I distinctly heard the word "intubate." No. *No* was my safe word. If I said no enough, perhaps the yelling would end. Or so I thought before the responder stuck a glass pipe in my mouth and yelled for me to take deep breaths and hold it. I would take a deep breath if I could. But I couldn't. Again yelling. This time to hold my breath. It was all very confusing, and throughout the entire event, I still couldn't breathe.

Did I say at one point I felt like a pin cushion? I would have complained except for some strange and nerve-racking reason I had the need to prioritize gasping for breath over communicating. And this interplay continued for some undisclosed amount of time until I knew that my whereabouts changed and I was no longer in that tube of a vehicle, bouncing around with that yelling 911 medic team. Now I was certain that I was on terra firma and a new and sterner voice was shouting at me. I started to feel relaxed. My muscles were relaxed. I never heard the word "sedated." Yet I immediately felt more aware of my body than I had since starting up the hill to the house while gasping for air. I thought it strange that with all that's going on with this breathing problem, I had a clear and impactful sensation of my muscles becoming relaxed.

I felt an increasing magnitude of localized muscle relaxation. And I was keenly aware of this sensation, not the lack of air sensation. The change surprised me to no end. As the relaxation took hold, it simulated a rising shock wave effect starting at my feet and rising slowly to my crown. The muscle-relaxing shock wave, starting at my legs, left in its wake limbs and torso relaxed, free of trouble. The shock wave escaped the constraints of my body and rose up above me. *This was different,* I thought realizing I no longer had a problem with my breathing. Once the effect rose up out of my head, I could no longer feel my body. The shock wave effect was replaced with a detached feeling, a suspending feeling. The feeling that I was suspended in time and space overtook me. I didn't move a muscle. I couldn't. I recalled no feeling in my body as if it were not my body but something alien and apart from any consciousness. I was about to hear the shouting of unidentified people with one of the voices being somewhat recognizable. When instead I heard a rustling of the breeze in the trees and the vision of the horse fences before me. I had no sensation, yet I knew still that I remained frozen in posture atop some bed or table while others clamored about me. The wave that originated in my legs upon what I thought was lower than my crown came to rest hovering above me. Any consideration of "above me" was thrown out with the wash as I soon realized that I was unable to think or to process what was now happening to my body or anything that constituted space and time.

The blurry figures surrounding me ceased their movement. I no longer heard shouts, voices, or commotion. I heard no normal background sounds. I had no sensation other than a rising preoccupation of something lifting upward and outward, escaping me. And there was silence. Silence? For the past thirty years, I have had the never-ending accompaniment of ringing in my ears. The ringing in my ears never abated, no matter how I tried to rectify my apparent hearing loss. Indeed, ten years ago the ringing in my ears increased in volume and tone, taking on the sounds of a tropical rain forest with its birds, monkeys, and insects all making their unique and individual clicking and buzzing sounds. Right now, there was no sound, only silence! I would have breathed a gasp of joy and relief to once again have silence without the tropical rain forest incessantly screaming in my ears, but I was not able to formulate or maintain a thought other than a sneaking suspicion that this was not a time to be rejoicing. I had no options. I was being pulled into the experience with my only purpose being to ride it out. Yet even without the ability to formulate a thought, I instinctively knew that at that very moment, I was leaving my body. Eyes open wide, physical me with adrenaline flowing, not a second spent in meditation or trance to prepare for leaving my body, and not a single intention to do so. Here I was, nevertheless, leaving my body.

Breaking the silence and reaching into me, a familiar voice sprang out. Not a word or a combination of sounds, but something familiar. Then came a long, calling yell and cry as if taking a cherished toy away from a baby. This wailing was the only sound I received and processed. And when it ended, there was once again no sound about me, just the silence. Then, out of some distant horizon, came a note. A note of music sung by a solitary voice, a single voice that was joined by a second and then a third and then more. The individual notes combined into a chord that hung in the air surrounding me as the sound came from nowhere. This single chord migrated in harmonic series to reveal a chorus of voices singing multiple chords, joining into one theme and one sequence. The sight I had of the lights, blurry, moving people-like objects, and pea green background was replaced with a soft and cooling glow. The glow blended into an uninterrupted white illumination—soft, gentle, and cooling illumination.

I felt a presence within the white glow that surrounded and encompassed me. Perhaps the glow was the presence I felt as it emanated life and vitality. I had no sensation of my body or mind. I had no conscious thought as I was suspended in this warming glow and presence. I had only my consciousness as I understood it, the seven decades that preceded the commencement of this day, today. The presence bid me, "Peace." It was a soft, loving, gentle command. Peace. I obeyed and rested within it. The presence, the glowing whiteness, resided within me and without, surrounding me, while enticing me, filling me with strength and calmness. Everything physical that I had associated with me up to that moment—my body, joints, aches, fatigue, and pains—was absent. I remained present there in the glow of permeating white, glowing light and realized, as a choir sang harmonic chords, that I was filled with calm and a sense of freedom. A breath overtook me, and like a sailor casting off mooring lines, I felt the loosening of all restraints and tethers. Restrained and tethered to what?

Death and Taxes

I never ceased marveling at where my spirit would bring me when I let it fly in meditation and trance to experience the duality of my life. This time, however, what cast its tethers were not only my spirit but also my consciousness as I knew myself. I was not having a momentary and unexpected trance thrust upon me by some instinctive practice that I didn't initiate. This was different. This was as physical as it was metaphysical. And within that peaceful, calming, and loving, glowing presence came wisps of other charismata. The presence then was many, all different from one another. As if I could tune a radio dial to the various identified frequencies, I surveyed the spectrum of the energy that evolved around and within me. My consciousness and mind wandered, sampling what the glow had to offer.

I thought I smelled a whiff of her perfume. I felt her touching my cheek and then a slight kiss on my lips. This was the touch and kiss of my dear spouse as given to me at our last meeting, when she passed from one life to the next. Another presence. A soft stroking hand on the crown of my head, followed by an easing of pressure upon my scalp, and the feel of warming energy that brought rejuvenation and health. That was the touch of my great-aunt Rose, who gifted me her ancient healing arts and took care of me when I was a young child riddled with sickness. The owner of a smiling face delivering a humorous push from an elbow, the smiling face of friends I've known. Then came the feel of the salt sea breezes and the swaying of a solid deck beneath my feet. I felt again at home upon the ocean of the unknown world, confident and eager to be about my business and mission. The lap of my grandmother while washing my face, holding me gently, looking into my eyes, smiling at me, while I was safe and secure. The feel of freedom standing on a mountaintop surveying the land below harmoniously conquered after huffing it up the mountain trail. Light passing through me, holding that moment on a wave and particle of light with the moment stamped and recorded, yet now also becoming that light. No longer a point on that beam but now the beam itself. My consciousness is now joined by others who call me brother. I have arrived. All is as it should be. Life is eternal, and I reside within the loving arms of those who call me kin and are one in the same. I am led from the glowing presence as if from a chamber to a bed. Sleep and repose. Gather myself. I enter the transition from life physical to life everlasting and am cleansed in the holy water and fire of the eternal forge. I am made whole, fashioned again into my eternal countenance. Rest. Become one again.

Death and Taxes

Purpose?

How could I possibly explain this? I have no frame of reference. How could I hope to relate my experiences of consciousness as I dwell resident in the other world? I don't have the vocabulary, but what is most notable is that we do not have the relational foundation of language, experience, and existence from this physical illusion to describe adequately the tale of this place where my true citizenship resides. The foundation goes missing. It was taken from us and hidden by the worldly powers that be, the creators of our culture and history. This, now before me, is the afterlife, where the spirit, soul, and consciousness go after they leave the body upon the completion of the physical life experience. Through my tale, I will attempt to create the text in humanistic, relatable terms. Yet the full story of my existence and being is perhaps for another day.

I rested as upon a bed of energies, meandering between particles of light. Something unknown held me anchored to a single cohesive consciousness. There were others about me, in attendance on me, and in company with me. Their company had a very stabilizing influence, and with their companionship, I knew that I was not alone. I felt stronger in being and spirit as I existed within this experience. I can best relate my sleep, now, to the state of mind I achieve in restful, deep meditation.

Spirit Guides and Angels

In meditation I empty my mind and free it from all thoughts with the intention of simply being at rest and being in the present moment. Still, thoughts do meander through my mind as I keep within the stillness of meditation. As I now lie resting on this bed of energy in a meditative state, here also impressions compete for my attention. The thoughts arrive as visions and elicit memories of events surrounding my recent earthly experience. The events signal emotions that I felt and the motivations that I held within when experiencing the corresponding occurrences. These are the scenes that I lived in this last physical sojourn. A vision of a thirty-two-foot sailing sloop was followed by the sight of a sleek thirty-eight-gun frigate under full sail with a following sea. I was attached to both; they are both related to my journey. Throughout my meditative lingering on this bed of energy, I maintained a constant flow of related sequences that told no tale in them yet were connected to me and my newly past living experience.

Other beings came and I felt their influence. These other consciousness individuals were familiar to me. Some were not so. I could not be certain. Their impact came to me as impressions radiating from some point of origin held tight through the cohesion of our souls' skins. They did not communicate with me. There were no words, thoughts, or symbols distributed between us. There were no messages or information given. There was only an imprint transferred, and the feeling of harmony that was evident; they and I were in harmony together in my current state, for I knew that each impression was connected to my life of Wayne Cesaro. Each had a frequency that signaled their identity during this last play on the world's stage. We were in celebration, and the gift of welcome played out as I bathed in the light of our loving co-experience. Here now were finally removed all earthly cares and afflictions. We were all beyond that now.

They came. Those who were close to me came as well as those who were not. Kin and friends, fans and rivals, as well as tormenters and bystanders who were impacted by the wake of my journey, they all came to bid me welcome while I slept on the bed of energy and became born into my world, returning to my true existence. As I rested, I grew in the strength of my genuine identity. My mind became clear as I shook off the shingles of my abandoned life that I once called Wayne Cesaro. I was coming now into my eternal being.

There were special moments that lingered. Impressions associated with those who were intimate were visited and made their presence known. I recalled a kiss on the lips from the one known as my dear spouse. But now she was in her full glory. No physical limitations burdened her. No trouble molested her. She was all loving while in strength and beauty and had about her representatives from the animal kingdom and a procession of sainted beings who were once sanctified on this world. I evoked a moment of humor as a worldly traveling brother in friendship paid his respects in the usual irreverent manner. And then I received an air of protection from the one who was my mother's father. I felt his radiating smile and approving nod. And so, it proceeded till every relationship undertaken with my fellows, as me here now was revisited, every myth of our world was dispelled, and every truth in nature validated. The questions I had about man's earthly existence were answered. The misconceptions I had were corrected. The influences and forces in play that shaped human history were uncovered and illuminated. The life was analyzed and measured for lessons learned and for new curricula to be developed.

I cannot relate this experience in terms of time. How long was I upon the bed of energy receiving greetings and impressions? I could not say. For now, for me, there were no longer the constraints of time. Indeed, I was the light and all that was in between and resided inside of the light, frozen between the pulse and particles. I was also the entire ray, from the beginning and origin to the terminus, of which there is no identifiable point. The light travels onward, never ending, and I was at its origin, ending, and at all points in between.

Death and Taxes

The experience ended. No signal did it provide as I was guided onward to the next parallel phase of transition as each aspect of process occurred simultaneously as opposed to sequentially. The procession of impressions and presences simply ceased, and all was quiet while I existed in a present, be-here-now state of mind. Then came the heralding. The choir erupted, and the procession began. Upon a chariot of fire came Raphael, archangel and pillar of creation, and with him a heavenly host of angels singing, joined in harmony and brotherhood. I was led to the chariot and lifted upon it by the bright shining ones who attend the archangel. And at that instant, I was one with Raphael as our consciousness merged. I was returned to the source and provided my heavenly robes, again connected to the wonder of creation. Yes. I was plugged back into the network, and all that existed in this world and all earthly worlds and heavenly dimensions again were under my purview. I could touch everything with a thought. I could survey all with one glance, whether past, present, or future. To be there, I simply had to think it.

There were other aspects to my connection with the host. Other angels flittered about me and followed my directions as I responded to the translated needs of those physical life forces that existed in complex happenstance. And so it was that I once again fulfilled my purpose of creation among the heavenly host.

Repeat the Cycle and Move the Wheel

Raphael, one of the pillars of creation, exists as a consciousness. This consciousness is comprised of many individual consciousnesses, personalities, entities, beings, or whatever one would call the individual sparks of creation that combined to comprise the archangel as he expresses his identity. I am but a tiny spark of the one. In that regard, I am an aspect of Raphael. My brothers and I are part and parcel of the expression in total known as Raphael. We are guided, focused, and directed through the core spirit of the archangel. We follow the patterns of our created purpose. That is not to say that there is no Raphael as an individual force. It is to say that what we consider the individual Raphael is akin to the mind of the body, while I am a component of that body. It would not be too far afield to consider me akin to a cell of the spinal cord relaying the mind's impulses to the body's organs and mechanisms, enabling the functionality and intention as directed by the mind's thought. The archangel can take on form and be an identified individual if need be. Doing so would require nothing more than directing the energy to do so. Think and the form shapes and is alive for others to experience within their relative level of understanding.

Death and Taxes

The energy projected from the archangel defines the individual. Know this individual by the acts of his work and by the energy he emanates. Healing and compassion are the hallmarks of the archangel. Now in my eternal being, I am joined with the archangel and taking up the purpose of my creation. I was created as the archangel was created, and with this shared purpose. I know no other way or manner of being. To understand true compassion and empathy with those of this world, I have undertaken to join them in their souls' journeys. I live the cycle as would their souls. I experience all that earthly existence has to offer from its beginning to its end. I secure an understanding of all the intricacies involved with being bound to this planet and its illusion of life. There is no risk for me, for I am eternal, and upon entering my eternal state after the death of the body incarnate, I am refreshed and reminded of where I am and of who I am. A spark, a portion of my consciousness, engages in the lesson of earthly, humanly life while my higher self remains anchored in the eternal life, working on my purpose. Upon the death of the body, my spark and fragment are then joined to my eternal being and consciousness. For you see; while living as the person Wayne Cesaro, my being continues to reside in my heavenly state. The spark of consciousness that resides within the spirit of Wayne is but a thought and an intention. While I live beside all humanity in the physical illusion, I remain as I am, have been, and always will be, among the heavenly host serving my purpose. This is a duality of life.

The souls engaged in the temporal human existence are many. Their origins are diverse. They include those of the angelic choir who undertake to serve man by living as one to understand firsthand what the life cycle requires. The angels send forth their energy, formed as a soul, to purposefully place themselves into the karmic wheel and undertake living a cycle. A cycle may take millions of years; the experience has its pitfalls. There are always pitfalls when becoming a part of the material illusion. The cycle has its opportunities also. The opportunities are not growth in the sense of becoming more spiritual or angelic. The growth opportunities are in understanding the challenges of man to render more effective service in unraveling the mysteries of advancing the earthly existence. We take up the baton when the circumstances for our growth are optimal and plunge again into the cycle by incarnating into another living being. We pick the circumstances of our birth, environment, family, point in earthly evolution, and societal development that will maximize our chances for reaching our intended goals of understanding. We do not enter the physical life in full power and authority of our office. We do not make it easy on ourselves. Quite the contrary, we make it challenging. How better to understand the human trial? We will always return to our permanent heavenly state. We will always merge with our full spirit and become one with it. We will always merge with our archangel and join the procession of heavenly beings, and we will always do so as if we never left. This is a piece of the puzzle of the duality.

I have always been fond of those souls and their spirits that are bound to the cycle of the earthly illusion. They are a hardy lot. Their existence since their creation is relatively short; short when speaking of eternity is still a long time. For example, in the order of creation of all universes, first there was the thought. Then there came the establishment of the four pillars of creation, who would assist with the administrative tasks of creating the heavens and the earths that we know of as the universes. The energy is contained and then released, and the core of earthly souls is created, all from the thought. They became one with the earth and tied to its evolution and life, from beginning to end. The created souls are the earth's keepers and shapers. They are the inhabitants of all societies that have existed and perished throughout the millions of years they have had this inhabitable earth. They are the ones who shall reign in all glory when the wheel has been successfully turned to the next and higher level of heavenly existence. These are the souls that hold my fondness and those that I primarily serve. It is for them that I have entered the cycle of this material illusion. I have participated in the reincarnation cycle now for the equivalent of five million years.

I look upon the earth and see the light of spirit reaching forever heavenly. The seekers of truth and love who would join with the heavenly host and the harmony of oneness are signaling. Calling. Searching. It doesn't matter where they are in the cycle of one civilization or another. It doesn't matter what their level of technology, peace, or prosperity, or lack thereof. There will always be the flickering of a spirit's call, seeking guidance and communion, wanting nothing more than to live in the glory of the oneness. There will always be those souls who enter again the fray of life's existence. To grow, progress, and become a living representative of love and harmony regardless of the circumstances or treatment, that is their goal. They are always determined, and they learn as they go. We are a wondrous lot and deserving of our most generous and loving service.

I go, soon, back into the physical life cycle. There is still much for me to do to become more effective. And there is much I can do to add to the positive energies that advance the human experience. The circumstances for my return are ripe. The clock on the earthly calendar has advanced by several thousand years. That is the time I chose for my next incarnation, although the era does not matter. I could very well have chosen the past from the perspective of my last earthly identity, known as Wayne Cesaro. But it is his world's future that I choose to experience next. I have incarnated many times throughout the last reckoning of civilized years. My presence on earth and my sequential participation was almost constant from the Middle Ages through to the fall of the current civilization. The intensity and rapidity of incarnation provided much fodder for growth, compassion, and identification with the human soul cycle. The conditions that are occurring now in the new civilization provide the greatest opportunity to influence societal development in a manner that may lead to successful and peaceful coexistence among the earth's future inhabitants.

I will once again enter the fray. With this experience, I will bring more of my knowledge. The life experience must be stronger and more resilient than the last one. This life expression must reach its full potential much earlier in age, as this will be quick and there will be but a short time to accomplish much.

The Surprise Awakening

No sooner did I prepare to jump off into an unknown whirlwind when I noticed the perspiration on my brow and received a sudden and mandatory urge to leave. Leave? Yes! Just leave and go elsewhere. All thoughts save for those associated with my current direction were replaced with the sudden and unavoidable urge to act. Something commands,

"Turn your head and look at me." I falter but comply. And I swear I'm not making this up: Everything around me blurs into a mass of light such that I cannot distinguish one color tone from another. I no longer register what I see before my eyes or my mind. I wonder if I blacked out. And out of this immediate blurring of all these myriads of colors turning into images, blurry images if you must know, I distinguish 1960s-era black-framed eyeglasses. And eyes. The eyes spoke to me, but I did not hear any words. The eyes are telling me to look at him.

"Look at me. Look at me!" he commands as a face takes form. A face that is physically close to me. One that is so close it's all I see; it fills my vision from right to left and top to bottom with nothing more to be seen. And to my relief and shock, the face is that of my favorite uncle, Ralphie. How could I possibly explain this? Uncle Ralph died ten years ago. But he's here in front of me right this instant with his face so close to me I can smell his cologne, Jade East. He is insistent on receiving my attention and wants it immediately. What is he saying? "Don't be a *chooch!* Tell your story!"

And with that, Uncle Ralphie was nowhere to be found, but instead, there was this whiskered, younger, hairless, and plumper man wearing glasses. His words to me, also being shouted just like all the others of his nature and those with him, were informing me that everything would be good. They were going to take care of me. Following some level of reassurance from this unknown whiskered, bespectacled, plump face, the word "sedative" was thrown out, and I have no memory of anything after that word until waking up in a semiprivate room in some medical facility.

My stepdaughter, Marie, disobeyed my relayed message to please see that the dogs, horses, and all at home was OK. Instead, she drove to the hospital ER directly. It was almost like she was already on the way to the hospital when she got the call from 911, she would later relate regarding her route running errands that pleasant Wednesday afternoon. Arriving at the emergency room and identifying herself, she went immediately to my room, where she was greeted with all the hysteria of this patient going into cardiac arrest. Yes. I was coding. She walked into the room, alarm sounding from some electrical machine indicating that a heartbeat had ceased. Standing around my bed at the time were the ER attending doctor and a nurse. I had no paperwork on file with this hospital, but everyone knew I was a DNR, or at least the 911 medics were to understand, or sort of knew. DNR stands for "Do not resuscitate." I always figured that if my body had it to the point that my heart ceased beating, then I was done. Otherwise, my heart wouldn't have stopped in the first place. Marie knew of my wishes, but again, she disobeyed me and shrieked, "I am the POA! Resuscitate him! Now! Now! Now."

The last "now" was much softer and less audible than the first two. When asked about resuscitating me being contrary to my expressed wishes, she said that she needed to give me a chance to stay if I wanted to. She figured that if I really did want to go, I'd go. She also stated that she would take care of the financial burden if I became a vegetable.

My cardiac failure was brought about by the whole mess of a heart attack that was thought to have occurred while my body was under extreme stress and exhaustion, fighting to breathe. The fight lasted from the second I started up my hill all the way till safe and tight in the local hospital ER medical-surgical bed. Marie arrived and identified herself as my personal representative, POA, and remaining family member in the western half of the country. She stepped in not long after the heart monitor alarm commenced. Her response was automatic. "Resuscitate him!" Evidently, I flatlined for about two minutes and twenty seconds.

Revived and sedated, they intubated me and hooked up a power-assisted ventilator till my lungs were stronger and better able to take the load of normal breathing. Yes. She disobeyed me by having them shock me with paddles and placing me on artificial life support. Her excuse was that she wanted to give me a chance to live. If I did not respond positive, then I'd be dead, and that was it. So, she gave it a try. And afterward, since

I was breathing on my own, she figured that they could keep me on the ventilator while I got stronger and the steroids did their work in healing the lungs.

Three days is what it took on the ventilator and steroids. Three days on a ventilator to strengthen the lungs, being injected with a steady stream of steroids. And my Marie took care of business like a pro.

Once admitted to the hospital and secured in the ICU, they subjected me to a battery of tests. I tested positive for RSV, pneumonia, and flu. You could have knocked me over with a feather when they told me. And for the remaining month, anyone could have knocked me over with a feather as I was that weak. I learned my lesson. I ceased cutting trees and had the wood-burning stove replaced with a propane stove. And I lived happily ever after.

Printed by Libri Plureos GmbH in Hamburg,
Germany

9 798869 182142